GOOD TEMPERED FOOD

Tamasin Day-Lewis

GOOD TEMPERED FOOD

Recipes to love, leave, and linger over

Photography by David Loftus

miramax books

DEDICATION

For the three loveliest children in the world, Miranda, Harry, and Charissa

Contents

Pandarus: He that will have a cake out of the wheat must tarry the grinding.

Troilus: Have I not tarried?

Pandarus: Ay, the grinding; but you must tarry the bolting.

Troilus: Have I not tarried?

Pandarus: Ay, the bolting; but you must tarry the leavening.

Troilus: Still have I tarried.

Pandarus: Ay, to the leavening; but here's yet in the word 'hereafter'
the kneading, the making of the cake, the heating of the oven,
and the baking; nay, you must stay the cooling too,
or you may chance to burn your lips.

Shakespeare, *Troilus and Cressida*

Introduction

IT SEEMS TO ME THAT THIS PASSAGE tells us as much about what's wrong with our attitude toward food today as it does about what, at best, it should be. We are not prepared to "tarry." In fact, in modern doctrine, the very idea of tarrying is stigmatic. We worship at the altar of the instant, we are governed and seduced by the words "easy," "fast," "quick," "simple." Leapfrog the process, vault over the preparation, skim, short cut, and bypass the stages that true cooking rather than assembling is all about, and you have bought into the culture that Pandarus was warning Troilus against around 400 years ago. In the absence of patience, of tarrying, fast food is your reward.

Look, I am no purist hardliner. There are days, if not weeks, when I crave easy food; a quickly frazzled bacon sandwich dribbling unsalted butter; pasta with handfuls of fresh herbs and raw fava beans from the garden thrown after them; a crab and avocado salad spritzed with lime, for which Phil, my fishmonger, has done the picking and dressing; a one-pan, flame-colored pipérade or Spanish omelet oozing a tangle of oily wilted onion and spinach and yesterday's potatoes. But none of these quite fits our notion of fast food, which is as much about provenance, or the lack of it, as it is about speed and convenience, two words which fill me with the same sense of gloom as "hygiene" when applied to food.

The very expression "fast food" is a misnomer, an insult, an indicator of something inferior—mere fuel to be ingested at speed, to provide energy, be convenient, serve a purpose. Does this equate with pleasure, goodness, love, care, attention, nurture? To the scents and smells of a fresh yeast loaf cooling on a rack, a stock simmering, a chicken roasting, a stew stewing quietly and unobtrusively in its own juices, the bitter whiff of January's Seville oranges filling the kitchen as they osmose to marmalade, clots of strawberries bubbling into jam, the raw depths of a garlicky aïoli, toast toasting, cookies baking. Food cooked slowly isn't better by definition, but every process, from conception, gestation, seeding, fruiting, to picking, plucking, peeling, paring, preparing is also about waiting. As is cooking itself. The alchemy of food, its transformation from raw to cooked, or raw to plate is about our transforming touch. Once we are no longer involved with that part of the process, once we don't how to perform the simple but satisfying tasks that even basic food demands, we are no longer cooks, nor are we heir to the traditions that food has been about since man first cooked it.

Somehow we have fallen for a myth, the notion that food that isn't fast prepared and fast cooked is inherently more difficult, more time consuming, more of a sweat, almost not worth the effort, or, at least, only worth the effort some of the time.

I lay the blame first at the feet of the supermarkets and fast-food outlets whose interests, and by that I mean profits, this is in; second, with the consumer, easily led, lazy, wanting to spend less rather than invest in quality, better nutritional value, taste, and sustainable methods of production; third, with the food manufacturers whose advertising, as dishonest as it is, is often brilliantly executed and faultless in its powers of seduction; and fourth, with the television chefs who are force-feeding their audience a diet that perpetuates the myth, telling people how quick and easy everything is, and choosing recipes that make-believe technique is unnecessary, time a luxury you can't afford, patience and attention to detail curious anachronisms from the past.

Well, I'm here to tell you that slow-cooked food, and what I like to call "good-tempered food," food that you can cook a bit of now, a bit of later, prepare today for tomorrow, or the next day or even next week, tinker with, macerate, freeze, finish, or reheat in another life, add to, subtract from, reincarnate, is what proper cooking is *really* all about. In fact, it's the chief pleasure of cooking, and if you find cooking pleasure enough to read about, buy into and experiment with, you're being short-changed if the writer is advising you exactly how to get the whole thing over and done with as fast as pulling a tooth, so the pain is past tense, and you can get on with the things that really give you pleasure.

This book is about reuniting you with that sense of pleasure in the kitchen; about setting aside time, just *thinking* about what you want to cook and eat. This is a hugely underrated pleasure in its own right—as can be the planning, shopping, reading cookbooks, deliberating, telephoning a friend for a recipe, or even that most evanescent of things, inspiration; checking out the cupboard, the pantry, the refrigerator, the vegetable garden.

Sometimes it is a chore, how could it not be? At the domestic level, feeding a

family is like a prolonged, never-ending military campaign; if one bit of the advance preparation goes AWOL or is forgotten, *disaster*, or, at least, a complete change of strategy is needed. But it's what you probably cope with already at least once a week. And what do you need most in a tricky culinary impasse? Time and imagination, although just one of these should do. And the knowledge that most food lends itself to this sort of crisis, even if it's "empty refrigerator" syndrome or "there's-nothing-I-feel-like-cooking," or an extra battalion has invited itself to supper.

Cooking is a test without the paper, the questions, or the answers, in the sense that you, the cook, are constantly trying to please a disparate bunch of people, who most often, being family, will not hold back on the criticism. You are coping with other pressures—budgetary constraints, an imperfect kitchen, no kitchen slaves to scrub, chop, wash up; but still, something as simple as a clove of garlic sizzling in good olive oil, shelling a tightly packed pea pod, smelling the readiness of the simplest of dishes can transport, relax, infuse with a degree of pleasure that the smallest of things can so cunningly do with the greatest of impact. Take the lid off a fat piece of pork belly that has been idling in the oven doing time for five, maybe six, maybe seven hours, steeped in its gluey juices, black breathed with the sweetness of molasses, brown sugar, star anise, and you should feel not far short of paradise.

Decide not to feel guilty if you are still slamming cupboard doors and searching for a 20-minute supper to cook when your children are mutinous with post-homework hunger and you are scanning the darker recesses of your memory and your refrigerator for a one-pot supper. I did just that last week, after four days in New York, arriving back jet-lagged to a yawningly empty kitchen and a lack of inspiration equaled only by my intense hunger. But I just didn't want to have to think or cook. The result: I picked the tiniest green embryos of fava beans from the garden, with handfuls of chives, mint, chervil, and thyme. I roasted some tiny, rather overripe, tomatoes in olive oil until split and deliciously weeping. Found some goat cheese and mozzarella lurking at the back of the refrigerator. Cooked some penne. Threw the tomatoes and their juices whole into the drained pasta, followed by chunks of the cheeses, more verdant olive oil, the very finely chopped herbs, salt, pepper, some zested lemon, and the raw fava beans. We ate it warm, rather than piping hot. It didn't feel like cooking, but it made me want to cook again. My youngest daughter Charissa eulogized over what felt like almost cheating, and thus was my appetite for the stove rekindled. It is, after all, appetite that induces pleasure and inspiration, and which, on contemplating the creating of something out of nothing, is all the better stimulated. The elaborate and the refined have their place, too, but food was always a necessity before it was a luxury, so maybe it is down to some ancient atavistic urge that the most satisfying of dishes are usually those that excite through their very simplicity and through the power of memory.

Let us not forget the simple art of roasting; and those of baking, poaching, pickling, preserving. More than that, that the greatest gift we can bestow on the next generation is educating them in the art, science, lore, tradition, and pragmatic experience of the kitchen. The quiet, unhurried, unchaotic ritual of preparation for the table, its simple repetitions, its satisfying processes, and its accompaniments—conversation, music, a glass of wine—savor them, enjoy them, afford them the time and respect they deserve. They are more than what life is all about, they are life itself.

TAMASIN DAY-LEWIS

a slow start

I

A spectacularly beautiful yet simple dish that I first ate at my Swedish friend Kristina von Wrede's house. The combination of sweet, sour, astringent, and salt, of textures from smooth to crisp and fresh, and the brilliance of the colors, make this dish both startling and original.

"Sun's Eye" or Sologa

FOR EACH SERVING:

3–4 anchovies, preferably the salted ones, rinsed and dried
1 tbsp capers or cornichons, chopped
1–2 tbsp white onion, finely chopped
2–3 tbsp pickled beet, and I do not mean the throat-gagging kind pickled in malt vinegar; white-wine vinegar please
2–3 tbsp flat-leaf parsley, chopped
1 raw egg yolk
a few drops of lemon juice (optional)

Chop all the ingredients one by one, keeping them separate. Arrange each plate, starting with a small circle of anchovies in the middle, so that all you can fit inside it is the egg yolk later. Then do the same with the capers or cornichons, so the circle abuts the anchovies, and outside that, the onions, then the beet then the parsley, over which you may sprinkle a bit of lemon juice. Finally put the egg yolk in the middle.

You eat the dish by breaking into the yolk and mixing it into the other ingredients. Would I be foolish in imagining this to be a good hangover cure, served with a homemade whole wheat or caraway roll?

Whole Wheat Caraway Rolls

MAKES ABOUT 20
preheat oven to 425°F

4 tbsp butter

1½ cups milk

2oz fresh yeast

1½ cups organic stoneground
   whole wheat flour to mix with
   1½ cups boiling water

1½ tsp sea salt

2 tbsp molasses sugar

2 cups organic stoneground
   whole wheat flour

1¾ cups plus 1 tbsp organic
   unbleached all-purpose flour

a handful of caraway seeds
   (optional)

Melt the butter in a pan. Pour in the milk and heat to lukewarm. Crumble the yeast into a bowl, pour in the liquid and stir until the yeast has dissolved. Add the 1½ cups flour and boiling water mixture, the salt and sugar, the 2 cups stoneground flour, and most of the all-purpose flour. Mix everything together into a pliable dough, then cover the bowl with a dish towel you have rinsed in boiling water and squeezed out, and leave the dough in a warm place to rise for about an hour.

Using the rest of the all-purpose flour, knead the dough with determination for about 7 minutes on a floured surface, then separate into two pieces. Cut each piece into 10 and shape them into rolls. Place them on two greased baking sheets, cover with dish towels, and leave for 30 minutes longer.

Bake in the middle of the oven for 10 minutes, then let the rolls cool on a wire rack under a dish towel. Serve warm.

Last year I purchased half a butchered Berkshire pig and armed with a copy of Jane Grigson's reissued classic *Charcuterie and French Pork Cookery*, I dreamed of raised pies, galantines, trotters, snouts, pig tails, and tongues. The pig came with a proper fatty overcoat, ideal for things like brawn and terrines, since the greatest enemy of the terrine is dryness, and good fatback and belly is of the essence. If you don't possess a grinder, any good butcher will grind the ingredients for you. Other than remembering how important the proportions of fat to lean, bacon to variety meat are, this is a simple and utterly beguiling dish, about as unlike the gray, chewy offerings of an inferior deli or the hideously pink commercial pâtés as you can imagine. When you turn out your browned, pink-middled, coarse-textured wonder, you will glow with pride.

Country Terrine

SERVES 10–12
preheat oven to 300°F

3 cups onions, roughly chopped
6 tbsp unsalted butter
1lb pork belly, rind and small
  bones removed, and coarsely
  ground through the largest
  hole of a grinder
12oz unsmoked organic bacon,
  ground
1lb pig liver, ground
6oz fatback, ground
¼ cup Cognac
¼ cup dry sherry
4 cloves of garlic, peeled and
  finely chopped
flat-leaf parsley, chopped
2 tsp olive oil
sprig of rosemary, finely chopped
a few sprigs of thyme
1 egg
½ tsp ground allspice
sea salt and white pepper

Gently cook the chopped onions in the butter until softened and golden, about 30 minutes, then put them on a plate to cool. Thoroughly mix all the ground meats and fat together with your hands in a big bowl until well amalgamated. Warm the alcohol in the pan you cooked the onions in, then set light to it with a taper and allow the alcohol to burn off.

Throw the onions and alcohol into the bowl of ground meats with the garlic and parsley. Heat the olive oil in a small skillet, throw in the rosemary and thyme, and allow them to soften (a couple of minutes). Pour them over the ground meat, add the beaten egg and the allspice, then season generously.

Scrape the mixture into a 5-cup terrine pan, cover with foil, and place in a roasting pan. Fill the pan three-quarters full with boiling water, then put into the oven for an hour. Uncover and check with a skewer poked down to the middle of the terrine. After 10 seconds, see if the skewer is hot on your tongue. The meat juices should be pink. Leave the foil off and return the pan to the oven for 15–30 minutes for the terrine to brown.

Remove from the oven, replace the foil or lid, and leave the terrine to cool. Place in the refrigerator until you want to eat it. It tastes even better if it is left for a couple of days.

This is one of the simplest and most delicious titbits of a dish I have ever cooked. It should be eaten straight from a communal plate, or even the skillet, your fingers oozing the pinkly sticky, buttery spicy juices, while you clutch a cold glass of something good with your free hand. The spices can all be ground an hour or so in advance and stirred together with the flour in the mortar. You may also de-vein the chicken livers in advance, leaving them whole, so all you need to do when your guests arrive or your family flock to the kitchen, is roll the livers in the spiced flour, heat your olive oil or butter, and cook them for about a couple of minutes a side. Beware, the spices spit, and do not allow the middles to turn from rosy softness to firm grayness. Tip hot with their oily juices on to a plate, and devour!

Spiced Chicken Livers

SERVES 4—6
as an appetizer with drinks, depending on greed and what's to follow

1lb organic chicken livers. I'm afraid I take a purist line here—only organic will do, since chemical residues collect in the liver and kidneys
1½ heaped tsp cumin seeds
1 tsp coriander seeds
the tip of a tsp of cayenne
1 tsp sea salt crystals
1 tsp black peppercorns
1–1½ tbsp all-purpose flour
olive oil or a good-size pat of unsalted butter

Cook the cumin and coriander in a small skillet over a gentle heat for 30 seconds to a minute, until the spices exude their scent. Tip into a mortar and crush with the sea salt and peppercorns. Add the cayenne, then the flour, and stir well together. Set aside.

Clean and de-vein the livers, keeping them whole, and removing any green patches. Pat them dry and keep in the refrigerator until about 30 minutes before you want to cook them.

Just before cooking, roll each liver in the spice mixture in the mortar and put on a plate. Heat a good pat of unsalted butter or olive oil, whichever you prefer, in a skillet—I prefer butter with a tiny addition of oil to discourage burning. Throw in the livers when the fat is hot. Allow one side to spit and crisp for a couple of minutes, turn over and repeat, then test with a knife point. When gorgeously oozily pink, slide the contents of the pan onto a white plate and consume.

This is a magical appetizer that I dreamed up as everyone was sitting down to dinner one night. I had already invented the spiced livers for a previous party. This time I offset their heat and spice with the bittersweet endives softened in what amounts to a warm salad dressing. You can serve the dish hot or warm. I cooked it in three or four minutes while people took their seats.

Spiced Chicken Livers on Wilted Endives

SERVES 6
*the ingredients for the chicken livers
as on page 19, plus:*

3 Belgium endives
4 tbsp best olive oil
1 tsp dark brown sugar
sea salt and black pepper
lemon juice to taste

While you fry the livers, cut the base off the endives, core them, and strip them into leaves. Heat the olive oil gently in a pan with the sugar, then throw in the endives and stir them in the warm oil. They will begin to wilt pretty quickly. Season, remove from the heat, and spritz on the lemon to taste.

Pile a few leaves onto each plate, add a few livers with their juices, then serve.

Look on broiled bell peppers as a base or foundation that can withstand pretty serious cosmetic enhancement and be easily transmogrified into something more glamorous if the need should arise. In the meanwhile, you can prepare pounds of red or yellow bell peppers, organic if possible—I am no fan of the hideous hydroponically grown numbers—when they are cheap and in season, and keep them in the refrigerator in jars *sott'olio*, under oil, for two or three months. Then you can use them as they are as an appetizer, layer a vermilion or yellow seam of them in sandwiches or bruschetta with a delicious goat cheese, or serve them as an accompaniment to cold pork. If you are going to eat them on their own, the following sauce, in which you can also abandon the peppers for up to a week, defines the word "alchemy."

Broiled Bell Peppers

SERVES 4 OR SO

4 red or yellow organic bell
    peppers
6 anchovy fillets
2 cloves of garlic
a handful of flat-leaf parsley
1 small, seeded dried chili
sea salt
best olive oil

Broil or char your peppers in the usual way. I only have an erratic overhead broiler, so I keep turning mine over with tongs until they are uniformly blackened and softened. Leave them to cool, then the skins should peel away easily. I am not of the plastic-bag school of pepper peeling. It is unnecessary, and I hate the idea of hot plastic melting into healthy organic peppers. Halve, core, and seed the peppers, then cut them lengthwise into thin strips.

Pound the anchovies in a mortar with the garlic, parsley, chili, and a little bit of salt, or chop them all together finely with a sharp knife or mezzaluna.

Put the mixture into a small pan with 4–5 tablespoons of olive oil, and heat very gently, mashing the mixture down as you go. Spoon over the peppers and let them marinate for at least 4 hours. Here's the best bit: The longer you leave them the better they get and up to a week in the refrigerator is just fine. You need good bread with a proper crust on it to accompany these.

Rillons are the big brother to rillettes, being whole, rather than shredded. Like goose or duck legs in the classic confit, large cubes of pork belly, which I buy from my organic butcher, are cooked very slowly in seasoned fat. When they have been cooled, the rillons can be stored for months beneath their snowy mantle of fat.

Rillons, or Confit of Pork Belly

SERVES 6—8
preheat oven to 400°F

2¼—4¼lb pork belly, the ribs
    removed
a generous tbsp of lard
some sprigs of thyme
2—3 cloves of garlic, bruised with
    the back of a knife (optional)
2 cups red wine
1 cup water
sea salt and black pepper

Cut the pork belly roughly into large cubes about 2 inches square, leaving the skin on. Heat the lard in a roomy pan and throw in the meat. Brown fast and hard, turning occasionally, then transfer to a large baking dish in which, ideally, the pieces should fit snugly in a single layer. Add the other ingredients, and put the dish in the oven. Check on it every 10 minutes, turning the pieces as you do. After about 30 minutes, the fat rendered from the pork should be at least half way up the meat, which will be browning nicely.

Turn the oven down to 350°F and cook the rillons for at least another hour, turning them once or twice. They are done when the skin is soft enough to chew without much effort.

Unlike most things, rillons are best served cold, straight from the refrigerator with some extra sea salt. Great with a glass of iced fino sherry. Toasted homemade mixed-grain bread is all the accompaniment you need.

Store the rillons for months in a sealed jar in a cool place, but if you think you are going to eat them within a couple of weeks, a plastic container in the refrigerator will do. The fat will help to keep the rillons moist, but if you don't like the taste of it, you can wipe it off before you serve them. This fat will set to a highly flavored lard, perfect for roasting potatoes and parsnips.

I have tried pork, duck, goose, and rabbit rillettes. All are delicious, as verified by the good people of the Sarthe region of northwest France, renowned for their extraordinary consumption of this delicacy. At 27½ pounds per person per year, it is a hundred times higher than the national average.

Rillettes de Tours

SERVES 4–6
as an appetizer or lunch dish,
or 8–10 as part of a cold table
preheat oven to 225°F

2¼lb pork belly
1½ cups dry white wine
4–6 cloves of garlic, crushed
nutmeg
sea salt and black pepper
1lb pork fat

Take the rind off the pork belly and put it to one side. Remove and discard the bones and cut the meat into 1-inch chunks. Put them into a Pyrex or nonaluminum dish. Pour the wine over them, then add the crushed garlic, a suspicion of nutmeg, and the seasoning. Cover and bake for at least 5 hours, or until the meat is virtually falling to pieces. Meanwhile, sprinkle the rind with salt and roast it in a hot oven, 400°F, until crisp. Leave to cool on a rack set over a plate to catch any residue.

Chop the rind finely. Melt the pork fat and strain it. Shred the meat roughly using two forks and mix it with its juices and the garlic; mix in the chopped, roasted rind and its juices. Pour into small pots or jars, or into one larger earthenware dish. When cool, pour the pork fat over the top to seal. Like the rillons, rillettes can be stored for months in a sealed jar in a cool place, or if you are going to eat them within a couple of weeks, you can keep them in a plastic container in the refrigerator.

Serve with a good crusty bread, some glossy green or black olives, a few cornichons, and a good bitter lettuce such as escarole or radicchio.

Everyone knows this wonderful northern Italian dish. I add crumbled feta and a sprig of thyme and serve quarters of the bell peppers like warm boats transporting their cargo of salty anchovy, garlic, olive oil, and herbed cheese. The perfect ambulant appetizer served with a glass of iced manzanilla sherry or rosé. You can prepare the *petits bateaux* in advance, then put them in the oven just before your guests arrive. Hot, warm, or cold, all are equally delicious.

Piemontese Bell Peppers

SERVES 4
preheat oven to 350°F

2 organic red bell peppers
2 large organic tomatoes
3 cloves of garlic
4–6 good-quality anchovy fillets
a sprig of thyme
best olive oil
a generous pat unsalted butter
some crumbled or cubed feta
   cheese, the best you can find
sea salt and black pepper

Halve the peppers and remove the seeds and innards, then halve them again and place them on a flat roasting tray like small boats. On each deck, place two tiny chunks of tomato, three thin slices of garlic, half a chopped anchovy in tiny bits, a sprinkling of thyme, and a splosh of best olive oil. Season, add a dot of butter, and bake in the oven for 40 minutes, or until the peppers are tender, but slightly resistant.

Add some crumbled bits of good feta cheese to the boats while still hot. Cool to whatever temperature you wish to serve them at and make sure you spoon back any escaped juices.

The therapeutic stuffing and rolling into rolls of this dish is as pleasurable as the eating, either hot, warm, or cold. You can eschew the meat and do a vegetarian version if you would rather. The soaking and draining of the grape leaves is hardly time consuming, and very much worth the effort. You can make the dish hours before you want to eat it and serve it at room temperature. The other joy is that you can use leftover cooked rice.

Stuffed Grape Leaves

MAKES 45—50

1 jar of grape leaves in brine
½ cup organic basmati rice, cooked and drained
½lb raw ground organic lamb
2 tomatoes, skinned, seeded, and chopped
1 small onion, peeled and very finely chopped
3 tbsp each of finely chopped mint, flat-leaf parsley, and celery leaves
4 tbsp pine nuts
¼ tsp ground cinnamon
¼ tsp ground allspice
2 tbsp tomato paste
6 cloves of garlic, cut into slivers
⅔ cup good olive oil and the same quantity of water
juice of 1½ lemons
sea salt and black pepper

Drain the grape leaves and put them in a bowl. Cover them with boiling water and soak for 20 minutes. Repeat the process twice more, but with cold water, before a final drain.

In a large bowl mix together the rice, ground lamb, tomatoes, onion, herbs, pine nuts, spices, and tomato paste. Season. Place a grape leaf on your countertop, vein side up, the stem edge nearest to you. Put a heaped teaspoon of the mixture in the middle of the leaf near the stem. Fold up over the filling, then fold both sides of the leaf toward the middle, and roll into a little cigar. Do the same with the remaining 49. Children are very adept at this sort of repetitive action if you have any on hand to bribe, but I find some comfort and relaxation in the leisurely performing of this sort of task, which is not going to ruin if the telephone rings.

Line a heavy-bottomed Dutch oven with a single layer of unstuffed grape leaves, slightly overlapping, so they come about a third of the way up the sides of the pan. Pack in the stuffed grape leaves, snuggled tightly together and one or two layers deep, placing occasional slivers of garlic between them. Add the olive oil, water, and lemon juice, and weight down with an upturned plate and a couple of weights.

Cook very gently on top of the stove for about 2 hours, until tender when pierced with a skewer. Check the liquid level after the first hour, you may need to add a bit more water. The sort of unhurried, uncomplicated, but tremendously satisfying, cooking that brings forth memories of the best kind of Greek taverna.

One of those delightfully old-style-trattoria dishes that is as substantial as you could wish for as an appetizer or main course. Why do things fall from fashion, only to be resuscitated as the emperor's new clothes? All I can say is there is always a place in my repertoire for a classic such as this, where there is a true marriage of texture and flavor, and not one ingredient too many.

Parmigiana di Melanzane

SERVES 4
preheat oven to 400°F

2¼lb eggplants
sea salt
1 buffalo mozzarella (do not buy
    the supermarket elastic-band
    kind on the grounds that no
    one will notice once it is
    cooked)
a few tbsp of good olive oil
14oz can of whole plum
    tomatoes, coarsely chopped,
    without their juice
1 clove of garlic, peeled and
    bruised with the back of a knife
handful of basil leaves
vegetable oil for frying, a non-
    intrusive-tasting one like
    peanut oil
black pepper
½ cup Parmesan cheese, freshly
    grated
2 eggs, hard boiled

Peel the eggplants, and cut them lengthwise into ¼-inch slices, like long tongues. Sprinkle them with sea salt and let them drain in a colander for a couple of hours before rinsing them and patting them dry on paper towels.

Chop the mozzarella into tiny cubes. Heat a splosh of olive oil in a pan and add the tomatoes, garlic, and basil leaves, which you have torn by hand. Season and cook down at a brisk heat for a few minutes, before pureeing through the coarse disk of a food mill or food processor, making sure that the basil gets through the holes.

Heat an inch of vegetable oil in a roomy, heavy-bottomed skillet and test by dropping in a tiny corner of bread; it should sizzle immediately. Then put in a single layer of eggplant slices and fry until golden brown on both sides, about 5 minutes. This method of salting, drying, and cooking in hot oil prevents the eggplants from absorbing copious quantities of fat and ending up hideously greasy, I promise.

Drain the eggplant slices on paper towels. Brush the bottom of a gratin dish with good olive oil, cover with a layer of eggplant, spread some of the tomato sauce on top, and dot with mozzarella. Season with black pepper and strew with some freshly grated Parmesan. Then top with a few slices of egg before repeating the process. Finish the dish with a layer of eggplant, on to which you dribble a bit of olive oil before baking for 25–30 minutes.

Allow to cool for a few minutes before serving—this dish emerges molten and bubbling from the oven and too hot to taste.

My first trip to Sicily this year was to the heights of Erice, a mountainous village shrouded in swirling mists, through which, when a skein occasionally parted, the valley floor and sea would appear far below. I was at a conference on molecular gastronomy, with a group of international physicists, chefs, food technologists, and writers, a sort of crosscultural soup, which was at once inspiring and huge fun. Unfortunately, we had no time to travel the island and taste its legendary food, so much of which arrived with the Saracens. But a couple of visits to Trapani for good fish and the daily fresh ricotta brought in by two of the most delightful scientists I have ever met, Ugo and Beatrice Palma, with wine from their estate, did more to encourage my taste for Sicilian food than the famous Sicilian lemons I have always bought whenever I come across them. This Sicilian dish is great as an appetizer or main course, or accompanies game or cold roast meat. Make it in advance, and eat it warm or cold.

Peperoni alla Siciliana

SERVES 4

4 red bell peppers
1 onion, finely sliced
2 cloves of garlic, chopped
3 tbsp best extra virgin olive oil
½ an organic vegetable bouillon cube
2 tbsp best balsamic vinegar, and by that, I mean an aged, velvety black number that is mellow rather than sharp. Mine is a 20-year-old.
a small bunch of fresh oregano
18 best glossy black olives, halved and pitted
4 anchovy fillets in olive oil
1½ tbsp salted capers, rinsed under cold water
sea salt and black pepper

Broil your peppers until they are uniformly blackened and softened. Leave them to cool, then the skins should peel away easily. Cut the prepared peppers into long strips.

Cook the onion, garlic, and olive oil gently in a covered pan, with a bit of salt and a couple of tablespoons of water. You want the onion to be softened to a puree. Remove the lid and carry on cooking until the onion is golden, which will take about 40 minutes. Add the strips of pepper, the crumbled bouillon cube and the balsamic vinegar. Cook, uncovered, for 30 minutes longer, stirring occasionally. You can always add an extra tablespoon or two of water if the mixture seems to be drying out.

Add all the other ingredients, and carry on slow cooking for 20 minutes at a very low temperature; anything more and the anchovies will turn bitter.

Serve the peppers warm or at room temperature, with good crusty bread or with game or cold roast meat as above.

Capers are a classic with skate and a black butter sauce. This is another Sicilian dish, a great accompaniment to a plain poached wing of skate, or served spooned out into some hollowed-out Pugliese bread, or alongside it, either for an appetizer or a picnic. It's that sweet-sour combination that does it for me. You can make the caponata a day in advance—indeed, it tastes better if you do—and leave it out of the refrigerator overnight to serve at room temperature. If you want to make it even farther in advance, it can be kept in the refrigerator for a few days and then brought back to room temperature before serving.

Caponata

SERVES 6

3lb eggplants
sea salt and black pepper
vegetable oil for frying
olive oil
1 heart or 3 stalks of celery
1 large onion, sliced
2 tsp dark brown sugar
1 clove of garlic, chopped
14oz can plum tomatoes
4 tbsp red-wine vinegar
3oz salted capers, rinsed
3oz good green olives, pitted
a handful of flat-leaf parsley,
    roughly chopped

Peel the eggplants, cut them into ¾-inch cubes. Sprinkle them with salt, weight them down with a plate, and leave them to drain in a colander for an hour. Squeeze them out, and dry them on paper towels.

Pour the vegetable oil into a skillet so you have a layer about 1 inch deep. When it is hot, drop in the cubes of eggplant and fry until brown all over, watching that they don't burn. Drain them on kitchen paper. Cut the celery into matchstick strips and fry them in the oil until they are crisped and golden.

Heat a splosh of good olive oil in another pan and throw in the sliced onion, garlic, and a teaspoon of the sugar. Cook for about 5 minutes until the onions begin to color, then add the canned tomatoes and the rest of the sugar. Season to taste. Cook briskly for a couple of minutes before adding the vinegar and capers. Halve the pitted olives and add them, with the eggplants and celery, to the tomato mixture. Cook gently for about 30 minutes, adjust the seasonings, and leave to cool.

When just warm and jammy, scatter some roughly chopped parsley over the dish and serve, or keep as suggested above.

Smoky Eggplant and White Bean Puree

SERVES 6
as an appetizer, more as part of a mezze

1 eggplant
olive oil
2 cloves of garlic
14oz can cannellini beans, or cook
    your own
1 tsp cumin and 1 tsp coriander
    seeds, roasted for 30 seconds in
    a pan until they exude their
    scent, then crushed in a mortar
1 tsp sea salt
½ tsp fresh chili paste, or make
    your own by crushing a seeded
    red chili with a bit of sea salt in
    a mortar
1 heaped tsp tahini
juice of half a lemon
a handful each of fresh mint and
    cilantro leaves
olive oil
pepper

Cut the eggplant in half lengthwise, make slits diagonally in the flesh, and brush with olive oil. If you have a griddle, brush oil over it lightly, then place the eggplant halves on it cut side down with the whole, unpeeled garlic. If not, cook them on a lightly oiled baking tray in a medium to hot oven (350° to 425°F). Cook until soft and beginning to char.

Scoop out the flesh of the eggplant and the garlic cloves into the food processor along with all the other ingredients. Process until smooth, and check the seasoning. Serve with some hot, griddled pita bread.

The word "glut," so emotive in its conjuring up a surfeit, a superabundance, the natural world gone mildly, but irresistibly and deliciously, out of control, was almost invented for the tomato. The correlation between the last flaming days of late summer and the arrival of this most versatile of fruits, their splash of scarlet a seasonal sunset or epilogue, should inspire you to make a homemade ketchup, a real Bloody Mary, jars of fresh tomato sauce, or a pipérade, one of the glories of the Basque country.

Pipérade, or Piperrada

SERVES 4

1¼lb organic red bell peppers
olive oil
1 onion, chopped
1 clove of garlic, chopped
1¼lb ripe, organic tomatoes,
    skinned and seeded
8 large organic eggs
4 slices of ham, such as Bayonne,
    pata negra, or prosciutto
sea salt and black pepper

Broil the peppers in the normal way, turning them every few minutes until the skins are black and charred all over. Allow the peppers to cool before peeling, removing the cores and seeds, and chopping them.

Heat a couple of tablespoons of olive oil in a skillet and gently sauté the chopped onion over gentle heat until golden, adding the chopped garlic toward the end. Chop the tomatoes, remove their cores, and add them to the pan with the peppers, cooking them down until you have a meltingly soft texture. Beat the eggs, season with pepper—I never add salt to eggs at the raw stage as it turns them watery—and pour them over the sauce, stirring everything together to make a sunset-colored mixture. Be patient, cook very slowly, moving the eggs a little until soft and slightly runny.

Fry the ham separately in a bit of olive oil until crisp, and serve it atop the eggs. I think warm with a hunk of good bread is preferable to hot.

An unshowy and versatile dish that you can eat in its own right as an appetizer or light lunch, or can serve with a broiled chicken breast or a pork chop as a more substantial main course. If you look snobbishly down on the much-maligned stuffed tomato, think again. I know you will reconsider if you try this dish. You can prepare the tomatoes several hours in advance before cooking.

Tomatoes Baked with Olives, Mustard, and Gruyère

SERVES 4
preheat oven to 425°F

8 ripe medium-size organic
    tomatoes
sea salt and black pepper
16 glossy, best black olives, pitted
a sprig of fresh thyme
1 tbsp black olive paste
1 tbsp Dijon mustard
a handful of bread crumbs made
    with day-old bread, white or
    whole wheat
1 cup grated Gruyère
olive oil

Cut the tomatoes in half horizontally and scoop out the seeds and cores with a teaspoon. Place them cut side up on a baking tray, season, and plop a pitted olive inside each half.

Rub a few thyme leaves from their sprig with your fingers into the olive paste, then stir in the mustard and brush it over the tomatoes. Mix the bread crumbs with half the grated Gruyère and use to stuff the tomatoes. Put the rest of the grated cheese on top and pour a slug of olive oil over each tomato half.

You are now ready to bake, but you can leave these prepared tomatoes for a few hours before cooking them if it suits you. Bake for 20 minutes and serve warm, with a good hunk of bread or a roll if you feel like it.

Why? Because it's worth it. And don't say a Bloody Mary isn't an appetizer. It's the best precursor to a fine sirloin of beef that I know, and it is my pre-Sunday lunch, post eight-mile-run-and-bath ritual, which I would have to be shaken not stirred out of to consider giving up. My most recent convert was my best friend Janie while filming a 15-part television series *Tamasin's Weekends*. Actually, that is only partly the truth. The whole crew and production team were instantly seduced. Janie, in her inimitable way, showed somewhat insulted and shocked surprise that for so many years she had been unaware of the heights this drink could reach, and vowed to try it out on her husband as soon as she got home. Remember that a good Bloody Mary's strength is down to the individual. Janie's first comment when I asked her what mine needed was "more vodka." I am not sure whether she regretted saying that as the alcohol is so successfully masked by the strength of the other ingredients. Once you have made the real McCoy, you will never go back to your old habits.

A Homemade Bloody Mary

MAKES 6—8 GLASSES

2½lb ripe organic tomatoes
2 small stalks of celery from the
    heart, with their leaves
a small bunch of fresh cilantro
a sprig each of thyme, flat-leaf
    parsley, and rosemary
1 tsp grated fresh horseradish, or
    a proprietary brand that is pure
    horseradish
1 tsp grated onion
juice of 2 lemons
a pinch of dark brown sugar
a pinch of sea salt
a few drops each of Tabasco and
    Worcestershire sauces
vodka, about a third of a bottle for
    this quantity should do
half a tray of ice cubes

If you have a pretty, freezer-safe glass jug, put it in the deep freeze for 30 minutes before you make your Bloody Mary—and the glasses if you have room. That way, everything has a rime of frosting when you serve it; quite beautiful.

Cut the tomatoes into halves or quarters, depending on their size. Blend everything except the alcohol in a food processor or blender, then push as much as you can through a strainer into a bowl, forcing it down hard with the back of a wooden spoon. Pour the cold vodka into the frosty jug, add the contents of the bowl, and mix well. Adjust the seasoning and serve the Bloody Mary in the cold glasses.

If there are any would-be virgins among you, keep back some of the Virgin Mary before you jug it and add the vodka.

This is almost not a recipe it is so simple; the sort of dish you can cook in front of friends over drinks and eat as an ambulant appetizer together, inspiring the conviviality of the table before you even get to it. Dunk a bit of bread in the sweet-sour juices, balsamic is perfect for small game, and do eat with your fingers—quail and cutlery don't go. I cook mine "long leg," that is, with the entrails still inside them, but if you are squeamish, don't.

Broiled Quail Flavoured with Balsamic Vinegar

SERVES 4
as an appetizer, 2 for a main course

4 quail
olive oil
sea salt
black pepper
best aged balsamic vinegar
chicken stock

Preheat the broiler. Place the birds on their sides in a large gratin dish, brush with olive oil, and rub with sea salt and black pepper. Cook for 5 minutes, then repeat the process with the other side. Finally, splosh about 4 teaspoons of best aged balsamic vinegar over each bird, add a tablespoon of chicken stock per bird to the dish, and blast the quails under the broiler for a final 5 minutes. Gently pull a leg away from the body and pierce at the joint to check the quail are cooked through, then rest them, turning them in their juice for 5 minutes before eating.

When blood oranges are in season, they make a thrillingly beautiful Sauce Maltese, but better still is the sharpness of a Seville orange. The sauce is, after all, just a delectable version of a hollandaise, so perfect with fish. The sweet-with-sweet combination of leeks and scallops is a fine marriage, sharpened by a puddle of the unctuous and glossy sauce.

Scallops and Steamed Leeks with Sauce Maltese

SERVES 4

8 large or 12 smaller scallops
3 tbsp white-wine or tarragon
    vinegar
2 tbsp water
10 white peppercorns
3 large organic egg yolks
¾ cup best unsalted butter,
    l'Escure or d'Isigny are my
    favorites
sea salt
Seville orange or orange and
    lemon juice, to taste
4 fat leeks or 16 slim wands of
    baby leeks, depending on the
    season

Trim the scallops, leaving their coral whole and separate. Slice the whites into three discs if the scallops are large, two if they are smaller. Season just before you cook them.

Put the vinegar, water, and peppercorns into a small pan and boil down to about a tablespoon of liquid, then pour it into a bowl and leave it to cool for a few minutes. Beat the egg yolks into the reduced liquid, then place the bowl over a pan of barely simmering water and stir, adding small pats of butter, bit by bit, as they melt in. If by any ghastly chance the mixture curdles, the remedy is the same as it is for mayonnaise: First hold your nerve, then try to bring it back by stirring in a tablespoon of scalding water. If that doesn't work, start with another egg yolk, whisk it, then add a tiny trickle of the curdled sauce, starting drop by drop, whisking hard as you go, until all is well. Once the sauce looks as thick and glossy as newly washed hair, remove from the heat, season with salt, and add the juice to taste. You can leave the sauce for an hour or so before you use it, then heat it through over barely simmering water, making absolutely sure you don't overheat it: Scrambled eggs is not the idea.

I steam my well-washed whites of leek whole if they are the baby ones. If it is later in the season and the leeks are thicker, either peel off any tough outer layers and steam them whole, or slice them finely to steam. You want them soft right through to the point of a knife. Keep them hot while you cook the scallops.

Cook the scallop whites on a hot griddle or pan you have lightly brushed with oil before heating, or in a skillet prepared the same way—a minute a side until just stiffened and opaque should do, introducing the whole corals for 30 seconds a side. Scatter the scallops over the leeks and hand around the sauce in a pitcher or pour it over each plate, according to your taste in such matters.

Poor man's food they may be—in the west of Ireland, when my friend John Kilcoyne was growing up, "herring choker" was an abusive term used by those in the town who thought their country brethren were not as well endowed as they were, intellectually speaking—but that does not stop herrings from being one of the jewels of the sea's harvest.

Broiled Herring
with Sweet Smoked Paprika and Cilantro

SERVES 2
preheat the broiler

1 herring per person as an
    appetizer, 2 as a main course,
    and ask your fishmonger to
    fillet them for you
coarse sea salt
2 pinches sweet smoked paprika
1 tbsp fresh cilantro, finely
    chopped
1 small clove of garlic, finely
    chopped
lemon juice

Place the herring, butterflied out and skin side up, on the broiler pan and scatter on a good sprinkling of coarse sea salt. Put the pan as close as you can get it under the preheated broiler. The skin will bubble up, and the salt will spit. Leave for about 3 minutes. Turn the fillets over, they should be almost tender when pierced with a skewer, and place back under the broiler for only 30 seconds or the flesh will dry out.

Remove the herring and place them on serving plates. Scatter a tiny pinch of the smoked paprika, some cilantro, and a morsel of garlic on each one. Spritz with lemon juice and serve with brown bread and butter.

I have always found it curious how oily fish—mackerel, smoked salmon, smoked eel—are made less rich by brown bread and butter. Curious but true.

This dish should be marinated for 18–24 hours before you serve it, leaving only the potato salad to do a couple of hours beforehand. It is really a fish "tartare" perfectly pickling the fish without cooking it, and the effect of the white-wine vinegar is to ameliorate the oiliness of the fish. A wonderful appetizer if you are catering for huge numbers, since it cooks itself and you can make it in advance.

Marinated Mackerel with Potato Salad

SERVES 6

6–8 mackerel fillets (ask your
  fishmonger to skin and fillet
  them, removing all bones)

For the marinade:
½ cup good green olive oil
½ cup dry white wine
¼ cup white-wine vinegar
½ cup water
2 tbsp Pernod
1 lemon, sliced
1 bay leaf
a few sprigs of parsley, dill, and
  thyme
1 carrot, finely sliced
1 stalk of celery, peeled and finely
  chopped
1 shallot, finely chopped
a generous pinch of dark brown
  sugar
sea salt and black pepper

For the potato salad:
1lb waxy all-purpose potatoes
1 shallot, finely chopped
¼ cup good olive oil
1 tbsp white-wine vinegar
2 tbsp of flat-leaf parsley,
  finely chopped
sea salt and black pepper

Cut the mackerel into long, thin strips, 3 x ½ inch. Put all the marinade ingredients together in a nonmetallic bowl, add the strips of fish, and submerge them. Cover the bowl with plastic wrap and refrigerate for at least 18 hours. Bring to room temperature before you serve.

An hour or two before you want to eat, prepare the potato salad. Boil the potatoes and peel them while still as hot as you can bear. Quarter or roughly chop. Pour the various components of the dressing—shallot, olive oil, white-wine vinegar, parsley, and seasoning—over the potatoes while they are still hot and turn them gently to coat them in the dressing. Place a layer of the potato salad on each plate, or on one large plate. Then place some mackerel with its accompanying juices, vegetables, and herbs onto the potato salad.

Short of catching them myself—as I do in the west of Ireland—the only shrimp I would consider using for this stupendous, timeless classic of a dish are Morecambe Bay brown shrimp. Local fishermen have been catching them off the Cumbrian coast of England for more than 100 years. The secret of this classic dish is all in the spicing: Too much discretion and it will be invisible; too much flamboyance and all subtlety is lost, just like life. And it is the balance and quality of the spices that is important, no one should predominate, indeed, you should be nudged into awareness of each of them individually. They should be proper blades of mace and fresh nutmegs that you use, alongside a restrained measure of cayenne. You want it to hit, but not hurt. Lecture over. This is a dish that will happily stand to attention in the refrigerator overnight or over two nights, and can then be turned out with its halo of set clarified butter and deep pink flesh to be eaten with warm mixed-grain toast and a glass of ice-cold fino sherry.

Potted Shrimp

SERVES 6

up to ¾ cup best unsalted butter, l'Escure or d'Isigny if possible
a small blade of mace
cayenne
fresh nutmeg
2½ cups peeled, cooked medium shrimp
sea salt and black pepper
lemon juice

First clarify the butter: Melt it slowly in a pan, leave it a couple of minutes, then pour the buttercup-yellow pure residue, minus the milky curdlike solids, into two small pans, half into each.

Crush the mace in a mortar and add it with the tip of a teaspoon of cayenne and a grating of nutmeg into one half of the warm butter. Taste and adjust the spicing, remembering that it has a bit of competing to do once you add the shrimp. Leave to infuse for 5–10 minutes, then stir in the shrimp. Season, spritz with a little lemon juice, and put the mixture into 6 ramekins, packed tightly down. Cool, then put in the refrigerator to set.

When set, pour a layer of clarified butter over the top of each ramekin, and return to the refrigerator to set again. Take the ramekins out of the refrigerator about 20 minutes before you want to serve them. Using a fine-pointed knife dipped in hot water, turn out each ramekin onto a plate. Serve with some hot mixed-grain toast.

I will not be moved on the subject of salmon. I will not buy and will never knowingly eat the farmed stuff. The breeding methods, cocktails of chemicals and antibiotics, danger to the wild fish when the farmed ones escape and breed with them (thus weakening the gene pool), and the horrors of sea lice upon these poor, caged apologies of creatures, whose taste and texture is limp, greasy and flabby, is enough to make me determined that salmon should remain a special, albeit expensive, SEASONAL—that heretical word in supermarket quarters—treat. Once a year is fine by me, although I usually manage a couple of extra salmon caught by obliging friends in the west of Ireland in the summer. But it beats me why we have to pretend that salmon is not a luxury food and that it should be available all the year around. Thus are bad eating habits, greed, and expectation manipulated by the food giants. Here is my recipe for fantastic ceviche, uncooked but pickled and preserved in its winey, citrusy marinade. To be eaten alongside a sambal of cucumber, fennel, and avocado, with or without brown bread and butter.

Ceviche of Wild Salmon with a Cucumber, Fennel, and Avocado Sambal

SERVES 6—8

1½lb wild salmon cut from the middle where it is fattest, skinned and filleted (an operation your fishmonger should perform willingly)
¾ cup dry white wine
juice of 1 lime
juice of half an orange
juice of half a lemon
1 small onion, sliced into thin rings
1 clove of garlic, sliced thinly

Using a very sharp knife, carve the salmon, taken straight from the refrigerator, into slices ¼ inch thick and put them into a container that has a lid; an old plastic ice cream container is ideal. Add all the other ingredients, cover, and refrigerate. Turn the salmon over from time to time.

It will be ready to eat after eight hours, but keeps well for two days if you remember to remove the onion and garlic after the first day so they don't overwhelm the salmon's flavor.

To serve, strain off the marinade and put a tablespoon of the sambal alongside the fish. Accompany with good wholewheat or soda bread if you like.

Cucumber, Avocado, and Fennel Sambal

MAKES ENOUGH FOR 6-8

½ cucumber
½ red bell pepper
the flesh of 1 avocado
1 bulb of fennel, cored
lemon juice
a tiny bit of sugar
olive oil
black pepper
dill, finely chopped

This works well with a crab soufflé or fishcakes too. Simply skin and seed half a cucumber and half a red bell pepper. Chop them, with the inside of a cored bulb of fennel, as finely as you can, so they are somewhere between dolls' size and minced.

Chop the flesh from an avocado into slightly bigger cubes, then sprinkle on some lemon juice and a little sugar. Turn in olive oil to taste. Finally add some black pepper and finely chopped dill.

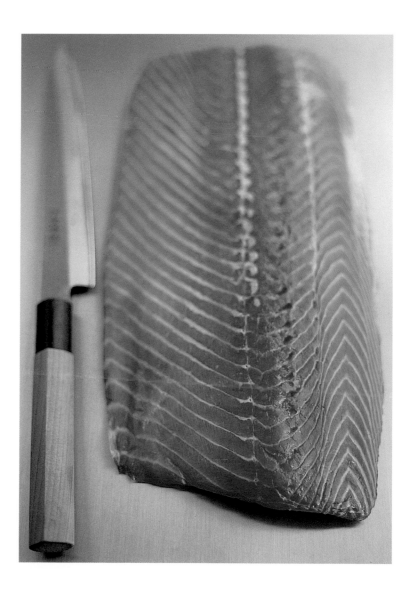

At the sharp-aired turn of the season, this dish—beloved of the Swedes with its earthy-sweet beet, sharp herring, and crème fraîche, and combination of raw, cooked, and pickled—captures and reflects the fall-to-winter shift. In medieval England such dishes were known as "salemine," which meant salty or highly seasoned, and referred to game as well as fish. They have transmuted over the centuries through "salmagundi" to the more modern "salmi." Either pickle your own herring with the very simple recipe given below or buy it from a specialist Swedish food store. If you are salting your own herring and pickling your own beets, you need to start making this dish three or four days before you want to eat it. If you've already pickled your beets and you can buy the herring from a store, start 24 hours before you want to serve the dish. Do not buy beet pickled in malt vinegar; it is too crude a substitute for white-wine vinegar.

Sillsalad

SERVES 6

10oz pickled herring fillets
4 medium-size pickled beets
4–6 waxy-fleshed all-purpose
    potatoes, depending on size,
    cooked, skinned, and cooled
2 tart eating apples
2–3 large cornichons or 4–5
    smaller ones
1 small onion, finely chopped
crème fraîche
fresh dill
black pepper

To PICKLE HERRING: Put the fish in a plastic bag with a cup of coarse sea salt to 2¼lb of herring, and store in a cool, dark place for 1–4 days. Remove the backbone, fillet the fish, and soak thoroughly in water to desalinate for 6–8 hours.

To PICKLE BEETS: Put whole, cooked beets in a jar and pour over white-wine vinegar and sugar, 4:1, to cover. Add one clove of garlic, a teaspoon of mustard seed, and 6 cloves. Screw the lid on and the flavor will be absorbed after two days.

To MAKE THE SALAD: Cut all the ingredients into rough ½-inch cubes and mix them together in a bowl. Add freshly ground pepper. Cover the salad and let it mature in the refrigerator for 24 hours.

When you're ready to serve, mix in some crème fraîche and chopped dill. Pile the salad onto a serving dish, sprinkle with some more chopped dill, and serve with some thinly sliced rye bread and butter.

As the author of *The Art of the Tart*, I have made my, and several other people's, fair share of tarts, to the extent that my publisher referred to me, during the gestatory period of the book, as "the Queen of Tarts." After the book was complete, I took a sabbatical. Neither a dessert nor a savory tart crossed the threshold of my stove for many months. Gradually the craving crept up on me, and first in line were these fabulous tomato and prosciutto tarts. I eased my way back into pastry making gently, by buying a sheet of the best puff pastry dough to make these tarts. Use a brand that is made with all butter; nothing else will do. Everything can be assembled before your guests arrive, to create as near a culinary heaven of a savory, ambulant appetizer to be consumed with drinks as this side of paradise allows. So, the only indulgence I crave is in repeating the recipe in this book.

Tomato and Prosciutto Tarts

MAKES 8 SMALL TARTS
preheat oven to 375°F

2¼lb best-quality puff pastry dough, of which you will need 10oz or so for this recipe and the rest you can freeze; make your own or use a brand that is all butter, nothing else will do
8 slices prosciutto
⅔ cup extra-virgin olive oil
3 cloves of garlic
black pepper
10 plum tomatoes, or about 40 organic cherry tomatoes
a handful of fresh basil and the same of either thyme or rosemary

Start with 10oz of puff pastry dough. Roll it out, and cut it out into eight 4-inch circles. Place them on a greased baking sheet and leave them in the refrigerator until you need them.

Tear the prosciutto roughly and put it in a food processor with half the olive oil, the garlic cloves, and pepper. Blitz for a few seconds to make a rough puree. Slice the plum tomatoes or halve the cherry tomatoes. Tear the basil leaves and add them to the remaining olive oil, but not more than 20 minutes before you are going to use them, or they will blacken.

Spoon a mound of the prosciutto mixture onto each tart crust, leaving a good-size edge free. Place a circle of tomatoes on top, brush with a little of the oil-and-basil mixture, and sprinkle with chopped thyme or rosemary. Cook for about 15 minutes, until the pastry is puffed up, golden, and cooked through. Put the tarts on a rack, brush with more of the oil-and-basil mixture, and serve them warm.

Slow-Roasted Tomato Tart

SERVES 6

For a 9-inch tart crust:
1 cup all-purpose flour
4 tbsp unsalted butter
pinch of sea salt
ice-cold water, 2–2½ tbsp
1 egg white

For the filling:
3lb ripe plum tomatoes
6 cloves of garlic, sliced wafer thin
5 tbsp olive oil
2 tbsp balsamic vinegar
salt and black pepper
a little sugar
3 egg yolks
⅔ cup crème fraîche
2 handfuls of basil leaves

Make the dough in the usual way, using the flour, butter, salt, and water. Place in a 9-inch loose-bottom tart pan and chill for at least 30 minutes before baking. Preheat the oven to 375°F. Line the tart shell with foil or parchment paper, then fill it with dried beans or ceramic pie weights. Bake the tart shell for 15 minutes, then remove the beans and foil or paper, and return to the oven for 5 minutes. Brush egg white over the pastry and leave it to cool. Turn the oven down to 300°F.

Place the tomatoes in a bowl and pour boiling water over them. Spike each one with the point of a knife and drain after a minute. Pour cold water over them and drain it off immediately; they will now be cool enough to handle. Slip the tomatoes out of their skins, slice them in half vertically and place them cut side up in a baking dish. Lay the garlic slices inside the tomato halves. Dribble the olive oil and balsamic vinegar into the halves and sprinkle with the salt, pepper, and a little sugar. Roast in the oven for about an hour, until shrunken and brown around the edges.

Arrange the roasted tomatoes in the tart shell, adding any juices from the baking dish. Mix together the egg yolks and crème fraîche and tear in the basil leaves. Season with salt and pepper, and pour the mixture over the tomatoes. Bake for 30–40 minutes, until the custard is set and light brown. Leave to stand for 10 minutes before turning out and serving.

This is a brilliant stand-in-the-kitchen-and-eat dish, which you can prepare in advance, cook in front of your friends, and serve straight from the pan with drinks. It is a dish most suited to a fish or vegetarian main course. I, for one, do not advocate meat-heavy dinners. You raise the temperature with the spice, then cool it with the guacamole, all in one mouthful.

Spiced Pork Meatballs with Guacamole

SERVES 8—10 AS A DISH-WITH-DRINKS

2½lb ground organic pork, fatty enough to stop the meatballs from drying out during the cooking
sea salt
1 red chili, finely chopped with its seeds
1 tbsp grated gingerroot
1 tbsp flat-leaf parsley, chopped
1 tbsp fresh cilantro, chopped
1 tsp fresh thyme, chopped
1 tbsp Dijon mustard
zest of a lemon, grated

Throw everything into a large bowl and mix together well with your fingers, making sure you don't rub your eyes afterward; chili is lethal. Form into small balls, the size of walnuts. At this point, you can refrigerate the meat for an hour or two until you need it. Remember, if you cover the meatballs and put them in the refrigerator, don't cook them until they come back to room temperature.

I cook mine on a griddle with no fat—there is enough in the meatballs—until crusted and crisped all over and cooked through to the stage where no pink juices flow out of the meat when you test it with a skewer.

The guacamole can be chilled for up to an hour before you want it, so all you need to do is spoon it over the meatballs, cold with hot, when they are cooked.

Guacamole

SERVES 8—10

3 ripe organic avocados
juice of 3 limes
1 chili, finely chopped, with its seeds
sea salt
a handful of fresh cilantro leaves, chopped

Mash the avocados on a plate with a fork until they are smooth, but with the odd lump for texture. Stir in the lime juice, chilies, and salt. Scrape into a bowl, cover, and chill for an hour. Stir in the cilantro, taste, and adjust the seasoning and citrus to taste. Lob spoons of the guacamole onto the pork meatballs hot from the griddle. If you want to eat this as a main course, you can make the pork balls into large, flat burgers, broil them in the same way, top them with guacamole, and put them over and under a good floury bun or tortilla.

This is a perfect fall dish, timely for the confluence of squash and porcini or chanterelles if, like me, you go out mushroom foraging. If you don't, you can use organic cremini or Portobello mushrooms.

Roasted Butternut Squash with Wild or Cremini Mushrooms and Cream

SERVES 4
preheat oven to 350°F

2 butternut squash, allow half a
    squash per person
butter and olive oil
2 cloves of garlic, crushed
    in a mortar with some
    sea salt to a paste
pepper
2 tsp rosemary or sage leaves,
    finely chopped
1¼ cups organic heavy cream
14oz mushrooms, but stick to one
    kind; to dilute the porcini or
    chanterelles with another
    mushroom is sacrilege
a handful of flat-leaf parsley,
    chopped

Cut the squash in half around their circumference, and seed. You will find that the seeds are contained in only one of the halves, but scoop out some space in both cavities. Put a generous lump of butter and a splosh of best olive oil in each cavity, with a bit of the garlic paste, the finely chopped rosemary or sage, and some black pepper. Reserve half the garlic for the mushrooms. Roast the squash until the flesh is soft, 30–40 minutes.

Brush the earth off the porcini, or clean the mushrooms with a damp cloth, before slicing them and frying them in a bit of olive oil until they begin to weep with juice. Add the garlic and cream and leave it to bubble, stirring as you go. Scatter the parsley over, season, and tip the contents of the pan into the squash cavities, stirring the cream into the butter. Leave to cool for a few minutes before you bring the squash to the table.

Richard Corrigan included this unusual, delicately spiced dish on the St. Patrick's Day menu we devised this year. It is beautifully "uncheffy," and most of the preparation can be done the day before, so all you need to do to serve is mix the cheeses and shallots, then arrange the plates with slices of wild smoked salmon. A lovely appetizer or lunch dish.

Smoked Salmon with Saffron-Braised Fennel

SERVES 4
preheat oven to 400°F

2 bulbs of fennel with the
    root left on
½ cup water
1 cup olive oil
3 star anise
a handful of green olives
    preserved in good olive oil,
    not brine, pitted and halved
a pinch of saffron
sea salt and black pepper
8 slices of smoked salmon,
    preferably wild
2 tbsp cream cheese
2 tbsp mascarpone cheese
1 tbsp minced shallots

Cut each fennel bulb in half, then each half into quarters or slices, depending on their size. Put them in a roasting pan or gratin dish with the water, olive oil, star anise, olives, saffron, and seasoning. Bring slowly to a boil, then cover with foil and cook in the oven until tender. Check with a skewer after 20 minutes. Cool and refrigerate—this can be done the day before.

Mix the cheeses with the finely chopped shallot. On each plate, arrange the fennel with a mound made out of a couple of the slices of smoked salmon, then add a spoonful of the cheese mixture. Serve with Irish soda bread.

Nothing last-minute about this dish, which makes a perfect cold appetizer or one of a series of dishes to serve at an al fresco lunch in the summer. My friend Brigid has brought this over to me in the casserole, the artichokes from her garden.

Globe Artichokes in an Overnight Balsamic and Shallot Dressing

SERVES 4

4 globe artichokes
½ lemon
2–3 shallots, peeled and finely
    chopped
good olive oil
balsamic vinegar, the best aged
    vinegar you can find, mellow
    and glossily black
sea salt and black pepper

Bring a large pan of water to a boil and acidulate it with half a squeezed lemon. Throw in your artichokes and cook without a lid at a rolling boil until you can easily pull an outside leaf away from its parent stem, 25–30 minutes. Remove and drain.

In a small pan, heat the finely chopped shallot very gently in some good olive oil until it is softened. Remove from the heat and whisk in the balsamic vinegar and seasoning to taste. Pour the warm dressing over the artichokes, and leave for as long as you can, preferably overnight. Before serving, spoon some of the escaped dressing over the artichokes.

Said to have been invented by a peasant for a hungry king, this dish has been cooked in Spain for at least 400 years. Every tapas bar seems to serve tortilla, with glasses of chilled fino or manzanilla, and although the classic rendering is made with potato, you can substitute onion, shrimp, bell peppers, spinach, chard, or what you will. I think tortillas make the perfect mouthful to accompany drinks, so absorbent are they, like blotting paper, arresting initial hunger pangs and any light-headedness concomitantly. The great thing, too, is that there is really no time of day I wouldn't serve a tortilla—late breakfast or brunch, lunch, on a picnic, in the early evening with drinks, or dinner itself. Tortilla can be served hot, warm, or cold.

Tortilla Española

SERVES 4

1lb potatoes, peeled and cut into
    small dice
6 large organic eggs
½ cup best olive oil
sea salt and black pepper

Do not use a voluminous skillet—you are making a cake of eggs, not a flat omelet. Heat the olive oil and, when it is hot, throw in the potatoes and coat them all over in the oil. Lower the heat and turn them gently every so often until they are cooked through. Remove the potatoes with a draining spoon and drain them on paper towels in a bowl.

Heat the olive oil in the pan again, with a bit extra if you need it. Meanwhile, beat the eggs with the pepper and pour them over the potatoes. Pour the mixture into the hot oil in the pan and cook over a high heat for a minute before turning the temperature down. Add salt and cook until there is no sign of liquid egg at the top of the mixture. Cover the pan with a plate and flip the tortilla over onto it. Add a splosh more olive oil to the pan, then slide the tortilla back into the pan, and cook for a couple of minutes longer.

Serve the tortilla hot or warm with a tomato sauce, on its own, or with a jar of Spanish piquillo peppers, roasted over beech wood. Or, eat it cold and cut into wedges, with a tomato salad. Once cooked, a tortilla will keep for a couple of days, and reheats well in a tomato sauce.

On my first night in Jerez in Spain, after flying into a pistachio-green and smoked-salmon sunset with Mark Sainsbury and Sam Clark of the lovely Moro restaurant in London, we were whisked off by our wonderful guide Bartolome Vergara to a tiny tapas bar. There we swiftly downed our glasses of chilled fino with dishes of tiny red mullet no bigger than leaves, and fava beans with Serrano ham, a wonderful combination.

Fava Beans with Serrano Ham

SERVES 6

2¼lb fava beans, fingernail size, not the giant toughies
6oz Serrano ham, prosciutto or organic back bacon
4 tbsp good olive oil
1 heaped cup minced mild onion
1 clove of garlic, finely chopped
4 large organic eggs
sea salt and black pepper
a handful of flat-leaf parsley, chopped

Cut or tear the ham into small strips and sauté it gently in the hot olive oil in a pan with the chopped onion until the onion is softened. Add the garlic and soften briefly. Throw in the fava beans, cover, turn down the heat, and cook until they are tender, 6–7 minutes.

Hard boil the eggs for about 7 minutes—I do not favor them being cooked until there is a grim black ring around a dried-up planetary orb—then shell and chop them.

Season the ham and beans, stir in the chopped egg and parsley, and serve warm.

A lovely Provençal hors-d'oeuvre, black, oily, salty—perfect to whet the most recalcitrant of appetites. Serve with a glass of chilled rosé.

Hard-Boiled Eggs with Tapenade

SERVES 6 OR MORE IF
THERE ARE OTHER
DISHES

6 large organic eggs
24 pitted black olives,
   the good Mediterranean
   ones kept in olive oil
10 anchovy fillets
   in olive oil
2 tbsp salted capers,
   rinsed on a slotted spoon under
   cold water
2oz best canned tuna
a scant teaspoon of
   Dijon mustard
olive oil
lemon juice
a few drops of eau de vie, Marc
   de Provence, if you have it,
   or Cognac
black pepper

Hard boil the eggs. Cut them in half lengthwise and scoop out the yolks to use in the tapenade.

Pound the egg yolks, black olives, anchovies, capers, tuna, and mustard together in a mortar. Then gradually amalgamate a couple of tablespoons of olive oil into the mixture, followed by a spritz of lemon and a breath of spirit. Season with pepper to taste; you will not need salt because of the salty ingredients.

With a teaspoon, fill the white egg cavities with the black tapenade. Serve cool. The tapenade will keep well for days and is equally good spread like a pâté on fingers of warm toast to be served with drinks.

This is an elaborate version of a Provençal anchoïade with the strength of a tapenade—magical, particularly on a hot day. Serve it with fingers of country bread, Pugliese or Boule de Meule are ideal, which you have brushed with olive oil and baked in the oven.

Anchoïade de Croze

SERVES 8

1 dried red chili
12 whole blanched almonds
12 anchovy fillets in olive oil
3 dried figs, roughly chopped
1 small onion, quartered
2 cloves of garlic, chopped
2 fronds of fennel
¼ cup mixed parsley, chives, and
    tarragon, roughly torn
olive oil
lemon juice
up to 1 tbsp orange-flower water

Put the chili, almonds, anchovies, figs, onion, garlic, fennel, and herbs in a food processor. Process to a thick paste, pouring in the olive oil in a steady stream, then adding the lemon juice and any extra olive oil to taste. Finally add the orange-flower water, a teaspoon or so to start with—it must scent not overwhelm.

Instead of serving the anchoïade on baked bread, you can oil the bottom of the bread, spread the anchoïade on the top, and bake in a hot oven for 10 minutes.

Canned simply will not do. I am not saying ever, but texturally you will not accomplish this dish unless you cook the chickpeas yourself. After all, soaking and cooking chickpeas has nothing to do with skill and time and everything to do with bothering, then leaving well alone. The effect of the libation of grassy, peppery olive oil upon hot, cooked chickpeas, or any other vegetable for that matter, is stimulant enough to the senses, releasing the scent of both and uniting them at the same time. When you stir in the chopped onion and parsley you complete the circle, scents and textures conjoined.

A Salad of Hot Chickpeas

SERVES 6

1⅓ cup organic dried chickpeas
an onion stuck with a
    couple of cloves
1 carrot, chopped
1 stalk celery, chopped
a sprig of thyme
a couple of fresh bay leaves
olive oil
a sprinkle of wine vinegar
sea salt
black pepper
1 small onion, sliced into thin
    rings
a little finely chopped red chili or
    8oz spinach (optional)
flat-leaf parsley, roughly chopped

Soak the chickpeas overnight in cold water. Next day, rinse them and just cover with fresh water in a large, flameproof earthenware casserole. Add the onion stuck with a couple of cloves, chopped carrot and celery, a sprig of thyme, and a couple of fresh bay leaves. Bring to a boil, skim for your life, then cover and allow to simmer at a mere burble for 2 hours.

Drain the chickpeas, turn them into an earthenware serving dish, and douse immediately with your best olive oil, a sprinkle of wine vinegar, and sea salt, which you must never add during the cooking because it will toughen the skins irredeemably. Add a good scrunch of black pepper and the onion, so finely sliced that the rings are papery thin and will wilt on contact with the hot chickpeas.

You can also add some finely chopped red chili if you feel like it or some spinach, the baby leaves if possible, which you throw in raw so that they wilt into the warm assembly. Finally, the parsley, a good green confetti of roughly chopped leaves. What could be simpler, yet more delicious?

A delicate summer appetizer or lunch you can leave in the refrigerator to set the night before you want it. How old-fashioned are the connotations of a cold mousse, but a light touch with the gelatin, the creaminess, the cucumber crunch, and the pale, sappy green of the finished dish are timeless and should not be consigned to the folklore of an earlier culinary era. At the last minute, peel some ribbons of cucumber with a potato peeler, sash length if possible, and drop them into the middle of the mousse.

Cold Cucumber and Ricotta Mousse

SERVES 8

1 organic cucumber, peeled, seeded, and diced small
1 heaped tsp sea salt
3 tbsp tarragon vinegar
½oz packet of powdered gelatin or the equivalent in leaf gelatin, my preference, see packet for instructions
1¼ cups organic heavy cream
2¼ cups fresh ricotta if you can get it, strained overnight through a strainer lined with cheesecloth, or ordinary ricotta from a supermarket that doesn't need straining
black pepper
a generous handful of chopped chives, parsley, and scallion

Mix the cucumber, salt, and vinegar thoroughly in a bowl. Turn the mixture into a colander, put a plate on top, and leave to drain for at least an hour. Remove the plate, and press down gently with a cloth.

Dissolve the gelatin in 6 tablespoons of very hot water, or as per the leaf gelatin directions in cold water, and cool to tepid. Make sure the gelatin is thoroughly dissolved, then whisk in the cream gradually until the mixture is smooth and very thick, but not stiff. Add the ricotta by passing it through the small disk of a food mill to aerate it as you go, then stir it in with the cucumber. Taste, and add a touch more tarragon vinegar and salt if you think it needs it, but do not make the taste too strong. Grind in the black pepper, then stir in the herbs and scallion. Turn into an oiled mold, and set in the refrigerator overnight.

Turn the mousse out onto a large plate just before you want it, by slipping the mold into a bowl of boiling water very briefly, then going around the edge of the mold with the point of a knife that you have dipped in hot water. Serve with wholewheat or caraway rolls (see page 16).

An old-fashioned ring mold is the thing I like best for making this tomato cream. You can heap some jumbo shrimp broiled with chili, garlic, and olive oil in the middle, or add some tepid fava beans that you have stewed in olive oil, adding a spritz of lemon and some chopped chives at the end, or simply some chopped tomatoes and cucumber. Or, you can surround the dish with eggs stuffed with tapenade (see page 58). Another forgotten dish that should reassert itself in the culinary canon. A sort of tremblingly set Virgin Mary if you think of the ingredients.

Tomato Cream

SERVES 8

organic tomatoes of a kind that
    really taste, although I
    shouldn't have to say that
gelatin
1 cup whipping cream
sea salt
Tabasco sauce
Worcestershire sauce
sugar

Skin, process, and sieve enough tomatoes to give you 1¾ cups Mix in the gelatin, dissolved as in the recipe on page 62, or according to the package directions. Add salt, Tabasco and Worcestershire sauces, and a little sugar to taste. The flavor should be strong, because the cream will mute it. You could also add some chopped tarragon, parsley, and scallion, or some chopped basil.

Chill until the mixture has thickened to the consistency of egg whites, then fold in the cream which you have whipped to stiffness, but not rigidity.

Check the seasoning again, scrape into an oiled mold, and set in the refrigerator overnight. Turn out and serve with chopped tomatoes dressed with herbs and oil.

The combination of garnet-hued beet, ivory sour cream, and green snipped chives is as beautiful as it is delicious. The tomatoes add a sour note to the earthy sweetness of the beets.

Chilled Beet Soup

SERVES 6

5 cups chicken stock
1lb small beets, cleaned, their
    whiskery bits left intact
3 or 4 good-size organic tomatoes,
    chopped
salt and fresh black pepper
lemon juice
⅔ cup sour cream
2 tbsp chopped chives

Bake the beets in individually wrapped foil packages in a hottish (375°F) oven until just tender when pierced with a skewer. Peel and cube them and add them to the hot stock, keeping one or two back to perk up the color later. Add the chopped tomatoes and keep the temperature at a blip for 20 minutes. Puree and strain the soup, then let it cool and chill in the refrigerator.

Grate the remaining beets. Season the soup to taste, add a spritz of lemon juice, and pour into bowls. Add a spoon of grated beets and one each of sour cream and chives to each bowl.

Iced Fava Bean Soup

SERVES 4

¾ cup chopped onion
4 tbsp unsalted butter
3 cups shelled tiny fava beans
4 cups chicken stock, really
    concentrated and jellied if
    possible
sea salt, black pepper, sugar
heavy cream (optional)
a few leaves of lovage, finely
    chopped, or sage if you don't
    have lovage

Cook the onion gently in the butter in a heavy-bottomed Dutch oven until softened, sprinkling on some sea salt to draw out the moisture. Add three-quarters of the beans, stir for a minute, and pour in the boiling chicken stock. Cook the soup at a simmer until the beans are done, about 5 minutes. Season with more salt, pepper, and a tiny bit of sugar.

Cook the rest of the beans even more briefly, by throwing them into boiling salted water for a couple of minutes, then draining and refreshing in cold water, and peeling them. Fiddly, but worth it—the baby emerald embryos lurking like jewels in the soup make all the difference. Puree the soup, strain it, and throw in the shelled beans, then leave to cool in a bowl in the refrigerator for several hours before you drink it. You can stir in a bit of cream if you want a rich soup, although I prefer not to. Sprinkle some lovage over each bowl when you serve it. You can eat this soup hot, in which case try frying the lovage leaves in a bit of butter until crisp, and then scattering them over the hot soup.

My cousin Deborah was horrified when she discovered I'd finished the manuscript for this book and she didn't feature. She has contributed to each of my books so far, and, more importantly, to my cooking and eating life since we were small, extremely greedy children. She remains one of the handful of people I most like to cook with, a rare attribute. We are totally simpatico in the kitchen, can communicate in shorthand, and can totally trust one another to come up with the goods with no fuss and plenty of fun. We have always joked that if our careers were scrapheaped, we'd always be able to earn a crust cooking a good dinner together. If it came to it, we would! This is the first of her three recipes for this book.

Green Salad Soup

SERVES 6

1 medium potato
4 tbsp butter
1 medium onion
8oz organic arugula
1lb baby spinach
8oz bunch watercress
2½–3 cups chicken or vegetable
 stock
1¼ cups milk
salt and black pepper to taste
a few toasted almonds
light cream

Peel and chop the potato into small dice. Chop the onion finely. Melt the butter in a large saucepan and sweat the onion and potato until soft and transparent over low heat for 5 to 10 minutes.

Add all the green leaves and sweat with the butter and onions until they have collapsed—about 5 minutes. Give them a stir from time to time. Add the stock and milk and simmer over a low heat for 10 minutes. Blitz the soup until you have a smooth puree, and add salt and pepper to taste.

Garnish with a few toasted almonds and a swirl of light cream on each bowl before serving. The soup can be served hot or cold, and with or without the garnish.

Predating Roman times, this ancient soup is said to have as many versions as there are mortars and pestles. If you are making it at the last minute, it can be whacked into the freezer for a 30-minute freeze down. If you have time, make it the day before you need it and leave it in the refrigerator overnight so the intense flavors mingle. On the day, just add a pitcher of cold water and stir to the desired texture and strength. I serve mine in glasses, but if you want to add little bits of chopped egg, olives, bell pepper, onions, or ham, serve the soup in bowls and let people spoon in the accompaniments. Use organic vegetables if you can.

Gazpacho

SERVES 6—8

1lb tomatoes, use organic canned
   tomatoes with their juice if you
   can't get good tomatoes
2 slices day-old white bread
   without the crusts
1 small onion, cut into chunks
2 cloves garlic, chopped
1½ red bell peppers
1 cucumber, half-peeled,
   quartered lengthwise, and
   seeded
2 tbsp best sherry vinegar
2 tbsp best olive oil
sea salt and cayenne
2½–3 cups very cold water
   straight from the refrigerator

Chop the tomatoes. I don't bother to skin them—you may prefer to—but I do halve and seed them. Hold the bread under cold water, then squeeze out the water and put it in the food processor with the onion, garlic, a teaspoon of sea salt, olive oil, and cayenne. The soup is meant to be piquant, not hot, so start with the tip of a teaspoon of cayenne, and correct at the end if it is not quite right. Blitz briefly to a pulp.

Add the cucumber, pepper, vinegar, and tomatoes and blitz until liquid. The mixture will be coarse rather than pureed. Pour into a bowl, cover, and chill as above. Just before serving, dilute with the refrigerator-cold water, stirring and tasting to the required texture and flavor. Adjust the seasoning and serve in tall glasses or bowls.

Dating back more than a thousand years to when the Moors ruled much of Spain, this is one of my favorite soups. Utterly unusual and subtle, it has an extraordinary ability to cool the imbiber on the hottest of days.

White Gazpacho, or Ajo Blanco con Uvas de Malaga

SERVES 4

1 cup organic Spanish almonds
8oz day-old organic white bread, the crusts removed
2 cloves of new season's garlic, peeled and chopped
sea salt
2–3 tbsp best olive oil
2 tbsp sherry vinegar
2½ cups water you have chilled in the refrigerator
a handful of seedless green grapes

Blanch the almonds briefly in hot water and pop them out of their skins. Process the almonds until ground or do it yourself in a mortar, if you are feeling purist and energetic.

Wet thick slices of bread under cold water, then squeeze it out. Tear it into chunks and throw it into the blender with the chopped garlic, salt, and olive oil. Puree, add the vinegar and almonds, and slowly pour in the cold water with the blender running. Process until smooth and creamy, then refrigerate for several hours.

Ladle into bowls and toss a few halved seedless green grapes into each one.

Sally Edwards, whose River Café in Taunton, Somerset, England, closed this summer, robbing a bunch of hard-line lunchers of the only star-in-the-diadem in what is a culinary desert, gave me this recipe when I wrote about her plans to go solo with a new café. They should have come to fruition by the time you read this book. In the meanwhile, several of her stunning recipes grace these pages and help the withdrawal symptoms for me at least, who now has no escape from the stove of a Saturday lunchtime. Sally makes her soup with a vegetable stock; I made my version with chicken stock. Experiment.

Thai Lettuce and Pea Soup

SERVES 6

1 tsp coriander seeds
1 tsp cumin seeds
2 medium onions,
    roughly chopped
1 tbsp olive oil
2 cloves of garlic,
    peeled and chopped
1 "thumb" fresh gingerroot,
    peeled and chopped or grated
½ tsp fresh chili paste or you can
    use some seeded red chili
    crushed in the mortar with a
    bit of salt
1 medium potato,
    peeled and cubed
1 vegetable bouillon cube,
    organic if possible, dissolved
    in 3 cups of hot water; or use
    3 cups of chicken stock
1 can coconut milk
2 cups fresh or frozen peas
1 head lettuce

Roast the coriander and cumin seeds briefly in a skillet for only 30 seconds or so until they exude their scent; any longer and they will burn.

Sauté the onion gently in a little olive oil. Add the garlic, ginger, spices, and chili and sauté for a few minutes longer until softened and translucent. Add the potato and stock, then simmer together for 25–30 minutes.

Add the coconut milk and bring back to a simmer. Add the peas and lettuce, and bring it back to a simmer before removing from the heat. Process in the blender, season, and serve.

With its swirl of vermilion rouille, this corn-yellow soup is a picture of fall and a bowl of balance: strong colors and flavors that neither suppress nor overwhelm each other.

Sweetcorn Soup with Rouille

SERVES 6

6 ears fresh corn
3 tbsp unsalted butter
1 medium onion, peeled and
   finely chopped
1 leek, white part only, washed
   and chopped
1 small carrot, peeled and diced
2 cloves of garlic, peeled and
   finely chopped
4 cups chicken, duck, or vegetable
   stock
6 tbsp heavy cream
sea salt, black pepper, sugar, and
   lemon juice
fresh cilantro, chopped (optional)

For the rouille:
7-oz jar pimentos, I prefer
   piquillo peppers
1 clove of garlic
2 red chili peppers, seeded
2 tbsp olive oil

Strip the kernels from the corn cobs with a sharp knife. Melt the butter, add the onion, and stew gently with the leek and carrot in a heavy-bottomed pan until translucent. Add the garlic about 10 minutes into the cooking. Pour the hot stock over, and carry on simmering for 10 minutes longer.

Add the kernels of corn, bring the soup back to a boil, then take the pan off the heat. Leave the pan for 5 minutes before pureeing in a blender. It will need a good 2 or 3 minutes before it is pureed enough to push it through a strainer. Then stir in the cream and season to taste with sugar and lemon as well as salt and pepper. If the corn is young and sweet enough, you will not need any sugar.

Make the rouille by simply placing the pimentos, garlic, chili, and olive oil in the blender with some seasoning and whizzing them to a scarlet paste to be dropped into the middle of the corn-yellow soup. Add a scattering of cilantro leaves over the summit, if you feel like it.

What an amenable root the parsnip is. It is enhanced by spicing, so it makes a stunning curried soup. It also allows its sweetness to be offset by a good, sharp cooking apple. I used the windfalls from under my apple tree in this fall concoction.

Parsnip and Baked Apple Soup

SERVES 6

1 small onion, peeled and finely
   chopped
5 cups peeled and diced parsnips,
1 large cooking apple
4 tbsp unsalted butter
4 cups chicken or vegetable stock
6 sage leaves, tied in a bundle with
   string
⅔ cup cream (optional)
salt, black pepper, flat-leaf parsley

Score the cooking apple around its circumference, core it, and bake it on a tray with ½ inch of water. Bake in a hot (400°F) oven until tender right through when pierced with a skewer.

Sweat the onion and parsnip in the butter gently for about 10 minutes, seasoning early on, then pour in the stock and sage, and simmer until tender. Remove the sage, puree the soup, adding the apple that you have peeled when it comes out of the oven, making sure there are no nasty tough bits around the core.

Check the seasoning, reheat with the cream, or without, and serve with a scattering of chopped parsley.

Cabbage and Bacon Soup

SERVES 4—6

2 tbsp butter
1 small onion, chopped
4oz organic thick bacon, snipped
    into strips
6 cups cabbage, cored and
    shredded
1 potato, peeled and diced
4 cups chicken stock
salt and black pepper
a few tbsp of light cream

Melt the butter and gently soften the onion and bacon. Stir in the cabbage and potato, then add the stock and bring to a boil. Simmer gently until the cabbage and potato are soft, about 30 minutes. Season, puree, reheat, adjust the seasoning, and stir in a few tablespoons of cream.

Sweet Potato and Cilantro Soup

SERVES 6

2 large onions, peeled and diced
½ in fresh gingerroot, grated
4 tbsp vegetable oil
4 large sweet potatoes, pink
    tinged if possible, peeled and
    diced
6 cups chicken or vegetable stock
1 cup cream of coconut
a handful of fresh cilantro,
    chopped
sea salt and black pepper

Heat the oil in a large pan and sweat the onions and ginger until softened but not colored. Add the sweet potatoes and stock, then bring to a boil. Simmer gently until the sweet potatoes are tender, and add the cream of coconut, cilantro, and salt and pepper to taste. Puree the soup in a blender or food processor, gently reheat, and adjust the seasoning if necessary before serving.

It seems that nearly every nation has a version of one-pot soup-stew; think of ribollita, pot au feu, borscht, for which you simmer in water whatever meat you happen to have and any legumes and vegetables you can find. The following recipe is Scottish; It is a soup of substance and address that is not really asking for anything to follow it. Quite the reverse, it is almost saying "I bet you can't eat anything else after this."

Barley Broth

SERVES 8

3lb neck of lamb or mutton
1 cup organic barley
1 cup split peas
2 carrots, diced
1 turnip, diced
1 rutabaga, diced
2 onions or fat leeks, diced
salt and black pepper
a handful of flat-leaf parsley,
    chopped

Put the meat in the bottom of a large, heavy-bottomed flameproof pot. Add 8–10 cups of water, then the barley and peas. Bring it to a boil slowly, skim until clear, then simmer slowly for an hour if it's mutton, 30 minutes if it's lamb. I mean so slowly that a bubble barely breaks the surface. Add the vegetables and continue simmering until the meat is really tender. This can take as long as an hour.

When the meat is cooked, remove it and the vegetables, barley, and split peas from the pot. Boil down the broth until you have a more intense flavor. Season, remove the meat from the bones, if you feel like a modicum of refinement, and return everything to the pot to heat through. Throw a good handful of chopped parsley into the pot and serve.

The mealy sweetness of sweet potato, with its beautiful orange flesh, and the sharp acidity of the cherry tomatoes with a smidgen of dark brown sugar to add minerally, treacly back notes, is an unexpectedly good combination in a soup. And the color is like an extravagantly unbelievable sunset.

Baked Sweet Potato and Roasted Cherry Tomato Soup

SERVES 6
preheat oven to 400°F

6 medium-size orange-fleshed
   sweet potatoes
1 onion
1lb or so of organic cherry
   tomatoes
a sprig of thyme
olive oil
a scrap of chili
a sprig of rosemary
4 cups chicken stock
1 heaped tsp dark brown sugar
sea salt, black pepper

Cut the sweet potatoes, in their skins, into chunks, about 3 per potato. Cut the onion into large chunks, and place both on a roasting tray. Splash a little olive oil over, scatter on some thyme leaves, some finely chopped rosemary, a scrap of finely chopped, seeded red chili, sea salt, and black pepper and turn the vegetables in the mixture to coat. Bake for about 30 minutes; the vegetables will not be hard when you test them, but they will not have reached softness through and through either.

Slide in the tomatoes, and a bit of extra olive oil if it looks as though there isn't enough to gloss them, and return the vegetables to the oven for 15–20 minutes, when everything should be done: the tomatoes weeping their luscious juices and beginning to split at the seams, the onion caramelized, and the sweet potatoes totally tender.

Skin the sweet potatoes while still as hot as you can stand and throw them into a food processor with everything else, including the stock which you have brought to a boil, and the dark brown sugar. Puree, then return to the pan. Bring back just to a boil and taste for seasoning and sweetness. If the tomatoes have made the soup too sharp, add a little more sugar before serving.

Every so often, only mild and delicate will do. There are times when I just do not feel like a gutsy, deep-flavored soup, but something pure and one note, reassuring in its simplicity and in the fact that it tastes of itself and its strength of character can stand alone. Florentine fennel with its slightly medicinal astringency is one such flavor that can support a pale but interesting soup. A much underused and undervalued vegetable.

Cream of Fennel Soup

SERVES 4

olive oil
butter
3 fennel bulbs, with their wispy fronds, but ruthlessly robbed of their tough skinned layers, chopped
1 small onion, chopped
1 tsp of dill seeds
salt, black pepper
4 cups chicken stock
a few tbsp light cream
lemon juice

Heat the oil and butter, a splosh of one, 2 tablespoons or so of t'other, in a heavy-bottomed pan. Add the fennel and onion, with about a teaspoon of dill seeds and some salt and pepper. Cover the pan and soften the vegetables gently for 15–20 minutes, peeking occasionally and giving an encouraging stir. Then add the hot stock and simmer until the vegetables are soft, about 15 minutes longer, before you push everything through the coarse disk of a food mill, my preference, or puree and strain.

Add a few tablespoons of cream, taste, adjust the seasoning and cream, and add a tiny spritz of lemon if you feel like cutting the creaminess a little. Reheat to boiling point, but do not let it boil. Serve hot.

You can, if you like, serve this soup with Parmesan "chips," or just *au natur* with a good roll or crusty French bread.

This soup does have guts, although they be vegetarian guts, and will quite happily stand alone as a main course. The flavors of chickpea, rosemary, and tomato predominate and then you add, at the last minute, some tiny pasta such as ditalini and finish with a sprinkling of grated Parmesan cheese. You can make the soup up to the point of cooking the pasta two or three days in advance and keep it in the refrigerator. You then reheat it, cook the ditalini, and serve with a bowl of Parmesan and a pile of soca pancakes.

Chickpea Soup with Pasta

SERVES 6

2 cups dried chickpeas, soaked overnight in plenty of water and 4 tsp baking soda
8½ cups vegetable stock, either homemade with 2 bulbs of fennel, 2 stalks of celery, a couple of onions and carrots, a leek, and a bunch of parsley and its stalks tied with a bay leaf, or an organic bouillon cube, or water
2 large sprigs of rosemary
6 cloves of garlic, peeled and bruised with the back of a knife
best olive oil
10oz organic tomatoes, skinned and seeded, or a 14oz can if there aren't any good ripe ones
1½ cups tiny pasta like ditalini
freshly grated Parmesan cheese
salt, black pepper

Drain and rinse the chickpeas. Put them in a large enamel pot and cover them with the vegetable stock or water. Add the sprigs of rosemary—preferably inside cheesecloth because they are not the easiest thing to fish out by their needles at the end—along with the garlicand 2 tablespoons of olive oil. Put the lid on the pot and bring to a boil. Lower the heat to an unpersistent simmer and cook for 2 hours before you check to see if the chickpeas are soft: They will harden if you lift the lid early in the cooking or salt them before they are cooked.

When the chickpeas are cooked, remove the garlic and rosemary and add the tomatoes, which you have put through a food mill or processed. Season and simmer for 10 minutes longer. Cook the pasta separately and add to the pan when it is *al dente*.

You can omit the pasta if you like, in which case, you can puree half the soup for texture before returning it to the pan. It would be too thick to serve like this with pasta.

Serve the soup in warm bowls, with some freshly grated Parmesan cheese to hand around.

These little pancakes, made from chickpea or gram flour, are simple to make and perfect to accompany the chickpea and pasta soup opposite. Gram flour is available from Asian food stores and good supermarkets.

Soca

MAKES 12

4oz chickpea or gram flour
1 tbsp fresh rosemary or sage,
   finely chopped
olive oil
1¼ cups water
sea salt

About 40 minutes before you want to serve the soup, mix the chickpea flour with a pinch of sea salt, a couple of teaspoons of rosemary, and a tablespoon of olive oil. Add enough water to give the mixture the consistency of light cream when you have whisked it well. Let it stand for 30 minutes.

Whisk again, then brush the bottom of a heavy skillet with olive oil. Heat until beginning to smoke, then drop a ladleful of the mixture into the pan, tilting the pan as you go to get a uniform covering. Sprinkle immediately with a little more chopped rosemary, fry for 2 to 3 minutes, then flip over and cook the other side.

Slide the cooked pancake on to a warm plate and keep warm while you make the other 11.

Another meal in a bowl, or precursor to something light, say steamed or poached fish. It is one of the few dishes that is always in favor with all three of my children, a distinct plus when one spends a lot of one's life feeling a little like a jaded short-order chef, struggling to keep up with the whims and mercurial fads of one's dependents.

Lentil and Pasta Soup with Smoked Bacon

SERVES 6

3 tbsp olive oil
2 small onions, finely chopped
6 cloves of garlic, finely chopped
2 stalks of celery, peeled and
    finely chopped
4oz organic bacon slices, snipped
    small
1⅓ cups Puy or Umbrian lentils,
    each the ultimate from their
    respective birthplaces
2 x 14oz cans organic tomatoes
5 cups chicken or vegetable stock,
    or water
3 sprigs of thyme and 2 fresh bay
    leaves
1⅓ cups small, tubular pasta, but
    not as minute as ditalini
sea salt and black pepper
a handful of flat-leaf parsley
1 cup Parmesan cheese, freshly
    grated

Heat the oil in a large, heavy-bottomed Dutch oven. Add the onions, celery, and bacon and cook slowly until softened and translucent. Introduce the garlic after about 10 minutes, so it doesn't become bitter. Add the lentils and stir to coat them in the oil and bacon fat. Add the tomatoes, chopping them down into the juice with a sharp knife. Bring up to a bubble, then pour the hot stock or water over. Add the thyme and bay, and bring to a boil. Cover and simmer for about 40 minutes, until the lentils are cooked. If the lentils are absorbing too much liquid, and beginning to look too thick for a soup, add a ladleful more of water whenever necessary. Season when the lentils are cooked through.

Cook the pasta separately until *al dente*, then add it to each soup bowl when ready. If you have enough soup left over to reheat, you need to cook fresh pasta for it, since pasta goes very soggy if it is left in soup and then reheated.

As with chickpea soup on page 80, this can be made a couple of days in advance, up to the point where you cook the pasta, and kept in the refrigerator until needed.

This is a classic Spanish soup, whose peasant ingredients and apparent simplicity belie its fragrance and subtlety. Garlic, chorizo, bread, and eggs—nourishment to the soul enlivened with sweet smoked paprika.

Sopa de Ajo

SERVES 4

a few tbsp of fruity olive oil

4 bulbs of garlic, broken into
cloves in their skins

3oz small organic chorizo

a sprig of thyme

the tip of a tsp of sweet smoked
paprika; it is as easy to overdo it
as it is with cayenne, beware

4 cups chicken stock

4 organic eggs

4 slices of country bread, Pugliese
or sourdough, toasted and torn
into rough bits

sea salt and black pepper

Heat 3–4 tablespoons of oil in a heavy-bottomed pan, then add the garlic and cook gently for about 20 minutes until the skins are golden and the flesh inside softened. Remove and squeeze out the innards as soon as the cloves are cool enough. Crush to a paste in a mortar with a little salt. Cut the chorizo into matchstick strips and fry in the oil until browned, then strip off the thyme and add it for a few seconds, followed by the garlic. Add the paprika and then pour over the hot chicken stock. Bring to a boil, then turn down to a simmer and season.

About 2 minutes before you want to eat, add the toasted bread and drop the eggs into the soup to poach. Serve immediately.

Golden saffron-infused liquid, ready for cooking a wonderful monkfish dish served with a spicy romesco sauce. Nothing complicated here but a spectacular result.

time to cook

2

It had to be good. The marathon culinary weekends undertaken by me and my friend George Morley when she comes to stay for the weekend have a lot to live up to. She is an outstanding cook, and as outstanding a scavenger of good recipes as I have come across, but then neither of us is entirely uncompetitive in that particular department. Last time she came to stay, I was in the throes of making a series for the BBC's new digital UK Food channel. A team of 15 was filming my weekends—alarmingly, every day became a weekend for 16 days. For once, I couldn't wait for Monday to mean Monday. George HAD to figure, she is one of the few cooks with whom it is a real pleasure to share a kitchen. On equal terms. Unfazed as ever, she arrived with her new-found recipe for bitter orange ice cream. Enough to make you swoon, despite the stress of it. In turn, she was treated to this dish and added a swag of her own, the most divine crushed Jersey potatoes with olive oil and thyme. I added the thyme—that is how things evolve when we start cooking. The result, we agreed, was up to standard, and that, in our most critical joint case, means quite something. Sunset-colored saffron and romesco; ivory potato; zucchini fried with pine nuts, golden raisins, and lemon juice. A feast of a dish. And her bitter orange ice cream, accompanied by tiny homemade hazelnut and orange cookies (mine), was a triumph.

You can make the gaudily brilliant sunset of a sauce an hour, even a day ahead, to dollop on top of the crocus-colored fish, which can be served hot, warm, or cold. Any leftover sauce can be kept for several days, versatile as it is, to eat with pork, chicken, vegetables, or fish. The fish needs 30 minutes or so to soak in its saffrony milk bath.

Monkfish Steeped in Saffron Milk with a Romesco Sauce

SERVES 5

For the romesco sauce:

2 tbsp whole blanched almonds

2 tbsp whole hazelnuts, roasted

8oz skinned and seeded tomatoes, or the equivalent from a can, with juice

2 cloves of garlic, finely chopped

6 tbsp best olive oil

a slice of stale bread, brown or white

2 tbsp red-wine vinegar

4 tbsp fino sherry

1 red chili, seeded and finely chopped, or cayenne to taste

For the monkfish:

2½lb piece of monkfish tail, taken from the thick end, on the bone

a generous pinch of saffron stamens

a few tbsp of milk

olive oil

sea salt and freshly ground pepper

FOR THE SAUCE: Roast the almonds briefly in a medium oven (about 350°F) until pale gold. Heat 4 tablespoons of the olive oil in a pan slowly, with the chopped garlic. When the oil is hot, remove and reserve the garlic and fry the bread briefly on both sides until crisp and golden. Remove from the pan, add 2 more tablespoons of oil and then the tomatoes and chili and stir until they are reduced and jammily thickened, 10–15 minutes. Grind the nuts in a food processor, or with a mortar for a better texture, then add the bread and garlic and continue to pound with the vinegar and sherry. Stir in the cooled tomato sauce, and serve in the mortar.

FOR THE MONKFISH: Cut the monkfish away from the bone, then cut each fillet into slices ¼ inch thick. Warm a few tablespoons of milk, then take the pan off the heat, add the saffron, cover, and leave to infuse for around 30 minutes. Put the fish in a single layer in a large dish and cover with the saffron milk. Heat some olive oil in a skillet, add the pieces of fish, and cook for a couple of minutes or so on each side. The point of a skewer should find the fish consistently soft right the way through when it is cooked. Season and keep the fish warm on a plate in the oven while you cook the the copious saffron-hued liquid to reduce it by about half. Pour it over the fish, and serve with the romesco sauce and the vegetables on the following page.

Griddled Zucchini

SERVES 4—6

6 small to medium zucchini
olive oil
lemon juice
sea salt and black pepper

Slice the zucchini lengthwise into long, thin tongues and brush both sides with olive oil. Heat your griddle or large skillet, having oiled it first, slap on the zucchini tongues and cook for a few minutes on each side until just resistant and branded with brown stripes. Remove, season, and spritz with a bit of lemon juice. Good served hot, warm, or cold.

Crushed New Potatoes with Olive Oil and Thyme

SERVES 4—6

2½lb new potatoes, scraped
best olive oil
2 or 3 sprigs of thyme
sea salt and crushed black pepper

Steam the new potatoes until tender. Tip them into a large earthenware dish or heavy pot with a few tablespoons of really verdant, grassy olive oil and crush briefly with a masher. Aim, as you wouldn't for mash, for a lumpy texture. Add the stripped thyme leaves and seasoning, then some more olive oil, and stir with a wooden spoon until softly lumpy and amalgamated.

The potatoes should taste of the oil, so it really is essential not to just use any old commercial olive oil, I use Seggiano or Ravida for this sort of dish.

Left: *Monkfish Steeped in Saffron Milk, with Griddled Zucchini*

This is wonderful with the monkfish and with much else besides. It is really a zucchini salad—it can be served as part of a vegetarian lunch or supper and eaten hot, warm, or cold. I serve it with the tomato and goat camembert tart from my book *The Art of the Tart,* or with pork, veal, or chicken. Don't worry about the zucchini being unevenly cooked. That, according to my friend George, is part of the charm of the dish—some are browned, some firm, some almost cooked to a pale green pulp.

Zucchini, Pine Nut, and Golden Raisin Salad

SERVES 4—6

6 medium zucchini
olive oil
a handful of golden raisins
a handful of pine nuts
2 cloves of garlic, peeled and
    finely chopped
lemon juice
sea salt and black pepper

Slice the zucchini into what my children refer to as money zucchini, and throw them into a heavy-bottomed skillet in which you have heated a few tablespoons of good olive oil. Cook, stirring as you go, until they are no longer completely firm and resistant. I hesitate to offer a time, because size and heat are the deciding factors, but around 7 minutes.

Then add the golden raisins, pine nuts, garlic, and plenty of seasoning. Let the pine nuts brown slightly before adding lemon juice to taste—use at least one whole lemon and possibly more. Cook everything together briefly to marry the flavors, then turn out onto a serving dish, preferably one of a contrasting color to show them off best.

There are movable feasts and interchangeable feasts. The next four dishes are the latter. You could use guinea fowl or pheasant instead of chicken. Just pay attention to the cooking times accordingly: cut up pheasants, say, are smaller than cut up chicken. If it is a whole bird you are cooking, always pierce the bird right through the leg with a skewer and wait for the juices to run clear.

I cut up a plump, small organic chicken to make this deliciously simple, but festive dish, and included the wings for succulence and glueiness. The sharpness of the vinegar was bubbled away and mellowed with a bit of dark brown sugar. I added little bits of butter at the end to gloss the sauce to a shiny caramel color. You do not always need to add wine to a stewed dish; indeed, the wine vinegar makes this dish less rich, but allows the flavor of the chicken and its exceptionally good texture to come through.

Pollo alla Cacciatore, or
Chicken Cooked with Red-Wine Vinegar and Herbs

SERVES 4

1 organic chicken, about
   3lb weight
2oz organic bacon slices
a sprig of rosemary, 4 sage leaves,
   2 fresh bay leaves, and a little
   bunch of thyme
olive oil and unsalted butter
4 or 5 Spanish piquillo peppers,
   cut in strips, or 1 dried chili
2 large cloves of garlic, peeled and
   bruised with the back of a knife
7 tbsp good red-wine vinegar
1 tsp sugar
4 tbsp butter
sea salt and pepper

Cut up the chicken so you have 4 pieces of leg, 4 pieces of breast, and 2 wings. Snip the bacon into small strips. With a mezzaluna or sharp knife, chop all the herbs together really finely and roll them into the bacon.

In a large, heavy-bottomed Dutch oven that will hold all the chicken pieces in a single layer and heat a generous splosh of good olive oil with a lump of butter, about 4 tbsp. Gently sauté the bacon and herb mixture with the dried chili if you are using it, and the cloves of garlic. Remove the chili and garlic once you sense the aroma of them has been released into the dish. Add the pieces of chicken, season, and brown properly on both sides for a total of 15 minutes. Add the strips of piquillo pepper at this stage if you are using them. Raise the heat and add the red-wine vinegar, then let it bubble furiously for a minute or so before adding ⅔ cup hot water.

Reduce the temperature to a gentle simmer, cover with a lid, and cook for 30 minutes longer, by which time the chicken will be tender when pierced with a skewer. Remove the chicken with all the herbs, peppers, and bacon to a heated dish and keep warm.

Boil down the juices for a few minutes with a teaspoon of sugar until they become more syrupy. Add some small pieces of butter to make the sauce glossy, check the seasoning, and pour the sauce over the chicken. Everyone can have half a breast and a piece of leg, and you still have the wings to suck on. I served this with brown jasmine rice and steamed ruby chard.

Organic guinea fowl are around 2½–3lb in weight, and I like mine hung for up to a week and uneviscerated. That way, the flesh begins to break down and tenderize, and the gamy flavor emerges without overwhelming. I threw both feet and giblets into the pot to help the juices along. I cooked this whole dish in about 45 minutes and it was sensational, the organic bacon adding flavor to the earthy lentils, and the Marsala, which I added in lieu of port, sweetening and fortifying the pan juices. Puy lentils are the best of the French, Umbrian the best of the Italian.

Guinea Fowl with Puy Lentils, Lardons, and Marsala

SERVES 4

a pat of butter

olive oil

1 guinea fowl, hung for a week,
    with its giblets and feet

sea salt and black pepper

a glass of Marsala (or port)

1⅓ cups Puy or Umbrian lentils,
    unsoaked

a fat clove of garlic, skinned and
    crushed with the back of a knife

a bay leaf

a bunch of fresh thyme

4oz organic bacon slices, cut into
    thin strips without the rind

3 large organic carrots, peeled and
    finely sliced

12 shallots, peeled, optional

a bit of heavy cream, optional

Heat a good-sized pat of butter and a generous splash of olive oil in a heavy-bottomed Dutch oven. When they begin to bubble, put the whole guinea fowl in the pot and brown it first on one side, then on the other for about 4 minutes a side.

In the meanwhile, wash the lentils and place them in another heavy-bottomed pot. Add the garlic, bay leaf, bunch of thyme, bacon, and a good scrunch of pepper, just cover with water, and bring to a boil. Skim, turn the heat to a simmer, cover with a lid, and continue to cook at a mild simmer, checking the pot from time to time, and adding a bit more water if the level gets too low.

After 20 minutes, bury the carrots and shallots, if you are using them, in the lentils and continue to cook until everything is softened and cooked through. Add some butter to the little bit of remaining liquid, season with salt and pepper, add a splosh of heavy cream if you are feeling so inclined, which I was, and keep the lentils hot.

Returning to the guinea fowl, brown each breast for 2 minutes before turning the bird over and sitting it on its back on the bottom of the pot. Season well and continue to cook gently for about 10 minutes. Add the giblets, feet, and Marsala, turn the bird on to its side again, cover the pot with a lid, and continue to cook for 7 minutes longer a side, followed by another few minutes breast up.

Pull a leg gently away from the bird sufficiently to see whether it still looks faintly raw and stick a skewer in to see if the juices still run red. If the answers are "no" and "no," pour the juices from the cavity into the pot as you remove the bird to a carving board, and let it rest for a few minutes. Place a shovelful—sorry, I am allergic to the word "bed"—of lentils on each plate. Give everyone half a leg and some breast, then pour over the pan juices. Mashed potato, and plenty of it, is a *sine qua non*.

There are dishes whose pedigree is so unimpeachable you cannot alter them one iota; they are true thoroughbreds. This particular one came into my hands through two generations of top-drawer cooks, Tim Withers of The George and Dragon in Wiltshire, England, whose dish it is, via the illustrious chef and food writer Simon Hopkinson. As Simon has noted, "One cup of tarragon may seem a lot but, believe me, it makes all the difference." I cannot implore you enough to try this dish: it is as good as it gets and there is no difficulty in its execution. Even if there were it would be worth it. Worthy of your most serious or celebratory of occasions.

Chicken Savoyarde

SERVES 6

For cooking the chicken:
4¼lb organic chicken
2 onions, peeled, and one of them stuck with 2 cloves
2 carrots, peeled and sliced in half lengthwise
3 stalks of celery, chopped in half
2 leeks, trimmed and well washed
2 bay leaves and 2 sprigs of thyme
salt

For the sauce and to finish:
4 tbsp butter
½ cup all-purpose flour
1¾ cups poaching stock
1¼ cups dry white wine
1 cup heavy cream
¾ cup grated Gruyère cheese
1 tbsp Dijon mustard
1 cup tarragon leaves, chopped
salt and pepper
½ cup fresh bread crumbs
¼ cup grated Parmesan cheese

Put the chicken in a large pot, and add the vegetables, herbs, and salt. Poach very gently for around an hour and a half, skimming off any scum that comes to the surface. Once cooked, lift out the bird and allow to cool. Strain the stock through a fine strainer and discard all solids. Leave to settle and lift off any surface fat using several sheets of absorbent paper towels.

Remove all meat from the chicken carcass (discarding skin and also removing all sinews from the drumsticks) and cut into large, bite-size pieces.

To make the sauce, melt the butter in a pan, add the flour, and cook for 3 minutes without browning. Gradually add the hot chicken poaching stock, white wine, and cream, and stir until thickened. Stir in the cheese, mustard, and tarragon, correct the seasoning, and simmer all together for about 20 minutes.

Preheat the oven to 450°F. Put the chicken in a buttered gratin dish, pour the sauce over, and sprinkle with the bread crumbs and Parmesan cheese. Bake in the preheated oven for 20–25 minutes until the dish is golden brown and bubbling around the edges. Eat with buttered new potatoes and a crisp green salad.

A small organic chicken, 2½ pounds or so, will feed four or more people, depending on whether the bird or the vegetables have the starring role.

Roasted Chicken and Leeks with Lemon and Tagliatelli

SERVES 4
preheat oven to 400°F

1 onion, peeled and quartered
1 organic lemon, quartered
2½lb organic chicken
1 onion, peeled and sliced
½ cup butter
sea salt
black pepper
8 leeks, cleaned and trimmed
olive oil
1lb 2oz tagliatelli
juice of a lemon and its finely
   zested rind

Quarter a peeled onion and a whole organic lemon and put alternate hunks inside the chicken. Place the bird on top of a peeled sliced onion in a roasting pan. Rub a generous amount of butter on the breast of the bird, and sprinkle over a good pinch of sea salt and a generous scrunch of black pepper.

Roast for 30 minutes, then baste the bird with the buttery juices and throw in the cleaned, trimmed leeks cut into short batons, roll them in the butter, and add a splosh of olive oil. Season. Return to the oven for 30 minutes longer. I add the chicken liver (from the chicken) to the roasting pan for the final 5 minutes cooking.

Meanwhile, bring a large pan of water to a boil. Test the chicken and leeks with a skewer to check they are cooked through. Transfer the chicken to a carving board to rest and leave for a further rush of fugitive juices to escape.

Cook your tagliatelli, about 4 ounces per person, none of that silly 2 ounce nonsense. When *al dente*, drain the pasta, leaving a bit of cooking water to lubricate it. Return it to the pot, then add a pat of butter, the meat juices, chicken liver and leeks, the juices from the bird's cavity, everything that has collected in the roasting pan, and the juice of a whole lemon and its zest.

Quickly carve hunks of hot flesh with their crispy, salty skin from the bird and throw them into the pot, mixing all the ingredients before you serve.

Tarragon and Garlic Chicken

SERVES 3–4

preheat oven to 400°F

1 organic chicken
4 tbsp unsalted butter
3 cloves of new season's garlic,
    crushed with the back of a knife
    and finely chopped
a bunch of French tarragon,
    chopped
spritz of lemon juice
sea salt and black pepper
1 lemon, quartered
1 small onion, quartered
olive oil

Push both hands under the skin of the chicken breast, easing it away from the flesh without tearing it, and do the same with the legs. Mash the butter with a fork and amalgamate with the garlic, tarragon, a spritz of lemon juice, and the seasoning.

Place a quarter of the herb butter on one breast under the skin, flattening it out with your fingers, then do the same with the other side and the legs. Put the lemon and onion inside the chicken, squeezing a little lemon juice over the breast first.

Pour a little good olive oil over the chicken, which you have placed breast up in a small roasting pan. Season the skin and cook for about 50 minutes, basting with the buttery juices two or three times. Remove from the oven and leave to rest for 10 minutes.

Pour the extra juices from the bird's cavity into the roasting pan, and carve. I served my chicken with rice made green with extra tarragon, and some spinach cooked briefly with no liquid, then turned into a béchamel sauce enriched with heavy cream.

Risotto slips easily into the category of food best described as soothing. Comforting as it is in the eating, it is the cooking, with the gradual, gentle application of hot stock and the repetitive, mesmeric stirring of the wooden spoon, that makes it a relaxing ritual that is also simplicity itself, IF you follow the rules. I had rather thought my leek and Vacherin Mont d'Or risotto was the pinnacle of my risotto making, but was overjoyed to be proved wrong when I encountered this recipe from the peerless Italian food writer Anna Del Conte. She, in turn, ascribes it to Giovanni Goria, of the Accademia Italiana della Cucina, via her friend Romana Bosco, who runs a cookery school in Turin. Whenever I have empty refrigerator syndrome, this is one of the few dishes I can still conjure out of the ether for six, eight, ten, even twelve. A house without lemons, good olive oil, Parmesan cheese, and risotto rice is an empty house indeed.

Risotto with Lemon

SERVES 4

4 tbsp unsalted butter
1 tbsp olive oil
2 shallots, minced
1 stalk of celery, minced
1½ cups Italian rice, such as
    arborio
4¼ cups homemade light meat or
    vegetable stock
5 or 6 fresh sage leaves
a small sprig of fresh rosemary
1 organic lemon, zest and juice
1 organic egg yolk
4 tbsp freshly grated Parmesan
    cheese
4 tbsp heavy cream
salt and black pepper

Heat half the butter, the oil, and the minced shallots and celery in a heavy saucepan and cook until the *soffritto* of shallot and celery is done, about 7 minutes. Mix in the rice and continue cooking and stirring until the rice is well coated in the fats and partly translucent.

While this is happening, heat the stock and keep it simmering all through the preparation of the dish. When the rice becomes shiny and partly translucent, pour in about ⅔ cup of the stock. Stir very thoroughly and cook until the rice has absorbed most of the stock. Add another small ladleful of simmering stock and continue in this manner until the rice is ready. You might not need all the stock. Good-quality Italian rice takes about 20 minutes to cook.

Meanwhile, chop the herbs and mix with the lemon zest, adding them to the risotto half way through the cooking. In a small bowl combine the egg yolk, the juice of half the lemon, the Parmesan cheese, cream, and a very generous grinding of black pepper. Mix well with a fork.

When the risotto is *al dente,* draw the pan off the heat and stir in the egg-and-cream mixture and the remaining butter. Cover the pan and leave to rest for 2 minutes or so. Check the seasoning, and that there is enough lemon juice, then give the risotto an energetic stir, transfer it to a heated dish or bowl, and serve at once with more grated Parmesan in a bowl if you wish.

Anna suggests that this dish is also a good accompaniment to costolette alla milanese, or chicken cut up, sautéed in butter, and cooked in a casserole in the oven with 1 cup heavy cream poured over—an old Milanese recipe.

Risottos do not stand around well, but I have found it absolutely fine to get the risotto to the halfway stage up to an hour before you want to serve it, then leave it with a ladleful of hot stock poured over it and a tight lid on it while you have your first course or drinks. Then carry on with another ladleful of stock, cooking the rice for its last 10 minutes. It is as good a first course as it is a main one if you are doing something more than a family lunch or supper.

Continuing with the lemony theme, here is a dish that wouldn't shame your smartest dinner. I take a sort of perverse pride in wowing people with dishes that use the very best ingredients transformed through the alchemy of the stove, yet are almost ludicrously easy in their execution. Remember Carême's dictum, "*faites simple.*" You can offer a bowl of home-made romesco sauce if you feel like it, it works wonderfully well with white fish. The cod—thick, whitely translucent, so tender that it falls away from the skin in giant flakes—is a dish that shuns embellishment, except the best grassy green olive oil. It doesn't even need spritzing with lemon—the Greek potatoes with which you marry the cod bring that, absorbing olive oil, lemon juice, and the scent of the herbs, and almost braising in their own juice.

Baked Cod with Greek Potatoes

SERVES 4
preheat oven to 400°F

For the potatoes:
2¼lb potatoes, cut long and thin, rather than chunky, into about 4 pieces if they are medium size
⅓ cups onion, peeled and finely chopped
6 cloves of garlic
a handful fresh thyme or oregano
salt and black pepper
1¼ cups best olive oil
the juice of 2 lemons

For the fish:
1 thick fillet of really fresh cod, about 2¼lb, and by thick, I mean 1–1½ in
olive oil
sea salt and black pepper

Put the peeled and sliced potatoes into a gratin dish or roasting pan so that they fit snugly in one layer. Throw in the onion and garlic, then the herbs stripped from their stems. Season and add the olive oil and lemon juice. Now add enough water barely to cover. Cook for 45 minutes before turning the potatoes over and cooking for another 45 minutes. An hour and a half should do it. Cook your fish during the last 15 minutes.

Butter a gratin dish thickly and lay your cod to rest in it, skin side down. Dribble some really fine olive oil over the top and season well. Bake for 15 minutes, then test with the point of a sharp knife or skewer. If it goes right through the flesh with ease and no resistance, the fish is done.

This dish works beautifully with "upscale" mushy peas. By that, I mean a packet of organic split green peas, which need washing but not soaking, and cooking for about 45 minutes to an hour in water that just covers them by ¼ inch or so. Do not salt until cooked, and skim them when they come to a boil, before turning them down to a simmer. When cooked, drain off a bit but not all of the remaining cooking water, add a good lump of unsalted butter, season, and serve with a bunch of fresh mint chopped and stirred in once they are off the heat.

The extraordinarily talented Stephen Markwick, chef/proprietor of Bristol's best restaurant, Markwick's, and ex-pupil of the great George Perry-Smith, was cooking this dish last time I steamed into his kitchen to watch him at work and write about him. He has quietly been going about his business for several decades, but his dedication to the kitchen and the pursuit of good cooking is as unstale as it is unfaltering. I have never tasted anything less than excellent when dining there, and have always been impressed by the way in which he has plowed his own furrow. Elizabeth David is an influence without being obtrusively and obviously so, Stephen is too creative for that, and times, after all, have moved on. Stephen serves this lovely dish as a first course with a few croutons of thinly sliced baguette brushed with a little olive oil and crisped in the oven. I think it is as successful as a main course served with plainly cooked rice. Slow braising renders the squid softly succulent, as does cooking it in a flash. Anything in between and you end up with something chewy and rubbery. It will wait around in the pot for you if need be, and it is as delectable warm as it is brought straight from the stove.

Braised Squid
with Leeks, Fennel, Orange, Chili, and Red Wine

SERVES 6 AS AN
APPETIZER, 4 AS A MAIN
preheat oven to 275°F

1 onion, peeled and sliced

4 cloves of garlic, peeled and
  sliced

1 leek, trimmed, sliced, and well
  washed

1 small bulb of fennel, sliced

2–3 tbsp olive oil

equal quantities of fennel seeds,
  dill seeds, and coriander seeds,
  ground together to make 1 tbsp
  in all

2 small, hot chilies, chopped

2¼lb cleaned squid, the body cut
  into rings, the wings into strips,
  and the tentacles left whole

zest and juice of 2 oranges

½ bottle red wine

a small handful of fresh cilantro
  leaves, chopped

to finish: a little extra grated
  orange zest and chopped garlic
  mixed together

In a heavy-bottomed Dutch oven, gently fry the onion, garlic, leek, and fennel together in the olive oil until soft. Add the ground seed mixture and the chilies, then stir in the squid. Stir around a little until the squid has stiffened and then introduce the zest and juice of 2 oranges and the red wine. Season well (squid absorbs a great deal of salt) and bring everything to a simmer. Cover and braise slowly in the oven for about 2 hours.

Stir in the chopped cilantro, sprinkle over the extra orange zest and garlic, and serve directly from the pot in either of the ways suggested in the introduction opposite.

I have been cooking hare, although all too infrequently, since I left university for my first job at Anglia Television in Norwich, England. There was a fine game shop in Norwich, which had lavish displays of everything of a furred and feathered nature, both in and outside the shop. Shoveller duck, the spoonbill with a shovel-like beak—muddied from its feeding from the bottom of ponds—widgeon, teal, snipe, glorious woodcock, braces of pheasant, pigeon, and partridge, hares, and the much-spurned meat of the postwar bunny. "Watership Down" the sign on the shop window read, "you've read the book, you've seen thc film, now try the pie." And I did. I cooked my way through as much of the winter repertoire as I could afford, learning as I did so from Jane Grigson, Elizabeth David, the shop, and the gradual gleamings of intuition my burgeoning experience suggested to me.

I never realized at the time quite how lucky I was to have stumbled on this rarest of shops, where you could order, for a kingly rather than princely sum to me, a newly ex-student, half a dozen saddles of hare with the blood and the innards if the fancy took you, and cook a civet with aillade entirely from this most prized part of the animal. I have to say, since the continuous tenancy of a family of hares in my west of Ireland field, that I have not looked in so gung-ho a fashion on bringing these beautiful creatures to table. Except in March, that is, when the mad March hares cavort with a sort of semicrazed abandon, often ending up as road kill, begging me to alight from my bike and sling the still warm ginger-faced victims across the handlebars to take home and gut in my shed. Like all good seasonal treats—once a year and honor is satisfied.

Civet of Hare with an Aillade

SERVES 4

preheat oven to 275°F

1 hare or rabbit, cut up
all-purpose flour, salt and pepper
goose fat or olive oil and butter
2 carrots, diced
2 onions, chopped
a few cloves of garlic
3 stalks of celery, strung and
 sliced

For the marinade:
1 bottle robust red wine
1 tbsp Cognac
2 tbsp olive oil
1 onion, thinly sliced
a few cloves of garlic, bruised
a couple of strips of orange zest
a couple of bay leaves
about 12 juniper berries, bruised
 rather than crushed
the same amount of peppercorns

For the aillade:
liver and kidneys of the hare
4 slices organic bacon, finely
 snipped
6 or 7 cloves of garlic, chopped
 into tiny dice
4 shallots, chopped into tiny dice
4 tbsp red-wine vinegar
a blade of mace
a sprig of thyme
salt and pepper

Mix the marinade ingredients and marinate the jointed hare for as long as it suits you, anything from one to three days.

Remove the hare from the marinade and dry the pieces thoroughly with paper towels, before rolling them in seasoned flour. I find shaking a few tablespoons of flour with some salt and pepper into a Ziploc bag, and sealing the hare inside it while you briefly toss it around is the best way to do the job unmessily, and without a surfeit of flour adhering to the pieces.

Heat some goose fat or olive oil and butter in a heavy-bottomed Dutch oven. Brown the two hind legs and the saddle cut into two portions for a few minutes on each side and then remove them to a plate.

Scrape up any crusty brown bits from the pan, add more fat if you need to, and gently sauté together the carrots, onions, garlic, and celery. When they have begun to soften, place the pieces of hare on the vegetables, season well with salt and pepper, strain the marinade over the meat, and bring gently to a simmer. Cover with a layer of parchment paper and a lid, and cook very gently for about two hours, either in the oven or on top of the stove.

Meanwhile, make your aillade. Chop the hare liver and kidneys and put them, with the bacon, garlic, and shallots, in a small pan with 4 tablespoons of red-wine vinegar, the blood of the hare, mace, and thyme and seasoning. Simmer at a whisper for a couple of hours, stirring occasionally to prevent anything from sticking. Pour the contents of the pan over the hare before serving. You might feel like offering a tart jelly as an accompaniment—rowan or crab apple work well.

The following day, you can add the ribs and fore legs to the pot of hare bones and remaining sauce, cover with water, having added the usual stock vegetables, and simmer for a couple of hours until you have the base for a wonderfully gamy hare soup.

I rarely cook boned roast meat. The Chinese have an expression, "the nearer the bone, the sweeter the meat," and, of course, the better the flavor. But opening out a roast of lamb or pork when the bone has been removed, flavoring it with something quite different, or piling it full of stuffing, is a different thing altogether, and can be a lovely variant to the standard Sunday roast. Pork marries beautifully with the *digestif* of a herb that is fennel seed, and the star anise, dill seed, Pernod, and oily orange zest work harmoniously together, particularly if rubbed well into the meat and left to penetrate for some time. If you can, buy organic pork with a thick coating of ivory fat.

Roast Boned Leg of Pork
with a Spiced Orange Rub and Orange Sweet Potatoes

SERVES 8
preheat oven to 400°F

For the marinade:
2 tsp fennel seeds
3 star anise
1 tsp dill seeds
sea salt and black pepper
2 crushed fresh bay leaves
a handful of fresh dill, chopped
zest of 2 organic oranges, grated
olive oil
2 tbsp Pernod

4¼lb boned leg of pork, untied
1 onion, sliced
sweet potatoes, 1 per person
    depending on size

If you can prepare this the night before, do; the maceration will tenderize and flavor more deeply. Crush the fennel seeds coarsely with the star anise, dill seeds, sea salt, black peppercorns, and bay in a mortar, then add the fresh dill and orange zest and stir in 2 or 3 tablespoons of olive oil. Rub the paste well into the opened-out pork where the bone has been removed and all over the outside of the meat and into the crevices where the fat has been slashed. Not easy, but pull it apart and try and push the paste into the gaps. Concentrate on the inside of the roast, the fat, and the ends. Splosh on a bit of Pernod and leave covered and in the refrigerator overnight or for as long as you've got.

Bring the meat to room temperature before you roll it up and tie it with string at 1-inch intervals. Place the joint on top of a sliced onion in a roasting pan. Sprinkle some sea salt over the fat and put it in the oven. After 40 minutes, baste and turn the oven down to 375°F. When the roast has been cooking for about an hour, chop each sweet potato, unpeeled, into 2 or 3 pieces, roll in the fat surrounding the meat, and cook with the roast for 40 minutes, turning them over at half time. The pork will need to rest, uncovered, for 20 minutes. Do not cover it, or you will jeopardize the brittle, mahogany-colored fat.

If you don't already know about this cut of meat, I suggest you become acquainted with it. It is the perfect cut for when you want to lavish on your guests or family something seriously uncheffy, but stunning, for lunch or dinner. You can scythe through the chine bones with a flourish, giving everyone a juicy, thick white loin chop on the bone. Next to it, sit a whole baked apple, which you have cored and scored around its circumference and stewed in the fatty juices from the meat and some tartly dry hard cider.

Roast Chined Loin of Pork
with Baked Apples and Cider Gravy

SERVES 6
preheat oven to 400°F

2 large onions
4¼lb chined loin of organic pork,
    preferably from an old breed
    with a good fat covering
plenty of coarse sea salt and
    freshly ground black pepper
6 large apples of the sort that
    don't collapse
6 fresh bay leaves
1¼–2½ cups good dry hard cider
cooking water from your
    vegetables

Peel and slice the onions thinly and place them on the bottom of a roasting pan. Sit the chined loin on the top, then sprinkle a goodly amount of salt over the top and some black pepper, and rub them in with your fingers. The joint will take 1½ hours to roast and another 15 minutes or so to rest on your carving board, under foil and a dish towel.

Half an hour before the end of cooking time, rigorously core your apples—you do not want to find tough bits—and tuck a bay leaf into the top of each hole. Score a line through the skin around the circumference of each apple with the point of a sharp knife, and place them upright in the roasting pan with the meat. Baste them with the meat juices and a good splosh of the cider and cook for the meat's final 30 minutes. The apples might burst, but you are not looking for cosmetic perfection here; the flavor and texture are all.

Keep the apples hot while you slice the fat horizontally off the roast in one piece, leaving as much of the fat as you can attached to the meat. Place the sheet of fat under a hot broiler and wait until it is molten brittle before returning it to the top of the meat. Do not cover the meat again or the fat will sog. Stir the meat juices and caramelized onion together in the roasting pan over high heat. Add the rest of the cider and, when it is bubbling, some water from whatever vegetables you have cooked. Reduce for a few minutes, then strain the gravy through a strainer into a pitcher standing in the sink, before pouring it into gravy boats.

Gravy. An emotive word. I remember as a child going to endless Sunday lunches with my parents, and being appalled at the floury taste of the gravy, the phoney, underfilled gravy boats, the cooks who thought a teaspoon of sauce was an "ample sufficiency" and didn't understand the concept of a lake of gravy. Or the importance of having enough left to make your shepherd's or cottage pie with on Monday. Flour in gravy is out of fashion, but is bound to be revived at a later date. Meanwhile, these are my golden rules—making a surfeit of gravy should go without saying.

Gravy

onions, peeled and sliced
water from parboiling potatoes
wine
seasoning

Roast your meat on a layer of peeled, sliced onions. The meaty juices will mingle with them, the onions will exude their flavor and juice in turn, and caramelize to a dark, crunchy, almost charred intensity. You have begun.

When you have laid your meat to rest on the carving board, whack the heat up, and put the roasting pan on top of the stove. Add a good splosh of whatever wine you happen to have open and let it seethe for a minute or two to burn off the alcohol. Take the potato water that you saved in a pitcher when you parboiled your potatoes and parsnips before roasting, and add it a little at a time, including the gorgeous, gluey, starchy bits at the bottom. These will help to thicken the gravy slightly without resorting to cornstarch. You can add any other vegetable water as well if you need, as you stir like crazy to release the oniony morsels from their sticking places. They will color the gravy a rich, burnished mahogany, so forget the horrors of fake browning.

Add more wine and seasoning to taste. Try Madeira or port with beef, really good cider with pork, white wine with chicken, or Marsala with veal. Remember to add the blood that has leaked into the carving tray to the gravy before you put it into your gravy boat or pitcher, or into a French dégraisseur that leaves the fat at the top as you pour. It's as simple as that.

According to legend, Jason returned with the Argonauts from Colchis in the Caucasus, which we now know as Georgia, with rather more than the golden fleece: He brought back the pheasant. Georgian recipes for pheasant include its being braised with walnuts, oranges, grapes, and pomegranate juice. The golden rule is to roast the plumper and more tender young birds, remembering that the hens are always better upholstered than the cocks, and braise or stew the oldsters. Geriatric birds should be put in the pot for soup. Sharp, seeded fruits like quince and apple are natural partners, as is the olive with its acetic back notes, and the endive's bitter leaves. But the Georgian way of sweetening and underscoring the flavor is most delectably exotic—a sticky coating of pomegranate molasses is cooked into the dish and it is finished with garnetlike jewels of pomegranate. I favor a bird hung for five to seven days, depending on the ambient temperature. A well-hung pheasant should taste gamy, not merely chickeny, but should not have taken on the greenish hue of incipient decomposition. To my mind, an overripe pleasure is a pleasure despoiled, but then what is taste if not subjective?

Pheasant and Pomegranates with Jeweled Bulgur

SERVES 4

6 pomegranates
2 pheasants
butter and olive oil
2 tbsp pure pomegranate
   molasses, good supermarkets
   and health-food stores stock
   bottles of it
1 lemon
4 tbsp butter, diced

For the bulgur:
1 medium onion, finely chopped
butter
1⅓ cups bulgur wheat
pheasant or game stock or, failing
   that, chicken stock
4 tbsp pine kernels
olive oil
salt and freshly ground pepper
a handful of fresh cilantro or flat-
   leaf parsley

Halve five of the pomegranates and squeeze the juice from them. You should end up with about ¾ cup juice. Remove the seeds from the last pomegranate, making sure you separate the bitter yellow skin from the jewels.

Brown the pheasant breasts skin-side down first, in a little butter and olive oil, then turn them over and repeat. Finally turn them skin-side down again, and pour the pomegranate molasses and juice over. Bring to a simmer, cover with buttered parchment paper and a lid, and cook exceedingly gently until tender and cooked through to pink. This should take about 10 minutes, but test with the point of a skewer that the juices are still running pink, rather than clear.

Remove from the heat, pour the juices into a pan, taste for sweetness, and add lemon juice to taste. Let the meat relax in a warm oven while you bring the sauce up to boiling point, adding the diced butter bit by bit off the heat, whisking as you go. Season to taste.

FOR THE BULGUR: Soften the onion in a good pat of butter, about 4 tablespoons, stir in the bulgur, and add enough stock to cover by about ¾ inch. Cover with a lid and simmer until the liquid has been absorbed, and the bulgur feels tender when fluffed up with a fork. Roast the pine kernels for a few minutes on a roasting tray in a hot oven, making sure they don't burn. Toss them into the bulgur, and fork them through, adding a good glug of olive oil and some salt and pepper as you do.

Place a hillock of bulgur on a warm serving plate, then scoop out a hollow in the middle. Scatter pomegranate seeds and fresh cilantro or parsley over the bulgur. Place the pheasant breasts in the middle, with the sauce flooded over them. A good, bitter Belgian endive or escarole and orange salad is the only accompaniment you will need.

This is how to cook the pheasant legs that you haven't used for the pheasant and pomegranates with bulgur on page 115. Legs lend themselves better to gentle stewing than they do to roasting or frying. Just make sure you use the best glossiest olives, kept in olive oil, not prepitted and brined. It is also important to remove the tendons properly, or ask your butcher to do so, when you are plucking and cutting up your pheasants. They do not make pleasant eating.

Pheasant Legs Stewed with Green and Black Olives

SERVES 4

4 pheasant legs
butter and olive oil
salt and freshly ground
    black pepper
2 young leeks, finely shredded
1 small carrot, finely sliced
1 clove of garlic, chopped
1 bay leaf
16 plump black olives, pitted
2 cups red wine
a measure of Cognac or Marc
16 plump green olives, pitted

Melt some butter and olive oil in a heavy-bottomed Dutch oven and very gently brown the pheasant legs all over. Transfer them to a plate and season.

Add the vegetables and garlic to the pan and soften gently. Add the bay leaf, pitted black olives, and the wine. Place the legs on top, cover with parchment paper and a lid, and stew at a murmur on top of the stove or in a medium oven, 350°F, until tender. Depending on the age and sex of the birds, this will be anywhere from 20–40 minutes, so check with a skewer that the flesh feels soft and yielding right through to the bone. The slower you cook pheasant legs, the more chance you have of them not toughening. Transfer the legs to a warm serving dish, and place them in a low oven.

Turn the heat up high until the juices in the pot are bubbling, pour the Cognac over, set light to it, and let the alcohol burn off. Put the vegetables through the coarse disk of a food mill, or mash them thoroughly, and return to the pan. Add the pitted green olives, heat through, and pour over the pheasant legs.

I think a dish of simple basmati rice, scented with the addition of whole coriander and fennel seeds, is the best accompaniment, with perhaps a salad of watercress and orange. The orange marries well with the olives and the pheasant.

Chinese Slow-Braised Pork Belly with Butter Beans

SERVES 4

preheat oven to 300°F

3 large onions, peeled and sliced
 into thin rings
piece of organic pork belly, with
 its rind on, weighing roughly
 1½lb
8oz dried lima beans soaked
 overnight in cold water with
 1 tsp baking soda
6 cloves of garlic, peeled and
 bruised with the back of a knife
a thumb of fresh gingerroot,
 peeled and sliced
3 star anise
1 heaped tbsp really good honey,
1 tbsp dark brown sugar
4–6 tbsp organic tamari sauce
white pepper

Put a layer of onions in the bottom of a heavy-bottomed Dutch oven and place the pork belly, rind-side up, on top of them. Surround with the soaked, drained beans, rest of the onions, garlic, gingerroot, star anise, honey, and dark brown sugar, and grind over some white pepper. Cover with cold water, a lot of which the beans will drink up as they cook. Bring slowly to a boil on top of the cooker, then cover with a layer of parchment paper and a lid, and put in the bottom of the oven for 3 hours.

Take out of the oven, add the tamari sauce, cover again, and cook for another hour or two. I have cooked this for as long as 5 hours. The reason why I don't add the tamari sauce at the beginning of cooking is that it might concentrate the saltiness.

Make some creamy mashed potato or cook some rice. Ladle the vegetables and juices into bowls and place a hunk of collapsed pork belly with its bones on top. You need to remove the rind before serving, but that too will peel off with ease. A thoroughly good dish.

If you, like me, are the kind of person who is put off by a shopping-list-length gallimaufry of ingredients, please think again with this dish. Just reading this recipe should have your taste buds standing to attention. The fresh, raw, zinging nature of the ingredients is everything you could desire when you want substance but lightness in equal measure, and to feel you are eating something that might, for once, be as good for you as it is delicious.

Oriental Noodle Salad

SERVES 4

1 clove of garlic, finely chopped
1 fresh red chili, seeded and diced
a finger of fresh gingerroot, grated
4 tsp fresh cilantro, chopped
4 tbsp organic shoyu sauce
olive oil
the juice of a lime
3 organic chicken breast halves, skin on, or chicken thighs; or use large raw jumbo shrimp, 3 or 4 per person
9oz organic spinach or plain egg noodles
1 large carrot
a handful of snow-peas
a handful of bean sprouts
5 or 6 raw cremini mushrooms
a bunch each of fresh mint and fresh cilantro

For the dressing:
3 organic lemons
3 organic limes
1 clove of garlic
a finger of gingerroot, grated
4 tsp honey
a piece of ginger in syrup and 1 tbsp of the syrup (optional)
olive oil
salt and pepper

Mix together the garlic, chili, ginger, cilantro, shoyu sauce, olive oil, and lime in a bowl. Add the chicken or shimp and leave to marinade. Cook the noodles as per directions on the package, then coat them lightly with sesame or olive oil so they won't stick.

Peel the carrot, then, with the peeler, ribbon it from top to bottom. Throw the ribbons into the bowl with the noodles. Thinly slice the snow-peas into strips, throw them into the bowl, and add the bean sprouts and mushrooms.

Remove the chicken or shrimp from the marinade. Pan-cook the chicken for 7 minutes a side or until cooked through; the shelled shrimp until pink and cooked through on both sides. Slice the chicken into long strips with the crisped skin and throw them into the bowl; the shrimp can go in whole.

To make the dressing, peel the citrus fruits thinly with a potato peeler so that you end up with no pith. Put the slices of peel with the juice of the fruit in a pan with the garlic, fresh ginger, and honey. Bring to a boil and reduce by a half until you have a lovely, syrupy sauce. Strain it into a bowl through a strainer, add the olive oil until you have a dressing you like the taste of, then add the finely chopped piece of ginger and its syrup and season to taste. Throw half the roughly chopped cilantro and mint into the salad, add the dressing, and toss with your fingers to amalgamate well. Throw in the rest of the herbs and serve.

Another of Sally's perfect lunchtime salads that you can experiment with, using red bell peppers, shallots, sweet potatoes, zucchini, or any of the good roasting squash such as red onion or butternut.

Roasted Eggplant, Red Onion, and Tomato Salad with Chickpeas, Feta, and Spinach

SERVES 4
preheat oven to 425°F

a handful of cooked chickpeas,
    I always make enough for
    hummus or soup at the same
    time
onion stuck with cloves
carrot
stalk of celery
sprig of thyme
2 fresh bay leaves
1 eggplant
2 red onions
4 large tomatoes
4 or 5 cloves of garlic
a sprig of fresh thyme
olive oil
a well-aged balsamic vinegar, you
    need something mellow and
    velvety, not sharp and rough
sea salt and black pepper
a handful of baby spinach leaves
4oz good sheep milk feta

Soak the chickpeas overnight in cold water. Next day, rinse them and just cover with fresh water in a large, flameproof earthenware casserole. Add an onion stuck with a couple of cloves, a chopped carrot and stick of celery, a sprig of thyme, and a couple of fresh bay leaves. Bring to a boil, skim, then leave to simmer at a mere burble for 2 hours under cover.

Cube the eggplant, peel the red onions and cut them into eighths, and halve the tomatoes. Place them on a roasting pan with the garlic and dribble olive oil over everything. Add the thyme and roast until everything is cooked through, 30–40 minutes. Remove from the oven and add a libation of olive oil and some balsamic vinegar to taste.

Place the roasted vegetables on a pretty, flat plate. Toss in the cooked chickpeas and the raw spinach, which will wilt gently in the warmth. Crumble the feta over. Season and serve.

Something of an annual event in our house, specific to the third week of November to be precise, Gladys's birthday. Gladys looked after my three children, Miranda, Harry, and Charissa, for nine years before she was felled by a stroke. She has been a third parent to them all, and is still very much part of our lives. Every year I cook her birthday dinner, and this steak and kidney pie is her absolute favorite. So much so, that she is given to asking for it again next year almost before the fork has been returned to the plate at the birthday dinner. I make the steak and kidney a day in advance; as with a good stew, this always improves the flavor. I leave it to cool to a rich, wine-dark meatiness, almost gelled with the nuggets of kidney. The stewing steak I buy is well hung, properly veined with fat, and comes with a quarter its weight in kidney—more can be overpowering. This is THE winter dish I would not do without: a traditional, a classic, which tweaking, however subtle or sparing, can neither improve nor embellish. I have, however, sometimes substituted venison steak for the beef steak. Although a leaner meat, the venison makes up for it with its powerful, gamy flavor. I add some crushed juniper berries to the venison version.

Steak and Kidney Pie

SERVES 4
preheat oven to 300°F

1½lb steak with about 6oz kidney
seasoned flour to coat, which you
    can do in a Ziploc bag
butter
3 small onions, chopped
3 large portobello mushrooms,
    or the equivalent weight in
    cremini mushrooms, wiped
    clean and sliced
2–3 ladlefuls of good chicken
    or game stock
1½ cups each of Marsala and port,
    or the equivalent in red wine of
    the decent, full-bodied variety
2 bay leaves, a sprig each of
    rosemary, thyme, and parsley,
    tied together or wrapped
    in cheesecloth

For the pastry:
preheat the oven to 375°F
1½ cups unbleached organic all-
    purpose flour
6 tbsp good cold unsalted butter
water
beaten egg, to glaze

Sauté the floured meat and kidneys in batches in a single layer in some butter in a heavy-bottomed Dutch oven until brown on all sides, a matter of a few minutes. Transfer the meat to a plate, scrape the crusty brown bits from the floor of the pan, add a bit more butter and sauté the onion gently until soft and translucent. Cook the mushrooms separately in a small pan in a bit of butter until they start to soften and weep with juice, then return the meat to the pan, add the mushrooms, tuck in the bouquet of herbs, season, and add the alcohol, letting it come to a simmer. Add the stock and bring back to a simmer. Cover with a layer of parchment paper and a lid and cook in the oven for 1½ hours. Cool overnight. You can cool the meat and leave it in the refrigerator for several days before using it.

There are several schools of thought on the pastry. Should it be puff, piecrust made with butter, or piecrust made with lard? I use piecrust with butter most often, but I have been known to veil my meat with a stratospherically light layer of puff pastry leaves—all French flour and L'Escure butter. Commercial pastry dough you can keep; that is where I draw my purist line anyway.

Make your dough in the usual way. Spoon the filling into the bottom of a deep, oval pie dish, placing a china blackbird or egg cup in the middle so the steam can be released. Brush the edge of the pie dish with water before sticking a thin strip of dough to it, all the way around. Brush the strip with beaten egg before cloaking the pie with your sheet of dough and indenting the edges with the tines of a fork to press them together. Use any leftover bits to decorate the top and brush the whole surface with beaten egg just before it goes into the oven. Bake for about 50 minutes. The top should look like golden enamel.

Serve with mustard, mashed potato, and cabbage blanched for 5 minutes then refreshed in cold water and stewed briefly with plenty of butter, salt, and pepper. Also some carrots cooked in chicken stock, butter, and a teaspoon of dark brown sugar at a rolling boil, until the liquid has evaporated and they are caramelized with the butter-and-sugar mixture.

If the recipe hadn't been Jane Grigson's, I'm pretty sure I wouldn't have stopped, looked, and cooked; after all, what is so special about sausages and cabbage? And just how effective can the alchemy of the two be, to transmute them into something so far from what the imagination can conceive of? The answer is, good enough for me to have cooked this dish several times each winter for nearly two decades. The two simple elements transcend their original state and unify so flawlessly that they want for nothing more; no extra can improve them. The long, slow cooking of the cabbage, leaching its intense juices into the finest organic pork sausages, which in turn exude their fat to coat and intensify the flavor of the cabbage, with only the addition of butter, salt, and pepper, is a process of stunning simplicity. The pink and green strata compact almost into a loaf or torte, and the whole, served with its copious juice, wants only for a baked potato, some coarsely bashed carrot and rutabaga, and a trekker's appetite. Never a problem. This is a dish to return to after abandoning it to its own devices for at least a couple of hours. Jane Grigson assigns the recipe to a French neighbor of hers, Madame Glon, who called it chou farci. You can use Savoy or Dutch cabbage.

Stuffed Cabbage in the Troo Style

SERVES 4
preheat oven to 300°F

3–4½lb cabbage
butter
1½lb best organic plain pork
   sausages
salt, pepper

Shred the cabbage into thin strips, coring it first, and blanch it in a huge vat of boiling, salted water for 5 minutes. Drain it in a colander and run cold water over it to prevent further cooking at this stage. Butter a deep baking dish.

   Slit the sausage skins and push out all the sausage meat onto a plate, discarding the skins. Place a third of the cabbage in the bottom of the dish and season. Press open the sausages and place half the sausage meat in a layer over the cabbage. Continue with a layer of cabbage and sausage, finishing with a layer of cabbage, seasoning each layer as you go, and dotting the top with butter. Cover tightly with a layer of parchment paper and a lid, and cook in the oven for 2–2½ hours. I have served the children at 7 o'clock, then reheated the dish for half an hour later in the evening, and it came to absolutely no grief at all.

When I was a child it seemed extraordinarily glamorous to eat salmon fishcakes for breakfast, but that is what my grandfather did, sitting at the head of an immaculately gleaming 18th-century oak refectory table. For a special treat, Rhoda, my grandmother's cook, would make a couple for me, too. They are still a treat, and will always remain so. Salmon fishcakes should be made with the leftovers from a perfectly moist salmon whose flesh has slightly gelled overnight, been flaked but not crushed to a pulp, and bound with some dry, smooth, unbuttery mashed potatoes and a healthy seasoning of flat-leaf parsley, coarsely ground pepper, and sea salt. These fishcakes are one of the small, select band of dishes that one can feel an urge for at any hour, breakfast, lunch, or supper, varying their accompaniment to suit the time of day. Even I can't envisage sauce tartare for breakfast.

Salmon Fishcakes with Crème Fraîche Tartare

SERVES 6

about 1lb 4 oz cooked salmon

about 2 cups cooked potatoes, mashed without milk and butter, but even half and half salmon and potato works if that is the quantity of fish you have left

sea salt and freshly ground black pepper

a handful of flat-leaf parsley, chopped

2 eggs, beaten

3oz stale whole wheat bread, baked in small squares in a low oven to dry out for 15 minutes, then whizzed to crumbs

vegetable or olive oil for frying

Mash the salmon into the potato roughly, so it still has coarse textured flakes and is not a homogenous puree. Season and throw in the parsley, then shape the mixture into cakes, ¾ inch thick, and place them on a large, flat plate. Keep them covered in the refrigerator for an hour or two to firm up, or longer if it is convenient.

Whisk the eggs on one large, flat plate, and spread the dried bread crumbs on another. Dip the fishcakes first in the egg on both sides, then turn them in the bread crumbs, making sure the sides are well crumbed, too. Place them on a third large plate. Heat a shallow film of oil, about 4 tablespoons, in a skillet over medium heat. Put the fishcakes in and fry for 4 minutes or so a side until golden brown. Drain on paper towels and serve, two per person, with a dollop of crème fraîche tartare.

This is a lighter tartare than the classic, but every bit as delicious; the sort of thing you have to dip your finger into, or scrape around the plate when you think no one is looking. It works well with white fish as well as fishcakes. It appeals to children, too—the usual version does not in my experience.

Crème Fraîche Tartare

MAKES ENOUGH FOR 6

1 organic egg yolk
1 tsp Dijon mustard
sea salt
Tabasco sauce
3–4 tbsp crème fraîche
2 tsp tarragon vinegar
1 tsp chopped tarragon
1 heaped tbsp chopped flat-leaf
    parsley
1 tsp chopped chives
1 tbsp rinsed capers, chopped
1 tbsp finely chopped cornichons

Beat the egg yolk with the mustard, sea salt, and a few dashes of Tabasco until emulsified. Add the crème fraîche, a tablespoon at a time, and a teaspoon of the tarragon vinegar, whisking well with a small balloon whisk. Whisk until thick, but pourable. Stir in the other ingredients with the second teaspoon of vinegar. Adjust the seasoning.

A charmoula is a feisty Moroccan spice rub, which lends itself as well to pork, lamb, or fish as it does to chicken, so play around accordingly. If you can slash the skin of the fish, flesh, or fowl and maximize penetration of the flavors, so much the better, and if you can be bothered to make your own preserved lemons, a simple and satisfying process, do. They will adorn your kitchen beautifully. I have made preserved lemons ever since seeing them grace the shelves of the doyenne of Middle Eastern and Jewish food, Claudia Roden. Seek out their company with turmeric and coriander; you will not be disappointed.

Chicken Charmoula with Preserved Lemons

SERVES 4
preheat oven to 400°F

For the chicken:
1 tsp cumin seeds
1 tsp coriander seeds
1 onion, peeled and chopped
3 cloves of garlic, peeled and
    chopped
1 tsp paprika
½ tsp dried gingerroot
a bunch each of flat-leaf parsley
    and cilantro
12 glossy black olives, pitted
1 preserved lemon
4 tbsp olive oil
salt, pepper, cayenne
4 organic chicken legs or 8 thighs

Briefly toast the cumin and coriander seeds in a small skillet over medium heat. By that, I mean until you smell toasted spice and they begin to brown, 30–60 seconds. Pound them together in a mortar. Put the onion and garlic with the herbs, spices, and dried ginger in a food processor. Blitz until they look finely chopped. Chop the olives and lemon more coarsely, and stir them into the mixture, then stir in a bit of olive oil to slacken the mixture to a paste. Season to taste with salt, pepper, and cayenne. Slap the paste all over the chicken pieces, down into the slashes, cover with plastic wrap, and place in the refrigerator for at least 2 hours, but overnight if you can.

Remove from the refrigerator and bring back to room temperature before cooking. Place the chicken in a roasting pan and roast in the preheated oven for about 30 minutes, or until the juices run clear when the meat is pierced to the center with a fork.

If you like, accompany with a bowl of sheep or Greek yogurt thinned with a spoonful of milk, into which you have stirred a teaspoon of toasted cumin seeds, some fresh, finely chopped cilantro, and salt and pepper.

I serve this dish with couscous steamed in chicken or game stock, then cooled to warm, when you might stir in the following spicy dressing. Feel free to add roasted, skinned red bell peppers and any other roasted vegetables you like to the couscous.

For the dressing:
1 clove of garlic, crushed to a
    paste with a bit of coarse sea salt
½ tsp ground cinnamon
½ tsp ground allspice
2 tbsp lemon juice
2 tbsp olive oil
sea salt and black pepper

Whisk the garlic, spices, and lemon juice together, then stir in the olive oil. Pour into the bottom of the serving bowl, then add the couscous and vegetables, and turn them through the oily dressing with your fingers until well amalgamated.

Preserved Lemons

MAKES 1 LARGE JAR

5 organic, thin-skinned lemons
about 5 tbsp salt
juice of at least 3 more lemons
1–2 tbsp olive oil

The preserved lemons must be made a month in advance of eating them. Scrub the lemons, then quarter them from the top to within ½ inch of the stem end, so the sections are still attached. Carefully open out each lemon and sprinkle it with about a teaspoon of sea salt. Close up and reshape the fruit. Put a tablespoon of salt in the bottom of a sterilized 2-cup jar with a rubber seal. Pack in the lemons, pushing them down well so they are squashed together, and sprinkling a little more salt in between the layers.

Leave the jar to stand in a warm place, like a sunny windowsill, for 3–4 days, when the juices will have been drawn out of the lemons. Press the lemons down again as much as you can, then pour in enough lemon juice to cover them completely. Before sealing the jar, pour a thin layer of olive oil on top of the juice to act as a protective film. Close the jar and leave to macerate and ripen for a month in a coolish place, when the lemons will be ready to eat. Don't worry if the lemon juice turns a bit cloudy at first because it will clear naturally. There is no need to refrigerate the lemons after opening.

To use preserved lemons, rinse them well under cold running water. Both the pulp and the peel can be used, although in most dishes the peel alone is called for; the juices can be used again to preserve a new batch of lemons, or try a splash in vinaigrettes, marinades, and aromatic spiced stews. Keeps for 2 years.

The Indians use yogurt in very different ways to us in their cooking. There is the famous "hung" yogurt that is suspended in cheesecloth or a strainer overnight until it becomes a set curd, and then there is their habit of mixing yogurt with water in place of buttermilk as a spiced drink. In Jaipur, this drink is ubiquitous because of the high temperatures; yogurt is used as a coolant, as I discovered on my trip there earlier in the year.

Yogurt is an indigenous part of Rajasthani cuisine, as is the high percentage of protein in the diet, which comes not from meat but from things such as legumes. Desert people are a strong race, with a lot of stamina. They have to be. They are always moving, the terrain is rugged, and it's a rough life with the camels, but nature seems to be on their side and provides them with the kind of food the body needs in extremes of temperature. They eat poppadoms at the end of a meal, not as we do at the beginning, to absorb the fat and oil from the rest of the food and to prevent the palate from feeling greasy. They use sugar to bring out salt, and salt to bring out sugar. They try to use the whole of a plant, preserving, drying, and pickling, as needs must in the desert. With cilantro, for example, the seeds, stems, roots, and leaves are all used, each because of their different properties.

As a lifetime hater of milk, thus of milky drinks, a glass of chaas was my ultimate tact test, knowing, as I did, that refusal was not an option. The addition of toasted cumin seeds and asafoetida (a bitter-tasting substance available in Indian markets), tipped crackling from the pan into the glass, were, with the additional spices, the sealant to my resolve. Indeed, one sip and I was converted. A whole glass later, I was begging for more. But this is hot-day food, or, should I say, drink. Then the body does actually crave the heat of the spice and the cool of the yogurt and that is when to make it.

Chaas, Yogurt Flavored
with Cumin, Asafoetida, and Green Cilantro

SERVES 6

1lb 2oz best organic live sheep or
    cow yogurt,
2¼ cups ice-cold water
3 tsp salt
½ tsp green chili, very finely
    chopped
oil
½ tsp finely chopped gingerroot
½ tsp cumin seeds
a pinch of asafoetida
½ tsp fresh cilantro leaves,
    chopped to tiny flecks

Simply whisk the yogurt with the ice-cold water, then add salt, chili, finely chopped gingerroot, and cilantro. Heat a splash of oil in a small skillet and toast the cumin seeds and asafoetida by throwing them into the oil for 30–60 seconds, when they will give off their characteristic, toasty spice smell. Tip the crackling spices into the yogurt drink, and serve at room temperature or chilled.

I have always felt about okra rather how I felt about milk drinks until my conversion. This is another myth that the magic of Jaipur dispelled. It was always the thought of the mucilaginous liquid leaking glueily, but irrevocably, from the green-taloned okra that put me off, but this trickiest of vegetables just needs a different sort of treatment, one that renders it crisp, dry, gloriously spiced, and with the texture more of a julienned fritto misto than a weeping pile of slime-green fingers. Look no farther and serve this with any of your favorite fish or curry dishes, or in a spiced green hillock as a *bonne bouche* with drinks.

Akri Bhindi, or Crisp Okra

SERVES 4

8oz fresh okra
scant 2oz onion
1oz red or green bell peppers. or a
    combination
scant ½ tsp fresh gingerroot,
    sliced into matchstick strips
½ tsp carom seeds
a pinch of asafoetida
a generous tsp of sea salt
½ tsp ground dried hot chili
1½ tbsp gram (chickpea) flour
2½ tbsp cornstarch
½ tsp chopped fresh cilantro
vegetable oil, enough to deep-fry

Cut the okra, onions, and bell peppers into thin julienne strips. Add all the ginger, spices, and flours and mix well with your fingers to coat the vegetables.

Heat the oil, then test that it is hot enough by dropping in a tiny bit of the mixture. If it fizzes and starts to brown immediately, get cooking. Fry the okra mixture until crisp and brown, then sprinkle with the cilantro and serve.

If anything could turn me vegetarian, the cooking of Rajasthan would be the strongest contender. Pickled, dried, preserved, or rehydrated vegetables, shoots, roots, flowers, and seeds are all used in the most ingenious assemblies. Legumes are cooked more imaginatively than I believed possible—such unknown delicacies as the sundried cakes of chickpeas that are like rock-hard dumplings until they are braised in liquid. The simplest of ingredients are made fragrant and desirable with a bit of mustard oil here, a *digestif* of fenugreek there, or a tempering of turmeric with its musty, fusty power assuaged by onion and clean-scented cumin. And, like this unusual Achari Paneer, many of the dishes can be cooked at home without your being driven frantic by an alien ingredients list. This is a lovely vegetarian dish—tiny quenelles of cottage cheese cooked briefly in pickling spices and mustard oil.

Achari Paneer

SERVES 4

2 tbsp mustard oil
a pinch of mustard seeds
a pinch of fenugreek seeds
a pinch of cumin seeds
4 tbsp minced onion
½ cup chopped tomatoes
½ tsp ground dried red chili
1 tsp ground coriander
1 cup best cottage cheese, strained
   and shaped into small walnut-
   size balls between two spoons
salt
sugar
lemon juice
a bunch of fresh cilantro,
   chopped

Heat the mustard oil in a pan and add the whole dry masala—mustard seeds, fenugreek, and cumin seeds—to temper. This takes only a minute or so and really brings out the flavor of the spices. Leave the seeds to crackle, then add the onions and sauté until brown. Add the tomatoes, and cook down for 10–15 minutes.

Add the ground chili and coriander, cook for a few more minutes, then drop in the paneer—the little balls of cottage cheese—coating them well in the spice mixture. Add salt, a pinch of sugar and a spritz of lemon juice to taste. Sprinkle some fresh cilantro over and serve. You can make the paneer mixture in advance and assemble all the spices and chopped onion and tomato an hour or two before you want to cook them.

Some pilau rice, sweetened and spiced with whole cloves, slices of ginger, golden raisins, toasted slivered almonds or pistachios, and turmeric, is the only other accompaniment you could want with an assortment of vegetarian dishes. Vegetable *thalis* are an indigenous part of Rajasthan cuisine. They are eaten from a communal plate, intended to reinforce the togetherness of people who either work or play together. *Thalis* are about "sharing, brotherhood and belonging" I was told by Jitin, the talented chef of the Oberoi's jewel of a hotel, Raj Vilas, in Jaipur. "We eat most food with our hand" he continued. "That is why Indians never burn their mouths, they burn their hand first!" This dahl is also a dish you can serve if you are cooking a fish or meat curry.

Moong Dahl Tarka, or
Yellow Lentils Tempered with Cumin and Garlic

SERVES 6

1 cup split lentils
a pinch of turmeric
salt
2 tbsp ghee or clarified butter
½ tsp cumin seeds
½ tsp garlic
½ cup finely chopped onion
2 tbsp chopped tomato
½ tsp ground red chili
½ tsp ground cumin
a handful of fresh cilantro,
    chopped

Wash the lentils, cover with water, and bring them to a boil. Remove the scum from the top with a draining spoon and some paper towels, and simmer. Add the turmeric and salt when the dahl have considerably softened and continue to cook until tender.

Heat the ghee in a pan, then add the whole cumin seeds and garlic, followed by the onions and tomato. Sauté them with the ground chili and cumin. When the mixture has become soft, add it to the lentils and heat through to boiling. Add a handful of fresh cilantro, check the seasoning, and serve.

High in the foothills of the Himalayas at Simla, where the climate is more temperate than Jaipur, the cooking wisdom is not dissimilar. I watch Rajiv, another talented chef, scorching whole tomatoes on the barbecue, mulching them into an instant chutney with pungent mustard oil, onion, ginger, ground Kashmiri chili , cumin, coriander, and a splash of sugar, a chunky sunset of an accompaniment for the powerfully spiced gravy that swamps his "Chaa Meat," slow-cooked goat, annealed by curd cheese and fresh cilantro leaves. Indians understand the effects of foods on the body. Excessive warmth is thought to be the cause of many maladies, so "heating" and "cooling" foods are balanced in an Indian meal. Yogurt, rice, and ghee are cooling to the body; meat and cashew nuts are heat inducing and consumed in moderation.

This dish of goat represents the Himachulis belief in a balanced meal. Black cardamom is used for savory dishes there, Rajiv is insistent that green cardamom is only used in desserts. I am trusted to roll out and stuff the "keema aur matter kulcha," leavened bread that we roll to Lycra stretchiness and stuff with black-cardamom-spiked ground lamb, or fresh peas with a suspicion of asafoetida. A typical lunch carried by the women to their husbands in the fields, and eaten simply with a dollop of fiery mango pickle. You can make the Chaa Meat with lamb or mutton instead of goat.

Chaa Meat

1 tsp salt
1 tsp paste made with crushed
   garlic and grated gingerroot
6 tbsp ricotta, a substitute for
   Indian curd cheese,
a couple of bay leaves.
2¼lb shoulder of lamb, mutton or
   goat, cubed
⅔ cup mustard oil
½ cup sliced onions
1 tsp chopped green chili
2 bay leaves
½ tsp coriander seeds, crushed
a pinch of ground turmeric
a pinch of ground coriander
a pinch of ground cumin
9 tbsp chickpea flour
salt
2¼ cups whisked yogurt
fresh cilantro leaves, chopped

Mix the salt, garlic-ginger paste, ricotta, and bay leaves to make the marinade. Add the cubes of lamb and leave for at least an hour.

When the lamb has marinated, put it in a heavy-bottomed pot, cover it with water, and bring it slowly to a boil. Simmer it gently until tender, 1–1½ hours.

Heat the mustard oil, add the sliced onions and chopped chili, and sauté. Add the whole spices and the meat and cook for a few minutes. Then add the ground spices and salt and simmer. Add the chickpea flour and cook briefly, then blend in the yogurt and continue cooking over a slow flame until the gravy is thick. Serve piping hot sprinkled with chopped cilantro leaves.

This is the simplest chutney in the world to prepare—up-front exotic, unusual, and highly versatile. Its sweet sharpness is a foil for any rich or fatty meats, and I think it takes the place of our own green gooseberry sauce with a humble herring or mackerel. Fillet the fish and broil skin side uppermost until charred and bubbling black. Do not cook the flesh side, its oiliness should not dry out, but you can slather and scorch it briefly with a spoonful of chutney on the flesh side if you prefer an integral dish to having your chutney on the side. Cape gooseberries are always available at Christmas time, so try this chutney with your cold goose or turkey, in or out of a sandwich.

Cape Gooseberry Chutney

MAKES A GOOD BOWLFUL

2 tbsp vegetable oil
¼ tsp mustard seeds
¼ tsp cumin seeds
4 tbsp chopped onion
1 tsp chopped fresh gingerroot
1 tsp chopped green chili
¼ tsp ground hot dried red chili
¼ tsp ground cumin
¼ tsp ground coriander
salt
14oz Cape gooseberries, hulled
½ tsp raw sugar

Heat the oil, then add the mustard and cumin seeds. After the mustard seeds have started to splutter, add the chopped onion. Cook until translucent, then add the other chopped ingredients. Cook for 2–3 minutes, add the ground spices and salt, and cook over low heat. Add the gooseberries and sugar. Gently sauté over low heat for a few minutes, making sure the gooseberries retain their shape and do not collapse. Cool.

A patrician, exquisite dish of marinated quail, which are submerged in a gravy sharpened and freshened with pastes of cilantro and mint leaves and the seeds of black cardamom. Rajiv was given the recipe for this dish by 80-year-old Madan Ram, who was the chef to the Ranas of Rampur Bushair. It has been eaten by rajahs and kings. Traditionally, the hunters brought back quail, boar, and partridge, and Madan got to work immediately with his cleaver and his spice box. I think the recipe would work as well with any small game bird, such as partridge, pigeon, snipe, or woodcock.

Bateyr Hara Masala

SERVES 4

8 quail
¾ cup paste of fresh cilantro
2 tbsp paste of fresh mint leaves
1 tsp pomegranate seeds
lemon juice

For the marinade:
2 tbsp wine vinegar
1½ tbsp ginger-garlic paste
1 tsp red chili paste (just crush a
    seeded red chili with a bit of salt
    in a mortar)
salt

For the gravy:
½ cup ghee or clarified butter
a pinch of black cardamom seeds
2–3 cloves and a bay leaf
2 tsp ginger-garlic paste
1 cup chopped onion
a pinch of dried ground hot red
    chili
1 tsp ground cumin
1 tsp ground coriander
⅓ tsp garam masala powder
1½ cups chopped tomato

Mix together the marinade ingredients, making the ginger-garlic paste with crushed garlic and grated gingerroot. Add a bit of salt and marinate the whole birds for at least an hour.

To make the gravy, heat the ghee in a pan, add the whole spices, and then the ginger-garlic paste. Add the chopped onion and cook over medium heat until soft and translucent. Add the spices and some more salt, and cook gently until the oil separates from the masala. Add the tomatoes.

Grill the quail on all sides on a barbecue, or under a broiler, until they're still a bit bloody, then add them to the gravy with the mint and cilantro pastes, and finish cooking. Pierce with a skewer, or insert a fine-bladed sharp knife; the flesh should be pink, but not look raw or feel tough. Finish the dish with the crushed pomegranate seeds and a squeeze of lemon juice. Eat with your fingers, you cannot do otherwise with quail.

Another lovely vegetarian side dish that you might prefer to serve with drinks. They are really little more than spiced potato and pea cakes. Garam masala and chat masala are both mixtures of spices. Garam masala contains cumin, cardamom, coriander, and other spices; chat masala is a mix of coriander, cumin, chilies, and dry ground mango .

Mater Tikki

SERVES I

½ tsp chopped fresh mint
½ tsp chopped fresh cilantro
½ tsp chopped fresh gingerroot
1 medium green chili
7oz potatoes, boiled and mashed
½ tsp garam masala
½ tsp chat masala
salt
½ tsp cumin seeds
2 tbsp fresh or frozen peas, blanched
lemon juice
1¼ cups vegetable oil

Mix together the chopped mint, cilantro, ginger, and chili and add to the mashed potato with both masalas and some salt. Heat a little oil in a small pan, then toast the cumin seeds for a few seconds till they exude their scent, before adding the peas and cooking gently until soft. Mash the cumin and peas together a little with a fork, adding the lemon juice and salt.

To make the tikkis, take lumps of the potato mixture and flatten them with the palm of one hand. Pop a bit of pea mixture into the middle and enclose it in the potato until you have a small potato cake. Use a little flour if the mixture is a bit damp and coat the palms of your hand with the flour so you can work the mixture with the heel of your palm. Heat the vegetable oil until a tiny bit of the mixture thrown in fizzes and begins to brown instantly. Drop in the tikkis and cook them for about 3 minutes a side. Drain and serve with minted yogurt and a few thinly sliced mild onion rings.

Prepare the tikkis an hour or two in advance if you like, spreading them out on a plate ready to fry.

A simple vegetarian dish of spiced potato and spinach, which you can serve as part of a vegetarian *thali,* or with fish or meat. If you have leftover cooked spinach and potato, or can contrive to cook extra and keep some back, you are on your way. Also very good to spruce up cold meat, turkey, or goose at Christmas, or roast pork or chicken on a Monday night. After the rich excesses of Christmas, a spiced lentil and spinach soup or vegetable dish fresh and warming with chili, cumin, coriander, and ginger is something I seem to crave.

Palak Aloo

SERVES 1

vegetable oil, a thin film
½ tsp cumin seeds
½ tsp finely chopped garlic
½ cup chopped onion
⅓ cup pureed and strained
    tomato
10oz spinach, briefly cooked and
    coarsely pureed
½ tsp ground cumin
½ tsp ground coriander
½ tsp garam masala
¼–½ tsp ground dried hot red
    chili, use at your discretion
1 heaped tsp chopped fresh
    cilantro
½ tsp gingerroot in matchstick
    strips
1 cup boiled potatoes cut into
    large chunks
salt

Heat the oil in a pan, then add the cumin seeds until they crackle, 30 seconds or so, before adding the finely chopped garlic. Add the chopped onion and cook until soft, then add the tomatoes and continue to cook. Add the spinach, then mix the ground spices, masala, chili, and cilantro with a couple of tablespoons of water, a brilliant trick to avoid the subtle spices burning while frying them. Add them with the ginger to the spinach mix and fry briefly. Add the potatoes and heat through, carefully stirring so they don't break up.

Do not be put off by the ingredients list, the process is simplicity itself, the spices all things you will keep in your cupboard if you are a keen cook. The result, a coolly elegant, subtly spiced, yogurt-based dish, is a perfect contrast to the sweet starchy potato dish opposite. Just remember to hang the yogurt the night before. I find a nylon strainer as effective as cheesecloth, which I don't always have when it's not the jam-making season.

Tadkeywala Dahi

SERVES I

tip of a tsp of turmeric, grate some root if you can get it
tip of a tsp ground dried hot red chili
1 tsp vegetable oil
¼ tsp mustard seeds
½ tsp coriander seeds
½ tsp cumin seeds
1 whole red chili
½ tsp garlic, crushed to a paste with a little salt
⅓ cup minced onions
⅓ cup finely chopped tomatoes
½ tsp chopped fresh cilantro
½ tsp chopped fresh mint
½ tsp fresh gingerroot in matchstick strips
salt
⅔ cup hung yogurt

Put the turmeric and chili in a bowl with a couple of spoons of water to prevent their burning. Heat the oil, add the mustard seeds, coriander and cumin seeds, and the whole red chili. Then add the turmeric and chili in water and the garlic paste and stir together. Add the onions, stir them in, and cook gently until they are soft. Add the tomatoes, continue cooking for a few minutes, then add the chopped fresh cilantro, mint, ginger, and salt.

Take the mixture off the heat, mix in the hung yogurt, and serve warm. You can also serve this alongside any plainly cooked white fish or chicken, alone with rice, or with a peshwari naan or a paratha to dip into the juices.

Three days in Bangkok recently taught me just how little I know about Thai food and its subtle variations in heat and style from the north to the south of the country. Watching fresh green coconuts being grated in the market, by women up to their elbows in the white, woody shavings, also made me realize that whatever I cooked on my return could only be an approximation. Chili, lemongrass, galanga, and coconut, fish sauce, shrimp paste, kaffir limes, cilantro, and garlic—the heat of Thai food is always ameliorated by the harmony procured by the addition of the salt, bitter, sweet, and citrus sharpness of the other ingredients. I didn't have galanga, kaffir limes, fresh coconut, lemongrass, or fish sauce when I made this, but fresh ginger, limes, a splosh of sherry, and creamed coconut in a block defied authenticity with bravura. Just what is cooking all about if you can't think substitution when faced with the inadequacies or shortfall of the depths of your refrigerator and cupboard?

My Thai Chicken

SERVES 4

vegetable oil, something
    unobtrusive such as peanut or
    grapeseed
4 large organic chicken breast
    halves without their skin, or
    any cut of chicken you happen
    to have
2 onions, finely chopped
5 cloves of garlic, finely sliced
2–3 red chilies of whatever
    strength you are comfortable
    with
2 fingers of fresh gingerroot sliced
    into matchstick strips
a splosh of dry sherry or fish
    sauce
grated zest of 2 limes, kaffir if you
    can find them, and the juice of
    both
8oz snow-peas, trimmed
1¼ cups chicken or game stock,
    I used pheasant
2–3 handfuls of frozen peas
a third of a packet of organic
    creamed coconut, it comes in a
    block
a large bunch of fresh cilantro
sea salt and black pepper

Heat the oil in a heavy-bottomed skillet, then put in the chicken breast halves and fry them for about 2 minutes a side until they are beginning to brown. Transfer to a plate, add a bit more oil, and gently fry the onion, garlic, chili, and ginger together until soft and translucent. Return the chicken to the pan, add a splosh of sherry or fish sauce, and allow it to bubble up briefly before you grate the lime zest over the chicken and squeeze in the juice. Season and simmer gently, turning the chicken over after about 7 minutes.

Meanwhile, throw the snow-peas into the boiling stock and cook for a couple of minutes. Reserve the stock and refresh the snow-peas under cold water in a colander so they don't cook any more at this stage.

Reheat the stock to boiling point, throw in the frozen peas, and cook them for 5 minutes. Remove the peas from the stock and put them in a bowl. Pour the hot stock onto the lump of creamed coconut and stir to help it dissolve completely, then pour it over the chicken. Cook gently for another 7 minutes, or until the chicken is cooked right through with the juices running clear when you pierce the flesh with a skewer. It is important the liquid does not boil at this stage or the coconut will separate. Finally toss in the snow-peas, peas, and half the fresh cilantro.

Turn out onto a large warm plate, and scatter on the rest of the fresh cilantro. I served my chicken with some plainly boiled green rice, a deliciously smoky Chinese variety, with a firm, slightly chewy texture.

My love affair with Spain is a recent one, nothing too exclusive, but something I am slowly cultivating, albeit in an *ad hoc* sort of way. What I do know, is that each trip I make there—filming the Labeque sisters, French pianists, in Barcelona; visiting the bodegas of Jerez, Sanlucar de Barrameda, and Santa Maria with Sam Clark, from the lovely restaurant Moro, whose recipe this is; looking at a fruit-growing estate in Seville in the hazy heat of picking time, when velvet-fuzzed bright apricots and sweetly acidic-scented, white nectarines are in abundance—has been a miniature of perfection, wonderful food, wine, music, and hosts. This dish is very Spanish in taste; complex, comforting, substantial, it needs no accompaniment other than a good glass of Rioja and a tomato salad.

Paella de Cerdo con Chorizo y Espinaca

SERVES 4

7 tbsp olive oil

12oz organic pork tenderloin, halved lengthwise, then sliced into ¼in strips

sea salt and black pepper

1 cup mild chorizo cut into little pieces

2 large Spanish onions, finely chopped

1 large green bell pepper, halved, seeded, and finely chopped

4 cloves of garlic, finely chopped

1 heaped cup paella rice, Calasparra is the one

1 tsp sweet smoked Spanish paprika

2 ñora peppers or dried peppers, not too hot

3½ cups hot chicken stock or water

18oz spinach, washed and drained

1 lemon, cut in wedges

In a 12–16 inch paella pan or skillet, heat the olive oil over high heat. Stir-fry the pork for a few seconds so it is still a little undercooked. Season with salt and pepper. Remove from the pan with a draining spoon and put to one side.

Turn down the heat to low and fry the chorizo for a minute. Add the chopped onion and green bell pepper and cook for 20 minutes, stirring occasionally. Add the garlic and continue cooking for 5–10 minutes longer. At this point the mixture should have caramelized and taste sweet. Stir the rice into the pan for a minute to coat it in the mixture. Up to this point everything can be cooked in advance.

The next stage requires about 20 minutes more cooking time. Add salt and pepper, for this is the time to season the rice perfectly. Add the paprika and ñora peppers, drained of their water, followed by the hot stock, and simmer for 15 minutes or until there is just a thin layer of liquid around the rice.

Meanwhile, in a large saucepan, briefly wilt the spinach with a little salt and put it to one side with the pork tenderloin. Evenly scatter the pork over the rice, followed by the spinach. With the back of a spoon, gently push the pork and spinach partially into the oily liquid that remains at the bottom of the pan. Tuck in the lemon wedges, cover the paella tightly with foil, and let it sit for 5 minutes before serving.

I have eaten a "white" daube several times at Lindsay House, the London restaurant of my favorite chef, Richard Corrigan. He understands the cheaper cuts of meat better anyone else I know, potting, curing, brining from snout to tail the cuts that many people reject nowadays, mostly out of the combined qualities of shameful ignorance and a feeling that anything that requires longer, slower cooking requires, absurdly, longer, slower preparation. Total myth. Pork shoulder, like shoulder of lamb, wins for taste over leg every day in my book, and lends itself perfectly to the gentle braise that should be at the heart of winter cooking. The sharpness of the apricots—I use unsulfured sticky dark ones, Richard doesn't, he goes for color—is an inspired touch over the more traditional use of prunes, a sweeter cousin. My interpretation of Richard's dish is just that, a bit of guesswork and poetic licence. If you want to eat the real thing, go to the restaurant.

Daube of Pork with Apricots

SERVES 8
preheat oven to 325°F

24 organic unsulfured apricots
freshly squeezed orange juice
sweet white wine
1 shoulder of pork, about 3lb 5oz

Marinade:
1 tbsp cumin seeds
½ tbsp fennel seeds
¼ cup honey
7 tbsp red-wine vinegar
8 cloves of garlic
4 sprigs of thyme, the leaves
   pulled from the stems
2¼ cups red wine
5 sprigs of mint, finely chopped
grated zest of an organic orange
sea salt and black pepper

olive oil
10 cups veal or beef stock

Soak the apricots in an equal amount of freshly squeezed orange juice and sweet white wine to cover.

Remove the rind of the pork and cut the meat into 4-ounce pieces. Mix the marinade ingredients together in a large bowl. Add the meat, mixing everything together well with your fingers, cover the bowl, and put it in the refrigerator for 24 hours. Remove the meat and pat it dry with paper towels, then brown it in batches in olive oil on all sides in a large heavy-bottomed Dutch oven. Transfer it to a plate.

Pour the marinade and meat juices into the pan and reduce over high heat to about half the original volume. Return the meat to the pot, cover it with the veal stock, a sheet of parchment paper, and a lid and cook for 2 hours in the oven.

Meanwhile, gently cook the apricots in their marinade until soft, but still holding their shape, and add them to the pork at the end of cooking.

Mashed potatoes, briefly cooked and refreshed buttered cabbage, perhaps a baked onion, what more could you want?

My cousin Deborah is as much of a culinary conjuror as I am when it comes to magicking up something of a feast from the peasant end of the spectrum of ingredients. Breast is one of the utterly undervalued and underused cuts of meat, be it lamb or veal. The tender, sweet delicacy of this cut of veal, with its gorgeous glueiness, defines the word comfort.

Stuffed Braised Breast of Veal

SERVES 8
preheat oven to 325°F

Stuffing:
4 tbsp butter
1 onion finely chopped
2oz pancetta, chopped
1⅓ cups cooked spinach, chopped
⅓ cup boiled rice
½ cup grated Parmesan cheese
1 large egg, beaten
a pinch of grated nutmeg
black pepper to taste

2½lb boned breast of veal
4 tbsp butter
splash of olive oil
2 stalks of celery, roughly
    chopped
2 carrots, roughly chopped
2 onions, roughly chopped
⅔ cup vermouth or white wine
1 lemon
2½ cups chicken stock
1 sprig each of thyme, rosemary,
    and parsley, and a bay leaf
1 tbsp crème fraîche
salt and pepper

First make the stuffing. Melt the butter and cook the onion until soft and transparent. Add the pancetta and cook through. In a bowl, mix the onions and pancetta with the spinach. Add the rice, Parmesan cheese, egg, nutmeg, and black pepper, and mix them together thoroughly.

Open up the breast of veal, sprinkle lightly with salt and black pepper. Spread the stuffing in the middle of the meat. Roll up the breast and tie with string along its length.

Melt the butter and olive oil in a Dutch oven large enough to hold the veal and vegetables. Brown the veal all over in the butter-and-oil mixture. Remove the veal from the Dutch oven and brown the vegetables. Add the herbs, the juice of the lemon and the skins of the lemon halves after they have been squeezed, the vermouth or white wine, and stock. Bring to a simmer. Add the veal, cover with a lid, and put in the middle of the oven. Baste and turn the meat several times during the cooking.

Check the veal after two hours. If it is tender when it is pierced with a fork, it will be cooked, if not leave for the extra half hour.

When it's done, remove the veal to a warm dish to rest while you make the sauce. Skim any fat off the pan juices and reduce if necessary over high heat until you have about 2 cups. Strain into a clean saucepan, check the seasoning, and whisk in a tablespoon of crème fraîche. Serve with the veal.

I always cook more legumes than I need. Mindful of their expansion I may be, but I am singularly incapable of emptying less than a package into the bowl to soak or, in the case of lentils, straight into the pan. It is probably because they so easily have two incarnations—and keep extremely well in the refrigerator as long as you remember to bring them back to room temperature before serving. This dish is perfect for a summer lunch, supper, or picnic and can be prepared in advance before being left to marinate for a couple of hours. Or, you can eat it warm as soon as you have made the dressing.

Puy Lentil, Feta, Roast Tomato, and Onion Salad Marinated in a Cilantro, Red Chili, and Ginger Dressing

SERVES 6
preheat oven to 400°F

2 cups Puy lentils
4 large organic tomatoes
2 onions, peeled and cut into 6
    pieces
olive oil
3 handfuls of baby spinach
6oz best sheep milk feta. Rinse the
    feta in cold water when you
    take it out of its brine.
3 cloves of garlic
1½in finger of fresh gingerroot
1 red chili, seeded
a large bunch of fresh cilantro
a generous tsp of Dijon mustard
olive oil
juice of 1½ lemons
sea salt and black pepper

Put the lentils in an enamel pot and just cover with water. Bring them to a boil, take any scum off the surface, then simmer them until cooked, about 40 minutes. The lentils do not need to be presoaked.

Meanwhile, halve the tomatoes and place them on a baking tray with the onions. Pour a generous libation of olive oil over and put the tray of vegetables in the oven to roast for about 30 minutes. The tomatoes should be weeping juice and soft, and the onions should have caramelly bits and also be soft. Drain the lentils and place them in a bowl with a splosh of good olive oil and the spinach, which will begin to wilt in their heat; stir until it has. Crumble the feta over the top.

Now make the dressing. Chop the garlic, ginger, and chili and put them in a food processor with the cilantro. Add the juices from the roasted tomatoes and onions, the mustard, then some more olive oil, about 5 tablespoons, and the lemon juice. Season and blitz. Taste and adjust anything that needs it. Place the warm tomatoes and onions in the salad and pour the dressing over, turning the whole salad when you have done so with your fingers. Serve or leave to marinate for a couple of hours and eat at room temperature.

Buy the thickest fillet of cod you can find. The Puy lentils need no soaking, so the whole dish can be made in 50 minutes. The marriage of lentils and bacon, pancetta, smoked ham, or prosciutto is as well known as it is delicious. The equation can be complicated and enhanced with cod, which partics well with both lentils and bacon, be they wrapped, over, under, or beside it. In fact, the cod is all the better for the smoky strength of the pig, which does nothing to undermine the fish's more subtle flavor, but everything to cod it up.

Roast Cod with Braised Puy Lentils and Roasted Vegetables

SERVES 2
preheat oven to 425°F

1 cup Puy lentils
1 bulb of fennel
1 onion
olive oil
a small sprig of fresh thyme
12 cherry tomatoes
1lb or so thick cod fillet
3 or 4 slices bacon
2 heaped tbsp crème fraîche

Just cover the lentils with water in a large, heavy bottomed pan. Bring them to a boil, cover, and turn down to a simmer. They will take about 40 minutes to cook.

Meanwhile, chop the fennel bulb in half and each half into thirds, cut the peeled onion into large chunks, and place both in a small roasting pan. Pour a slug of olive oil over the top, season, add the sprig of thyme, and put in the oven to roast.

After 20 minutes, add the tomatoes. All the vegetables should be soft after another 20 minutes, but pierce with a skewer to test. Put the cod in a gratin dish, pour a good couple of tablespoons of olive oil over the top, season well, and cook in the hot oven for 12 minutes before piercing with a skewer. The flesh should be unresistant right the way through.

While the fish is cooking, snip the bacon into tiny strips and fry them in a little pan until brown on both sides. Drain the lentils, then add the bacon. Tip in the roasted vegetables with their juice, and the crème fraîche.

Serve the cod alongside or on top of the lentils. You might wish to serve some creamy mashed potatoes, too.

Baked Turbot with Sauce Bretonne

SERVES 6
preheat oven to 400°F

5–6lb turbot
a small bunch of chervil
    and flat-leaf parsley, chopped
4 tbsp unsalted butter
⅔ cup white wine
sea salt and black pepper

For the sauce:
4 organic egg yolks
2 tsp Dijon mustard
a few drops of tarragon vinegar,
    if you don't have any, use
    white-wine vinegar with a
    teaspoon of fresh tarragon
2 tbsp watercress, chopped
2 tbsp chopped chervil, chopped
½ cup unsalted butter, melted,
    and the creamy solids removed
sea salt and pepper

Stuff the fish with the herbs. Grease a large roasting pan with butter, and place the fish in it. Pour the white wine over, dot the fish with butter, and season. Cover the fish with a sheet of parchment paper and bake for about 25 minutes before testing it with a skewer right the way through. How long it will take depends on the thickness of the fish, so if it is only a tiny bit resistant at its thickest point, check it again in 5 minutes. It is not difficult—fish are not temperamental or more difficult to master than meat, but there is less leeway between being cooked and overcooked. Roughly 10 minutes before you are going to test the fish, start making your sauce.

Stir together the egg yolks, salt, and pepper with the Dijon mustard. Add a few drops of the tarragon vinegar, then add the watercress and chervil and slowly stir in the melted butter, a few drops at a time to start with, as you would for mayonnaise. The sauce will hold if you place it over a bowl of hot water, but do not make it in advance—you want the herbs to be green and fresh tasting. You can experiment with other herbs like chives, flat-leaf parsley, and dill, the best herb if you want to try the sauce with a piece of poached salmon or sea trout.

A perfectly beautiful pale salad, lightly bound with a herb mayonnaise. Each ingredient adds a different texture and flavor; the whole is a dish of gentle subtlety requiring absolutely nothing else. When I first made it, my youngest daughter Charissa and I ate the whole bowlful.

New Potato, Chicken, Green Bean, Egg, and Avocado Salad in a Herb Mayonnaise

SERVES 2

2 handfuls of green beans
12–14oz small waxy new
  potatoes, scraped, boiled, and
  still warm
1 organic Hass avocado
2 organic eggs
1 cup or so of leftover chicken,
  without the skin, pulled along
  the grain into ¼in strips
homemade mayonnaise made
  with an egg yolk, half olive oil,
  half sunflower oil, lemon juice,
  and salt, with a handful of
  snipped chives, finely chopped
  flat-leaf parsley and 6 finely
  chopped lovage leaves if you
  have them, stirred in

Soak the green beans in cold water for an hour to invigorate them. Trim and throw them, a handful at a time, into a large pan of rapidly boiling, well-salted water. Do not put a lid on the pan or throw all the beans in at once, so lowering the temperature of the water to below boiling. If you do, the beans will turn out khaki rather than sparkling green. Cook until they have just lost their bite. Resistant green beans are horrid, the French never fell for the bizarre *al dente* bean habit we seemed to embrace 10 years ago. Plunge the beans immediately into cold water to arrest the cooking, drain them, and chop into thirds.

Meanwhile, softly hard-boil the eggs, halve them, and cut each half into three. Slice the larger cooked potatoes in half, leave the pebble-sized ones whole. Cut the avocado into slices.

Place everything in a roomy, pretty bowl. Pour the herbed mayonnaise over, and turn the salad lightly so nothing gets broken up. Serve while the beans and potatoes still have a memory of warmth about them.

You can use loin of venison for this dish if you prefer, taking it off the bone and marinating it in red wine for a couple of days. Wild roe deer does have an incomparable flavor, but it is not always possible to lay your hands on it. The best unintensively reared venison I can get comes from Graeme Wallace out on the Blackdown Hills. I find that keeping his medallions of venison in the wrapping in my refrigerator for two to three weeks improves both the flavor and texture. I want game, not beef. The sweet-sour, aniseedy-earthy, creamy-perfumed elements of the subtext are powerful foils to the venison.

Medallions of Venison with Spiced Beet, Cornichons, Tarragon, and Sour Cream

SERVES 4

2 shallots
butter
6 juniper berries, crushed
1 heaped tsp red-currant jelly
¼ cup port
½ cup red wine
1¼ cups game or chicken stock
1½lb or so of venison medallions, at least ½in thick
¼ cup sour cream
4 or 5 cornichons
fresh tarragon, finely chopped
2 or 3 medium beet, scrubbed, root ends still attached, wrapped in foil, and baked in a medium oven (350°F)
2 tbsp unsalted butter
well-aged balsamic vinegar

Chop the shallots finely and sweat them in a little butter with the crushed juniper berries until soft, before adding the red-currant jelly, port, and red wine. Reduce them by about a half, then add the stock and again reduce by a half.

While this is happening, cook the medallions in a pan with a little melted butter, turning them frequently and making absolutely sure you don't overcook them. Dried-out venison is not one of the great pleasures of life; tender, pink, stickily oozing venison is. Check with the point of a skewer—you want a little blood, but the meat should feel soft right through, after about 3 minutes a side. Season.

When the stock has reduced, finish it with a generous tablespoon of sour cream, some finely sliced cornichons, and a little finely chopped tarragon. The beet you can cook in advance, peel when it is not too hot, and grate. Then all you need to do is heat it through in a bit of butter, salt and pepper, and a little aged balsamic vinegar.

Roe deer produces the best-flavored venison, in a different league from red. It needs to be well aged and then marinated, before being covered in a protective coating of fat. It has so little fat of its own that it dries out disastrously without it. I think roast venison works much better with mashed potatoes than roast, and a coarse mash of carrot and rutabaga. You can then serve roasted parsnips for texture. A great dish for a party of eight or more. The fatback is not worth eating. Don't be tempted to use smoked bacon—its flavor is too pervasive.

Roast Haunch of Venison

SERVES 8

a haunch of venison
1 bottle good red wine
2 tbsp olive oil
brandy
1 tsp juniper berries, bruised
1 tsp black peppercorns
organic fatback
3 onions, sliced
1 tbsp elder and blackberry jelly
    or any sharp jelly

My haunch weighed more than 5lb. I kept it in the refrigerator for four days—longer would have been fine—before putting it on a large, shallow plate in a coolish place for two days, with a marinade of the wine, olive oil, a measure of brandy, and some juniper berries and black peppercorns. Again, a few days longer would have been fine. I basted or turned it over from time to time, and kept it under plastic wrap.

When you're ready to cook the venison, preheat the oven to 400°F. Season and cover the whole of the top of the haunch with slices of fatback, place it on a bed of sliced onions in a roasting pan, and roast it for two hours.

Transfer the meat to a carving dish, cover it with foil, and leave it to rest for 25 minutes, allowing the juices to work their way back through to the edge of the meat from the middle. I made a ruby-red gravy from the marinade stirred into the caramelized onions with a tablespoon of elder and blackberry jelly.

I am not suggesting Christmas Eve is the only time you eat this dish, it is too good for that, but I always cook a special fish dish then in both anticipation and dread of the monstrous meat fest that ensues. This Christmas Eve we had lightly smoked eel fillets for lunch with a homemade horseradish cream and granary toast. With them, I served shot glasses of the first of my late-bottled damson and mulberry gin. In the evening I roasted enormously thick hake steaks on the bone, hence the charnel house oven temperature, and cooked poor pan's potatoes, the Spanish patatas a lo pobre. The latter is a oily, garlicky potato dish that I make with both red and green bell peppers, decanting the excess deliciously scented olive oil into a jar to use for cooking stewing meat, onions, fish, or any dish that can carry the robust flavors.

Roast Hake Steaks with Poor Man's Potatoes

SERVES 4
preheat oven to 450°F

For the potatoes:
1 cup best extra virgin olive oil
3 large onions, sliced thinly
5–6 cloves garlic, sliced thickly
3 bell peppers, red and green, I
   usually use two red to one
   green, the red are more
   digestible
3 or 4 fresh bay leaves
2¼lb firm waxy-fleshed potatoes
a couple of handfuls of cherry
   tomatoes (optional)
sea salt and black pepper

4 extra-thick hake steaks on the
   bone, mine were about 1½ in
   thick
olive oil
sea salt and black pepper

In a large heavy-bottomed pan, heat 5 tablespoons of the olive oil, then add the finely sliced onion and some salt to help release the juice. Cook gently for about 20 minutes, stirring occasionally, until softened and translucent. Add the sliced garlic, roughly chopped peppers, and the bay leaves, which you can break up a bit to release their flavor, and cook for 15 minutes longer.

Cut the potatoes lengthwise, then cut each slice into two or three chunks and salt them lightly. Add the rest of the olive oil to the pan and when it has heated up, throw in the potatoes and the tomatoes if you are using them. Leave everything to simmer for 40–50 minutes, by which time the potatoes will have cooked through completely when you pierce them with a skewer. Drain the oil through a strainer into a pitcher, enough will have adhered to coat the vegetables without them swimming, and all the flavors will have married most pleasingly.

About 15–20 minutes before the potatoes are ready, brush the hake steaks on both sides with olive oil, put them in a gratin dish, and season. Put the fish in the oven, and test it after 15 minutes with the point of a skewer through its thickest part. The flesh should not resist you at all and be flaky, translucent, and juicy without having softened to a pulp. The potatoes will keep in a warm oven if there is any discrepancy over timing. If you use cherry tomatoes, you will have no need of another vegetable.

I am so easily led, but I suspect that is the fate or the temperament of many a keen cook. This is the third book I have written to include a recipe for Irish stew, and just in case anyone has even noticed and feels short-changed, they have all been different. This latest is my under-the-influence version of how Richard Corrigan, the divine Irish chef of Lindsay House, in London, and I cooked it when he came down to appear in my recent television series for U.K. Food. We managed what amounted to a four-course thesis on the merits and demerits of everything from scrag to middle neck of lamb; whether barley should or shouldn't be used (and, I might say, another major influence, Simon Hopkinson, to whom I gossiped subsequently on the subject of Richard's theory, disagreed totally); stock versus water; and which vegetables and herbs.

I am now convinced that Richard is right, although I don't know whether I'll always be bothered to bring the meat to a boil first and discard the water, and plunge the potatoes into the stew 40 minutes or so before the dish is ready, rather than burying them at the outset as I have always done. But Richard has managed to shame me into not using barley any more, as he thinks it's a starch too far with the potato. Simon differs, but then he's not Irish, although Richard's reasons are textural rather than to do with authenticity. And I actually taught him something, a first and probably a last! He took one look at my organic scrag, cut into thick, bony, fatty chunks, and said that he'd been trying to get meat that looked as good as mine but had never succeeded.

Irish Stew

SERVES 6

3lb 5oz organic scrag (middle
   neck) of lamb
4 onions, sliced
3 cups carrots, cut into thick disks
3 stalks of celery, cut into short
   lengths
a bouquet of fresh herbs
2¼lb baking potatoes
sea salt and black pepper

Cover the meat with water in a large, heavy-bottomed pot and bring it slowly to a boil. Transfer the meat to a plate, throw out the scummy water, and start again—put the vegetables at the bottom of the pot, tuck in the bouquet, place the meat on top of the vegetables, and just cover with water, or tuck in the potatoes before covering with water. I think I will continue to cook the potatoes in the pot from the start, since they help the water to become thickened and starchy. Season, bring to a boil, cover with a lid, and cook at a gentle blip for a couple of hours.

Then, Richard's thickening trick: Remove a good couple of ladles of potato, vegetable, and juice, mash to a coarse pulp with a potato masher, and return to the pot. Consume in large quantities, perhaps with some colcannon. Even better the next day if you leave the dish to cool, skim off the congealed meat fat, and reheat when you want it.

Colcannon

SERVES 6—8

2¼lb green cabbage, finely
   chopped
2 small leeks, finely chopped
⅔—1¼ cups milk
2¼lb potatoes, roughly chopped
salt and pepper
a pinch of grated nutmeg
½ cup butter

Simmer the cabbage and leeks in just enough milk to cover, until soft. Boil the potatoes until tender, drain, and mash them, then season to taste with salt, pepper, and nutmeg. Add the cabbage, leek, and milk mixture. Place in a deep, warm serving dish, make a well in the middle, and pour in the melted butter. Serve the vegetables with spoonfuls of the butter.

This is for an older leg, a hogget rather than a tasteless and underage youth, or indeed for a real oldster—a ruby-red leg of mutton.

Leg of Lamb Braised Slowly with Haricot Beans

SERVES 8

preheat oven to 450°F

3 cups haricot or flageolet beans,
    soaked overnight
butter and olive oil
1 leg of lamb
a small ladleful of brandy
8oz fatback, snipped into strips,
    rind removed
2 carrots, peeled and diced
2 stalks of celery, peeled and sliced
2 onions, peeled and chopped
3 leeks, cleaned and sliced
12 whole cloves of garlic, peeled
a bunch of fresh rosemary,
    thyme, and bay tied together
½ bottle white wine
4–6 cups chicken stock
sea salt and black pepper

Drain the beans, just cover them with fresh water, and bring them to a boil. Remove any scum with a draining spoon and paper towels, then simmer for an hour. They will be undercooked. Drain them, but keep their liquid.

Heat a generous pat of butter and a good slug of olive oil in a large, heavy-bottomed pot. Season, then gently brown the leg of lamb on all sides. Pour the brandy into the pot, warm it, then set light to it with a taper, letting it flame and crackle until the alcohol has burned off.

Put the leg and all the juices into a roasting pan. Add a bit more fat and oil to the pot and brown the fatback, adding the vegetables and garlic when the fat begins to run. When the vegetables have began to soften, scrape the contents of the pot into the roasting pan, add the bouquet of herbs, beans, and enough wine and stock, which you have heated together, to cover the vegetables but not the meat. Add some of the bean liquid if you need to.

Cover the pan with foil and cook in the oven for 3½ to 4 hours, turning every 40 minutes or so. Adjust the seasoning and cut the lamb into thick slices, heaping each plate with mashed potatoes, vegetables, beans, and juices as you go.

Every year I feel impelled to come up with a different solution for the remains of our lovely, organic Bronze turkey; pies, risottos, and fricassés have all had their year, as have pulled and deviled turkey, and turkey curry. This year I made the most successful dish yet, spurred on by the thought that the friends we were having over to supper would consider cold turkey, if not exactly an insult, perhaps something unexpected in the originality and expectation department. This is something to do when you really want to finish the bird, since I do not believe in removing the meat from the carcass until the point you are going to eat it: It dries out more quickly away from the bone. So, remove all the meat you can and make a huge pot or two of turkey stock the afternoon of the gratin supper. The sauce you are going to swathe the bird in is unctuously creamy, but made less so with equal quantities of hot stock. You can prepare the dish, right up to the heating up and blasting under the broiler, a bit earlier in the afternoon. White and dark meats should be used in as equal quantities as possible. I fed seven people, with second helpings for those who wanted them.

A Gratin of Turkey… or Chicken, Guinea Fowl, Pheasant

SERVES 7

4 tbsp butter

2 heaped tbsp all-purpose flour

1¼ cups or so of rich full-fat milk

10–12 tbsp heavy cream

12–14 tbsp turkey stock, but you may need more of all three: milk, cream, and stock

nutmeg, sea salt, and pepper

4 tbsp coarsely grated Parmesan cheese

2¼lb cooked turkey meat, pulled along the grain into roughly equal-size pieces

2–3 handfuls of fresh bread crumbs

another tbsp or two of coarsely grated Parmesan cheese,

Melt the butter, then stir in the flour off the heat. Return to the stove, add half the hot milk, and whisk it in. Add the rest of the milk, continuing to whisk until you have a satin-smooth, but far too thick, blanket of sauce, about 5 minutes. Add the cream and the hot turkey stock, half of each at a time, and continue to whisk. Season, being sparing with the salt at this stage because the Parmesan is salty, and cook very, very gently for about 20 minutes on a heat diffuser if you have one. You should no longer be able to smell flour when it has been cooking long enough. You want a thick, velvety, pouring consistency, so if the sauce still looks too solid, add some more cream and stock, and whisk them in. Off the heat, whisk in the Parmesan and adjust the seasoning.

Pour a layer of sauce into a large gratin dish, just to coat the bottom of the dish. Add the turkey, pour the rest of the sauce over, sprinkle with bread crumbs and Parmesan, and cook in a hot oven (400°F) for 15 minutes. Finish under the broiler until bubbling and golden. If you are making this in advance, leave the dish to cool before you sprinkle it with bread crumbs and cheese.

A traditional Provençal bourride is a rich fish stew enlivened and enriched with dollops of aïoli, a pungent with-garlic-and-green-olive-oil mayonnaise that is stirred into it at the last minute. I think this dish lends itself equally well to being made with chicken. The bird is cut up and braised in strong herbs and saffron, the juices acidic with tomato and white wine. The acid balance is then rescued and somehow brought back from the brink at the last moment by the emulsification of the garlic, egg yolk, and oil.

A Bourride of Chicken

SERVES 6

For the chicken:
olive oil
2 cups well washed, trimmed and sliced leeks, the whites only
6 or 7 carrots, thinly sliced
2 medium onions, thinly sliced
3 cloves of garlic, finely chopped
14oz can whole organic tomatoes
1 decent-sized organic chicken, skinned and jointed, each leg cut into 2 pieces. Leave the wings on the carcass for stock
3 strips of orange peel
a good pinch of saffron filaments
a few sprigs of fresh thyme, bay leaves, and marjoram or oregano
⅔ cup dry white wine
sea salt and fresh black pepper

Heat some olive oil in a heavy-bottomed Dutch oven, then add the leeks, carrots, and onions and sweat them gently for 10 minutes. Add the garlic and a can of tomatoes, chopping them down into the pan as you go. Stir everything together, then add the pieces of chicken, orange peel, saffron, a couple of sprigs each of the herbs, stripped from their stems, and a couple of bay leaves.

Simmer very gently for another 10 minutes. Add the wine and bring back to boiling point. Cover with a layer of parchment paper and a lid, and simmer on top of the cooker until the chicken is tender and the juice runs clear when the flesh is pierced with a skewer, 20–25 minutes.

You can get the dish to this point an hour or so in advance, then just warm it through when you're ready to eat. You can also make the aïoli in advance and merely effect the heating through and their ultimate marriage when you are ready to do so.

For the aïoli:
4 large cloves of garlic, peeled
sea salt
1 organic egg yolk
2/3–1¼ cup best extra-virgin,
    cold-pressed green olive oil,
    you need this intensity and
    fruitiness for *le vrai aïoli*
lemon juice

Pound the garlic in a mortar with a little bit of sea salt, add the egg yolk, and stir it in with a wooden spoon. Start pouring the olive oil in a drop at a time, stirring continuously until the liquid begins to emulsify to yellow ointment. Then you can pour in a slow, steady stream, making sure that your stirring incorporates the oil as quickly as it descends into the bowl. Add lemon juice to taste at the end.

If you are going to keep the aïoli for an hour or two before using, pour a thin film of olive oil over its surface to prevent a crust forming. You can stir this oil back into the aïoli when you are ready to drop it into the bourride.

To add the aïoli to the dish, put a couple of ladles of the hot sauce into a bowl. Whisk in the aïoli quickly with a balloon whisk, then put it back into the pan off the heat, and whisk it in more before you serve it. A few plain boiled potatoes are all you need to crush into the bourride, followed by a green salad.

This dish is a true classic. It is perfect at an al fresco summer lunch, with a huge white spoon planted into the thickly sticky ointment of aïoli.

It is not the ingredients that are sufficiently different for me to have the nerve to give you this recipe, it is the technique. Or techniques, since I am also giving you a completely unorthodox version, given to me by Heston Blumenthal, a talented chef. Heston's is as scientifically unimpeachable as a recipe can be and, since he is in cahoots with Peter Barham, a physics professor at Bristol University, England, he is in something of an unparallel universe to my own. I first met Heston and Peter at a hifalutin' sounding conference on molecular gastronomy at Erice in Sicily earlier in the year. What I learned, in a reductionist nutshell, was to question the methodology of everything I had ever cooked, because there was probably a better way of doing it scientifically speaking. And that I should never have ignored the huge part that science plays in the cooking of good food in such a comprehensive way. You do not have to be a scientist to understand the reasons and methods behind the processes. Scientists, food technologists, food writers, and chefs all gathered together for three days to try to understand better what happens to food when we subject it to the alchemy of cooking, to try to define taste and texture and what we mean by them; and to cast aside some of our insular prejudices.

Mashed Potato—My Mash

SERVES 3

one large or two medium
   potatoes per person. Choose a
   floury-textured, absorbent
   variety rather than a firm, waxy
   one
½ cup whole milk
6 tbsp unsalted butter
seasoning

My favorite potato for mash is the "salad blue." Not only does it have the right floury texture, it is a deep violet color, making, after the paling effects of the milk and butter, a thrillingly exotic parma violet-colored mash. Quantity is down to the individual, but my Irish blood is clearly dominant judging by the amount I and my family seem to get through.

Mash is both vehicle, background, and food in its own right. It should be cooked as carefully and with as much attention as whatever else is going to grace your plate, which it often isn't. There is absolutely no excuse in my book for watery, lumpy, slack, or under-seasoned mash, even less for butter-free mash, unless you are being ersatz Provençal and pouring in a glug of olive oil. Low-fat spreads and skimmed milk are not what mash is all about. And if you are worried about the butter quota, just eat less mash, ergo you eat less butter.

Peel the potatoes, cut them into large chunks. and cover them with water in a pan. Sprinkle in some salt, and bring them to a boil with the lid on. Turn down the temperature to a leisurely simmer and cook until you can pierce them right through with a skewer without resistance. No hard edges but not so cooked that they are beginning to collapse. Drain the potatoes, then put a clean dish towel over the top of the pan, and force the lid down as hard as you can for 5 minutes, just as you would to absorb the steam when you have been cooking rice.

Turn the potatoes into a food mill with the coarse disk in place, and gently heat about ½ cup full-cream milk with a good lump of unsalted butter, about 6 tablespoons for 3 people, in the pan in which you cooked the potatoes. Mouli the potatoes into the pan as the milk heats and the butter melts, then season to taste. Over gentle heat, stir the potato, milk, and butter well together with a wooden spoon, altering the texture and flavor if it is not quite right by adding more butter and/or milk and seasoning.

You will realize when you begin to stir, just how smooth this precious kitchen gadget renders your potatoes. If you do not have a food mill, might I suggest they are invaluable? Soups have more texture and body when put through a food mill than if you swirl them to oblivion in a blender, and your mashed potato will be peerless. Enough said.

Well not quite. Richard Corrigan passes his potatoes through a potato ricer twice, and probably uses half the amount of butter to potato. Sublime and sublimely rich. It is brought to the table in little copper pans. I always ask for more, despite the butter content; I just can't help myself, it is the best.

Heston's Mashed Potatoes

potatoes, Belle de Fontenay,
   Bintje or Charlottes are
   particularly good for mash, but
   Desireé can work well, too
butter, a third the weight of your
   potatoes or less
milk
white pepper

Peel and slice the potatoes into 1-inch chunks. Soak them in hot water, around 150°F, for 30 minutes, keeping the water at as constant a temperature as you can. Presoaking fixes the starch molecules, making an even network of gelatinized starch surrounded by water. In effect, you've stopped free starch molecules running around.

After 30 minutes, put the potatoes under cold running water until cold—they will look opaque—then put them into a pan of barely simmering salted water. Cook them at a blip—if the water boils too much they will break up—for about 30 minutes, until the point of a knife goes in without resistance. Drain the potatoes, put them back in the pan with a cloth under the lid, and shake them while they dry out.

Then put them through a potato ricer or the finest disk of a food mill onto diced, cold butter in a bowl. Heston uses a third the weight of butter to potato, you may wish to use less. He then pushes them through a drum strainer twice; you can use the food mill. Forcing the potatoes down rather than from side to side, stops them from going gluey. By this method, you have gelatinized the starch and made an emulsion, rather like mayonnaise.

To finish, put the mash in a pan and warm some milk in another pan. Pour the milk over your potato base a bit at a time, over gentle heat, whisking it as you go, until you achieve the desired texture. Add freshly ground white pepper at the end.

You can keep this base in the refrigerator until you need it. Never before have I come across a scientific way of making mash that means you can keep it in the refrigerator for up to four days without its being beyond redemption. I never put mash in the refrigerator full stop, but having gelatinized the starch, it will not come to grief, as long as you bring it back to room temperature before heating it through gently as above.

Another utterly unorthodox yet scientifically proven way of cooking this classic dish to perfection. You can cook this version the day before and merely heat it through when you want it, without it separating into an oily, unappetizing mass. First buy your mandolin, preferably of the strong plastic Japanese.

Heston's Pommes Dauphinoise

SERVES 2
preheat oven to 225°F

1lb potatoes
⅔ cup milk
1 sliced clove of garlic
a sprig of thyme and a bay leaf
some nutmeg, cayenne, and salt
7 tbsp cream
6–10 tbsp unsalted butter

Slice the potatoes on your mandolin straight into a gratin dish containing the milk, which should cover the potatoes, so you might need another ⅔ cup. Add the garlic, herbs, spices, and salt, err on the generous side with the salt as the potatoes draw it in, and bring it up to a simmer. Simmer for 5 minutes, making sure the potatoes do not stick to the bottom of the pan, then remove the thyme and bay leaf. The potato starch thickens the milk, so you can use less cream.

Then add the cream and unsalted butter, depending on your taste, and place the gratin dish on a baking tray in the oven for 4 hours under a tightly wrapped foil lid. After each hour, if you can remember, remove the foil lid and press down the potatoes with a spatula to bring the liquid back up to the surface. When you remove the dish from the oven, there will be liquid covering the top of the potatoes. Leave the dish overnight in the refrigerator with the foil cover on, and a couple of weights on top of it, and the potatoes will reabsorb the liquid.

When you want to use the potatoes, remove the gratin dish from the refrigerator in time to bring them up to room temperature. Preheat the oven again and heat the dish through for 20 minutes, then place it under the broiler until it is golden and bubbling

the advance party

3

Some dishes are made for parties, and the best of them, if you are the party giver, are the ones that simply demand to be prepared in advance. Jambon persillé, a beautiful pink and green mosaic, Jackson Pollock of a dish, is one of them. When my first attempt plopped out of its glass bowl onto a plate, glistening rosy-pink chunks and grassy-green seams glued with the transparently binding jelly from the trotters, I did stop for a minute to marvel. It tasted as stunning as it looked. Make this dish the day before you need it.

Jambon Persillé

SERVES 12
it really isn't worth making less, but it keeps well in the refrigerator

5½lb boneless pork shoulder, tied
4 organic pig's feet, split
a bunch each of tarragon, thyme, and parsley
12 black peppercorns
6 juniper berries, bruised
1 bottle of dry white wine
6 tbsp chopped flat-leaf parsley
2 cloves of garlic, crushed
2 tbsp tarragon vinegar
grated nutmeg
pepper

Cut the pork shoulder into three large chunks, still tied, and place in a heavy-bottomed pot with the pig's feet, herbs, spices, and wine. Top up with water if you need, just to cover the meat completely. Bring to a boil slowly, scum rigorously, and continue cooking at a mere blip for 2 hours. Transfer the pork to a plate and leave it to cool. Remove the herbs, then continue to boil the liquid and trotters for 30 minutes longer. Strain into a large bowl and cool quickly. Once the liquid is cool, skim off as much of the white fat as possible.

Don't cut the meat until the stock has completely cooled, or it will dry out. Leaving some but not all of the fat on it, cut the meat into ½-inch cubes. Place them in the bottom of a large, glass bowl. Some people use a terrine, but I think a great circular domed mosaic is more breathtaking. Add the parsley, crushed garlic, and tarragon vinegar to the cooled liquid, then the nutmeg and pepper, and tip everything over the pork. Stir to mix the parsley in with the pork. The pork should be completely covered. Keep any extra liquid to use as jellied stock. Cover the bowl with plastic wrap and put it in the refrigerator overnight.

When it has set, spoon off the white fat down to the darker jelly. Remove the bowl from the refrigerator 30 minutes before you want to eat. Immediately before serving, dunk the bowl into boiling water for about 15 seconds. Turn the jambon persillé out onto a plain white dish. Serve it with mustard, cornichons, buttered new potatoes, and a plain romaine lettuce salad, or with homemade bread and best butter.

When, last summer, the nearest bakery to me that makes anything faintly resembling a decent loaf erased three-quarters of its loaves from its repertoire, it was clearly time to take action. Hobbs House bakery at Chipping Sodbury doesn't deliver its wondrous bread this far south of Bristol. And my infrequent trips to Baker and Spice in London are utterly spoiling when they happen, but make the thought of being despoiled the rest of the time with inferior supermarket pap—for which you are paying for air and water rather than flour and time—distinctly unappealing.

Bread, a work in progress

The world falls into two camps at this point: Those who make their own bread and those, like me, who don't. Or didn't. As I write this, I realize my early weeks as a bread-making novice have now turned into months. Seven months. And bar the odd loaf bought hungrily from the two impeccable sources mentioned above, I have kept up this new pursuit as doggedly as the running I started nearly two years ago. In fact, the two are not altogether unallied. Training for my first marathon earlier in the year gave me a prodigious appetite for carbohydrates, and turned me into a breakfaster. Homemade bread, toasted, with homemade crab-apple or bramble jelly in the fall and early winter, later followed by Seville orange marmalade—my other new-found skill—is now a habit it would be difficult to break.

Literature on the subject of bread making is so extensive as to be seriously off-putting to the beginner, even a relatively experienced cook like myself. What you want is a simple, crusted loaf that has a fine texture and flavor, and is not gluey, taut-grained, crumbly, spongy, or leaden. You want it to work the first and every subsequent time, instilling confidence, a sense of achievement, and the feeling that finally, finally, one has the sort of kitchen that smells how a kitchen should. There is no better scent than that of a fresh, yeast loaf rising, cooking, and cooling before you eat it—still warm, nutty, crusty, with a just-too-large-to-be-decent slab of deliquescent unsalted butter.

The last few months have taught me many things. First, it is perfectly possible to fit bread making into the most hectic of schedules, and without being a martyr to the cause. It does not demand the sort of attention that many supposedly simpler dishes do. I can leave it to rise and go out running AM or make and eat dinner as it rises PM. If you bake three loaves at a time and freeze one or two, depending on the size of your family, bread making does not become a chore, it stays a delight. Every bag of flour you buy, albeit the same make as the last one you bought, is different, so you need to feel what you're doing, not just follow directions. That takes experience, but all the bread I've baked has been better than supermarket bread, and most of it has been REALLY good. The ambient temperature makes a difference.

So-called "fresh" yeast isn't always fresh. I have been sold dead yeast on a number of occasions. Always inspect the package before you walk away. If it is pale and crumbly, rather than rubbery, and in a homogenous, springy block, do not accept it. Some recipes say one ounce of yeast per one pound loaf, some say one-and-a-half ounces per three one-pound loaves. I have made both. My son was complaining at the over-yeasty taste of the bread with the larger concentration, when I found the second recipe on another bag of flour, which, incidentally, reversed the kneading and knocking-back processes from my original recipe. Less yeast, and kneading after the first mixing rather than the second, work much better, both for texture and taste.

As for the kneading, four or five minutes is not enough. You have to knead vigorously for eight to ten minutes, and only then, in my experience, will your loaf not turn into a compressed breezeblock. It is the only hard work throughout the process, and its rigors are both comforting and enjoyable if you are prepared to find them so, which I decidedly am. No bread-making machine or dough hook I've used has done it for me so far, and the dried yeast you use in machines does not make bread of the taste or texture that you are making homemade bread for in the first place. Circular loaves baked in a low-sided pan work the best as you get the highest surface area of crisp crust, but don't make a loaf in a too-big pan, because the loaf will spread sideways during the rise as well as upward.

Experiment. Once you have cracked the making of a basic loaf, change it. I have made the following over the last seven months: whole wheat and rye bread; a spelt loaf with handfuls of millet thrown into it—spelt is an early Egyptian flour made of a durum-type wheat; granary bread with two-thirds malted grain granary flour, either Dove's or Shipton Mill if you can find them, both organic, and one-third white or whole wheat flour added; 100 percent whole wheat bread with a handful of sunflower seeds, poppy seeds, or sesame seeds—or all of them—the tops brushed with milk just before baking, and one of each of the above seeds scattered on each of the three loaves; white bread made with hard, unbleached organic flour, with and without the addition of any or all of the three seeds.

I find producing a homemade loaf at any meal brings about a quite extraordinary reaction. It is not nostalgia exactly, because most of us were not lucky enough to be brought up on homemade bread. But it is nostalgia for what might have been and could obviously be, when the beholder sees the apparent ease with which the warm, yeasted offering is brought to the table, as though it were just an ordinary part of the proceedings and of keeping a good table. It sort of makes it seem possible, which I now know it is, without being a slave to it.

Malted Grain Loaf

MAKES THREE LOAVES

I leave it to you to vary the flavor with the different flours and seeds

8 cups organic malted grain flour

4 cups hard organic whole wheat flour

1 tbsp sea salt

1½oz fresh yeast or 3 packages active dry yeast

3 heaped tsp dark brown sugar

4 cups hand-hot water; it should neither feel boiling, nor tepid

3 tbsp extra-virgin olive oil

sesame, sunflower, or poppy seeds and a little milk for the top of the loaves

Put the flours out into a very large mixing bowl and add the salt. Boil a kettle, and put about 1 cup of boiling water in a measuring cup, topping up to the 2-cup mark with water from the cold tap. The water should now feel hand hot. Drop in the dark brown sugar and fresh yeast and stir vigorously for a few seconds until the liquid looks creamy. Leave it for 15 minutes to rise. I still find this as absorbing as I did when I baked my first loaf, the living organism fizzing, popping, bubbling, and the sudden rush and rise in volume like a geyser with a will of its own inhabiting the cup.

Pour the contents of the cup into the flour, add 1¾ cups of hand-hot water, then pour in the three tablespoons of olive oil. With one hand, start working the wet dough together until it coheres completely into a ball, then remove it from the bowl on to the work surface and start kneading. Sometimes the dough will appear too dry to work, sometimes too wet and claggy. Simply add a little more water for the former, and sprinkle with a little more flour for the latter; the dough should not feel sticky. After you have started working the dough vigorously with both hands on the work surface, you will, from time to time, probably need to shake a little more flour onto the work surface. The dough will elongate into a sausage each time you work it, which you need to furl back into a ball shape each time before repeating the process.

After 10 minutes, place the ball back in the bowl and cover the top with a clean linen dish towel, which you have wet in hot water and wrung out. Leave at the side of the stove for about an hour, or until it has swollen to about twice its original volume and appears light and spongy.

Set the oven to 450°F to warm up. Brush the insides of your bread pans with olive oil. Turn the dough out onto the work surface, and divide it into 3 pieces with a sharp knife. Knock the air out of each piece for 3 or 4 minutes, without kneading it, and place each loaf in its pan.

Re-cover with a hot, damp cloth, and leave in the warmth close by or on top of the stove for 20–25 minutes. Brush the top of each loaf with a little milk and sprinkle over a handful of seeds. Put two loaves together on a higher shelf and one on a lower. Set the timer for 35 minutes, but it could take 40. You want a distinctive hollow sound when you tap the base of the bread while turning it out on to a rack with a metal spatula. Allow it to cool

for at least 40 minutes; bread is steamy, doughy, and indigestible if you eat it too soon. These basic principles apply to all the other types of loaves I listed, and to rolls, which naturally take less time to cook. When you are using an all-purpose flour and wish to add seeds to the actual bread mix to make it more interesting, throwing in a handful of all three types of seeds—such as sunflower, sesame, and poppy—seems to work beautifully.

Progress...

Since writing the above beginners' treatise, my baking technique has advanced dramatically after a highly informative day with master miller John Lister of Shipton Mill in Gloucestershire, England. It appears that the rise of the commercial loaf, in both senses, is the result of two things. Post-19th century, came the discovery that brewer's yeast could enable the baker to prove the loaf quicker and quicker, using more and more yeast. Then, in the 1950s, came the Chorleywood bread process. They discovered that one of the key elements of good bread is putting in energy. "Kneading is not for fun, it is to condition the dough," John told me. "Then came the discovery that there are chemicals which can achieve this in a very short time, you can do the mix in 20 seconds, and that 20 seconds is the equivalent to 11 kilowatt hours of energy. It will prove in minutes, but high-speed bread is totally different to the hand-baked loaf. You are trading time for the mechanical input of energy and chemicals. You can make things bread shaped, but they are not bread. The fermentation process is the most important part of bread making. If you remove this process, how can you still call it bread? Imagine if the French took fermentation out of wine making and still called it wine. Fermentation is the critical part, it transforms wheat flours from inedible to edible. If you allow time for the fermentation to happen properly, the bread starts to digest the proteins in the wheat and transform them from indigestible to digestible. People might be put off by having to leave their bread to rise for 24 hours, but you just leave it alone in a warm place and it's ready. Bread NEEDS fermentation, it is the crucial element that changes it from raw to cooked. A long fermentation means the yeast produces sugars, and converts the carbohydrates into sugars so that they can multiply faster, then the sugars caramelize and you get a beautiful colored crust that you can recognize immediately."

Not only beautiful to look at, this bread has the texture that no instantly made loaf has, and a crust that you really have to chew—crisp, crusty, and almost cracks like an egg shell when you cut it. Good bread is also about the wheat the miller buys, the art of blending it, how it comes out slightly toasted from between the millstones in a process that, again, you cannot speed up. "Every time I try to make things more complex I come back to the simple best four loaves and change the process. Look at Monsieur Poilâne, he only makes one loaf. It's about best wheats, the simplest process and really understanding fermentation. It's a lifetime's work, just focusing on those aspects," John told me. So don't expect to achieve instant perfection. Just enjoy, as I do, the mysterious part of the process that is responsible for every batch you bake being wholly unlike the one you last baked. It is eternally fascinating to me how ambient temperature, the amount and age of yeast and flour, the warmth of your hands, and the strength you exert that particular day during the kneading, as well as many other things that I am only just beginning to learn to analyze, can affect the finished loaf.

Here is a sensationally good white loaf made with Shipton Mill's hard white flour, a handful of their newly toasted, deliciously oily wheatgerm, and an overnight or overday rise to maximize the fermentation. I now make bread on a terracotta stone. It should be a thick one, according to John, but my pizza stone does two loaves beautifully. It radiates the heat evenly and there are no pan sides to give you a less-crusty crust. Heat transfer is critical during baking, and stones radiate heat in a totally different way to a metal pan. I also throw in a splash of water or squirt it into the oven with my iron spray—the steam helps to caramelize the surface of the loaf. I think it works best after the loaf has been in the oven for 10 minutes, but see what you think. If you can't source Shipton Mill flours, use a top-quality organic, stoneground flour.

White Loaf

MAKES TWO LOAVES

8 cups traditional organic, hard white flour
3 tsp fine sea salt
1½oz compressed yeast or 3 packages active dry yeast
2½ cups warm water at 85°F in summer, 105°F in winter. To guess it, it needs to be hand hot, not boiling

Allow approximately 14½ hours from the time you start the dough to baking your bread. Dissolve a piece of yeast the size of a pea in ½ cup of warm water. I stir the yeast in with a tiny whisk in a pitcher. Leave it for 10 minutes, then add it to 1½ cups of the flour to which you have added half a teaspoonful of fine sea salt. Mix the dough a little with your fingers until it just coheres, then cover it with a dish towel soaked in cold water and wrung out—this prevents a skin forming. Leave it for 12 hours at room temperature in the kitchen. I have left it a couple of hours longer when convenient and it has not come to any harm.

Twelve hours later, dissolve the remaining yeast in ½ cup of warm water, whisking it as before. Leave it for 10–15 minutes in the warmth of the kitchen. It won't froth up as it does with a quick-rise bread when you add sugar to the yeast and water at this stage.

Mix the rest of the flour with the remaining salt and throw in a handful of wheatgerm. Add the starter dough, which will be spongy, to the mixture, then the yeasty liquid followed by the remaining 1¾ cups of warm water. Work it in the bowl with your fingers until it coheres, then transfer it to the work surface and knead energetically for 8–10 minutes.

Put it back in the large bowl, cover with the damp cloth again, and leave it for an hour to rise: it will double in volume. Put the dough back on the work surface, seize it, and bash the air out, then leave it uncovered for 15 minutes.

Divide the dough into two pieces with a knife and bash out the air again. Form each piece into a ball and cover with a damp cloth for 50 minutes. It will double in size again. Preheat the oven to 425°F and put the baking stone on the middle shelf to heat up. Snip a little decorative hole or two in the middle of the top of each loaf, scatter a tiny bit of flour over and, with a flat spatula, plop the loaves onto the hot stone. After 10 minutes, spray or throw a little water into the oven until the steam hisses. The loaves will need 35–40 minutes, check that the bottoms sound hollow before leaving them to cool for an hour on a rack.

Below: *White loaf*

Eric Treuille and Rosie Kindersley, his wife, are the new owner-managers of my favorite playing-truant shop, Books for Cooks, in Notting Hill, London. Eric has a lovely version of focaccia with thyme, Gruyère, and crème fraîche, the centerpiece of a light lunch that needs no more than a Provençal tomato salad or roasted tomato soup. Eric suggests making and kneading the dough and leaving it to rise in the refrigerator all day or all night, for 8–12 hours, before letting it stand at room temperature, punching it down, and shaping it.

Focaccia with Potato, Thyme, Gruyère, and Crème Fraîche

MAKES I LARGE LOAF
preheat oven to 400°F

For the dough:
4 cups hard white flour
2 tsp sea salt
1⅓ cup tepid water
2 tsp active-dry yeast

For the topping;
18oz baby potatoes
1 cup grated Gruyère
2 tsp fresh thyme leaves
sea salt and black pepper
4 tbsp crème fraîche
coarse salt to sprinkle

Put the flour in a bowl, make a well in the middle, and put the salt on the raised ridge of flour around the side. Pour the water into the well and sprinkle the yeast over. Leave for 5 minutes to soften, then stir to dissolve. Draw in enough of the flour to make a soft paste. Cover with a cloth and leave to sponge for 20 minutes until bubbly and slightly puffed up. Draw in the rest of the flour to make a rough, sticky dough. Turn out onto a lightly floured surface and knead for 10 minutes until smooth, light, and elastic. Put back into the bowl, cover with a cloth, and leave until doubled in size, about 1½ hours.

Cut the potatoes into ¼-inch slices. Bring a pan of salted water to a boil, add the potatoes, and bring back to a boil. Cook until the centers are just tender when pricked with the tip of a knife, about 5 minutes, drain well, and cool. Deflate the dough by pressing down with the palm of your hand. Roll out into a flat round, about 9 inches across, and place on an oiled baking sheet. Spread about half the cheese evenly on top of the bread dough, arrange the potatoes on top, scatter with thyme, and sprinkle with a little salt and pepper. Cover with a cloth and leave until risen, about 30 minutes. Dot teaspoons of crème fraîche over the potatoes and scatter on the remaining cheese.

Bake for about 30 minutes or until the potato topping is crisp and golden and the bread sounds hollow when tapped underneath. Cool on a wire rack. Serve warm or at room temperature, sprinkled with coarse salt and cut into wedges.

Falafel are one of the national dishes of Egypt, where they are made with dried white fava beans and chickpeas. I make mine with chickpeas alone, and have long pondered the curious fact that deep-fried foods accompanied by cooling yogurt or tahini sauce are perfect in the heat. I often serve falafel at large gatherings, winter and summer—they are the perfect food to eat in your fingers while you drink. Remember to soak the chickpeas overnight and you can then keep the prepared mixture for up to 24 hours in the refrigerator before you use it. On the subject of canned chickpeas, I'm afraid the answer is no. It is hardly a bother to soak your own, which in this recipe are whizzed to a gritty rawness in the food processor. You could not emulate the texture with the canned kind; they are mushy and the taste is not so good. Falafel also make a perfect outdoor lunch or picnic food, clutched inside a pita bread with some salad and a yogurty, minted, cucumber-studded dressing.

Falafel

MAKES ABOUT 30

2 cups dry organic chickpeas, soaked overnight

a medium onion, minced, nothing bigger, or the juice from the onion prevents the falafel from adhering when they are cooking

4 cloves of garlic, chopped

2 green chilies, seeded and finely chopped

a handful of flat-leaf parsley, chopped

a handful of fresh cilantro, chopped

2 tsp cumin seeds

2 tsp coriander seeds, ground with the cumin in a mortar

sea salt and black pepper

an unobtrusive oil for frying, peanut or grapeseed

Drain the soaked chickpeas and dry them. Put them in a food processor with the onion, garlic, chili, chopped herbs, ground spices, and seasoning. Blitz to a pulp, but don't expect the mixture to be smooth; the chickpeas will give it a grainy texture. Take walnut-sized quantities of the mixture and shape it into patties. You can use the falafel immediately, or put them on plates and keep them in the refrigerator.

Heat the oil. About 2 cups will be enough if you decide to fry the falafel waist deep before turning them over and cooking on the other side. I did this very successfully. Otherwise, use double the quantity of oil and deep-fry. Either way, drop in a bit of the mixture to test whether it's hot enough. It will resurface bubbling furiously if the oil is to temperature. Don't cook too many patties in one go, or you will reduce the temperature of the oil. Cook until a deep golden brown, about two minutes a side if you are turning them over, then transfer them to a plate and drain them well with paper towels, top and bottom.

Serve with some tahini sauce or a bowl of Greek-style yogurt. Thin the yogurt with a little milk and stir in a teaspoon of tempered, ground cumin, a clove of crushed garlic, and some salt and pepper.

A gloriously Mediterranean-colored mosaic of a dish that you can prepare up to the point of cooking in advance if you are going to serve it hot, and finish completely if you are going to serve it cold. I love the meatiness of monkfish, which lends itself so well to roasting, and the fact that the copious juices the fish exudes are tantamount to self-basting; most convenient. The saffron, scarlet, and emerald green colors are set off brilliantly by the fish's white background, and the fish juices are suffused with the scent of lemons, thyme, and cracked black peppercorns. The joy of this dish, too, is that the fish, stuffed with roasted red bell peppers and anchovies and tied like a package with string, takes no more than five minutes to prepare for the oven. Ask your fishmonger to skin and take out the backbone of the monkfish for you, leaving the fillets on each side still attached.

Above and below: *Roast Stuffed Monkfish*

Roast Stuffed Monkfish with a Lemon and Caper Sauce

SERVES 10

preheat oven to 400°F

5lb monkfish, a single tail if
  possible. Ask your fishmonger
  to remove the bone, leaving the
  fillets on either side still
  attached

1 tbsp each of thyme, black
  peppercorns, and sea salt

a pinch of saffron threads, soaked
  in a tablespoon or two of warm
  water for 10 minutes

2oz can of anchovies in olive oil,
  drained, or 2oz salted anchovies
  washed and despined under
  cold water

2 roasted, seeded, and peeled red
  bell peppers, or buy a jar of
  wood-roasted Spanish piquillo
  peppers

3–4 tbsp best olive oil

4 tbsp unsalted butter

1 lemon

a handful of flat-leaf parsley,
  chopped

2 tbsp capers, drained, then rinsed
  in a draining spoon under cold
  water

Put the thyme, peppercorns, and salt in a mortar and crush until coarsely ground. Open the fish like a book and spread the anchovies and red bell peppers evenly over both surfaces. Pour over the saffrony liquor, then half the olive oil. Close the fish together, and hold it while a friend or child ties string around it at 1-inch intervals, to make 10 portions.

Scatter the seasoning mixture in a roasting pan, roll the fish in it to coat, then pour on the rest of the olive oil. Put the fish in the middle of the oven for about 35 minutes to roast. Check with the point of a skewer that it has cooked right through and is not resistant in the middle. Transfer it to a hot serving dish if you are going to serve it hot and rest it, shrouded in foil, while you make the sauce.

Boil the remaining liquid in the roasting pan down to about half the quantity you started with. Meanwhile, peel the lemon, removing all the pith with the blade of a sharp knife, and divide the fruit into segments. In a small skillet, melt the butter gently until it begins to turn brown and nutty, add the pieces of lemon, then throw in the drained capers. Add the fish liquid and stir it in, then pour it over the fish, and strew over the parsley before you carve the fish into tranches 1 inch thick. Remember to remove the string before serving.

If you are serving the fish cold, do not offer the butter sauce. You can make the sauce with olive oil instead or omit it, merely pouring over the reduced liquid while the fish is cooling.

The English fishcake, alone and palely loitering in its mild, parsleyed, potatoey way, has always lent itself to a good spicing. Children demand ketchup, although in my youth there was the horror of anchovy essence that came in a dismal yukky pink bottle and was shaken with abandon into what I imagine was a béchamel sauce. And then along came people like the wonderful Kiwi chef Peter Gordon, broiling scallops and dressing them with crème fraîche, sweet chili, lime, and cilantro, or painting them with his scrumptious tomato chili jam, with its anchovied undertones of fish sauce. I make and keep a permanent home for this condiment in my refrigerator since discovering it. The jam works as well with pork, white fish, and vegetables as it does slathered on Montgomery Cheddar or an oozing goat cheese bruschetta.

I've always been of the opinion that a good kedgeree deserves a generous spicing of garam masala, and that a salmon fishcake is never better than when it is accompanied by almost its own weight, or at least size, of crème fraîche tartare. Hardly sacrilegious, then, to apply heat, citrusy spice and musky sweet-sharp undertones to cod, which is capable of absorbing them to great and good effect. You can make the cod-cake mixture well in advance and keep it covered in the refrigerator until frying time. The dipping sauce keeps equally well and should be served cold. These cod cakes also make a sensational first course, in which case they will feed four.

Cod Cakes with Kaffir Lime Leaves and Thai Dipping Sauce

SERVES 2 AS A MAIN DISH

1 shallot
2 cloves of garlic
2 small hot red chilies, seeded and
    chopped
a handful of fresh cilantro leaves,
    coarsely chopped
8 kaffir lime leaves, cut into strips
1 tbsp Thai fish sauce (*nam pla*)
sea salt
1lb cod fillet

Peel and chop the shallot and peel and crush the garlic cloves. Place the shallot, garlic, chilies and cilantro in a food processor with the lime leaves and fish sauce and blitz. Scrape into a bowl and season with sea salt. Throw the cod in chunks into the processor and blitz to a paste, but not to a sludge. Tip the fish into the spice bowl and mix everything together thoroughly.

Form the mixture into eight flat patties—you can flour your palms a little to prevent sticking—and put them covered in the refrigerator until an hour before you want to use them.

For the dipping sauce:

6 tbsp rice vinegar

4 tbsp light brown sugar

1 tbsp organic shoyu sauce

1 small red and 1 small green
  chili, seeded and finely chopped

1 tbsp cilantro leaves, very finely
  chopped

juice of 2 kaffir limes or 1 lime

peanut or grape seed oil for frying

Heat the vinegar and sugar in a small pan until the sugar has dissolved and the mixture is syrupy, then stir in the shoyu sauce. Leave it to cool before adding the chilies, cilantro, and lime juice. Chill.

Heat about 6 tablespoons of oil in a skillet. Fry the codcakes, a few at a time, until golden on each side, about 4 minutes. Drain them on paper towels and serve them with the dipping sauce. I have made much smaller patties for an appetizer and cooked them for a little less time. They are just as successful and good for serving with drinks when you need something easy to pick up in your fingers.

Ketchup equals Heinz, but this is the real McCoy and well worth the effort, if only to do justice to a particularly fine sausage or a fishcake. It is different, rather in the way that home-baked beans are an entirely different dish to the canned version and instant coffee is quite unlike fresh.

Homemade Ketchup

MAKES SEVERAL BOTTLES

2 cloves

1 bay leaf

a small piece of cinnamon bark

1 cup apple vinegar

8 tbsp light brown sugar

1 tsp celery seeds

½ tsp ground mace

¼ tsp ground coriander

3lb 5oz ripe tomatoes

½ tsp sea salt

1 tsp English mustard powder

1 clove of garlic

Tabasco sauce

1 tbsp tomato paste

Tie the cloves, bay leaf, and cinnamon together in a bit of cheesecloth. Put the vinegar and sugar in a heavy-bottomed enamel pan and bring to a simmer. Add all the other ingredients and bring to a boil, stirring to prevent anything from sticking to the bottom of the pan. Reduce to a simmer and let the mixture blip away for about 40 minutes, stirring occasionally.

Remove the spice bag, puree the sauce, and strain into a bowl. Cool, then pour through a funnel into sterilized bottles. The ketchup will keep for up to a month in the refrigerator. Something to do at the tomato glut time of year, particularly if you have quantities of your own to pick.

Now that those two fabulous salt beef bars in London's Great Windmill Street are no more, and Bloom's in the Whitechapel Road has gone the same way, access to a warm, ruby-red, salt beef sandwich, with its marrow-soft yellow fat, sharp gherkin, and rye bread, is strictly limited, unless you decide to make your own. This you can do quite simply, knowing that if you have the urge, it will take five to ten days between making the salt beef and tasting the first satisfying slice that you cut from the joint. Some things are as enjoyable in the anticipation as they are in the immediate consumption.

Salt Beef

SERVES 10 OR MORE

4½–6½lb piece of organic beef, brisket, silverside foreflank, or shin
1 bouquet garni
1 of each of the following, chopped: carrot, onion, celery stick, leek
1 garlic bulb cut in half across the middle

For the brine:
5½ qt water
2 cups packed light brown sugar
2¼lb coarse salt
1 tsp black peppercorns
1 tsp juniper berries
5 cloves
2 bay leaves
a sprig of thyme
a bunch of parsley stems
5oz saltpeter (optional)
  Leave it out if you want to stay organic, but the meat will be grayer as a result, without the through-and-through pink that saltpeter assures

Put all the ingredients for the brine in a large saucepan and stir well over low heat until the sugar and salt have dissolved. Bring to a boil, allow to bubble for 1–2 minutes, then remove from the heat and leave until absolutely cool. Cover your piece of beef completely with the cold brine, weighting it down if necessary. Leave the meat in the brine for 5–10 days in the refrigerator. If the joint weighs under 6½lb, do not leave it in the brine for more than a week, or it will be too pickled.

Before cooking, remove the meat from the brine and soak it in cold water for 24 hours, changing the water a couple of times. Put the meat in a pan with the bouquet garni, vegetables, and garlic, cover it with cold water, and bring to a boil. Poach at a gentle simmer—a 6½lb piece will take about 2½ hours.

Serve the salt beef hot, with plenty of mashed potatoes and cabbage, horseradish, and English mustard, or eat it warm or cold in a sandwich made with strong, freshly made English mustard, cornichons, and rye bread.

When Simon Hopkinson alerted me to Elizabeth David's Grillade des Mariniers du Rhône, made with lean beef, in her magical book *An Omelette and a Glass of Wine*, I got thinking. The sharp wine vinegar and salty anchovies would surely work spectacularly well with lamb, using a cut like the breast that can tolerate hours of gentle stewing before cooling overnight and skimming off its thick crust of snowy fat. It did indeed suit this notoriously fat, gluey, almost gelatinous cut of lamb to perfection, the affinity between lamb and anchovy being one I'm sure you know about. I usually push fillets of anchovy into the nicked fat of shoulder of lamb, with garlic and rosemary before roasting it. The result is not fishy, but lends a miraculous depth of flavor to the meat. My children are pretty vociferous in their hatred of this small, silver, salt-of-the-sea fish, but they have yet to guess and raise hell.

Don't be shy of serving a cheap cut of meat at a party. I served this at one of my publisher's dinners, at which the Michelin-starred chef Richard Corrigan was a guest. I had been determined not to serve him food that smacked of a restaurant kitchen, it is not my style; and I fear it has induced much of the sense of inadequacy that seems, at present, to stalk the home kitchen. Anyway, this is just the sort of cut that Richard has helped put back on the carnassial map. He adored the dish, and the organic lamb breast from Swaddles Green Farm to feed 12 people cost £8. Honor and satisfaction in one.

Another dish to make a day before you need it. You can double the quantity and make two giant pots with the minimum of extra effort if you are feeding a large party.

Grillade of Lamb Breast

SERVES 6

preheat oven to 275°F

3 cups peeled and finely sliced
   onion

2 organic lamb breasts, boned

2 tbsp unsalted butter

1 heaped tsp all-purpose flour

2 tbsp chopped flat-leaf parsley

a clove of garlic, minced

3 tbsp olive oil

1 tbsp red-wine vinegar

4 anchovy fillets

sea salt and freshly ground black
   pepper

Put half the onions in a layer in the bottom of a heavy-bottomed, but not too deep, earthenware casserole. Place the breasts, laid out flat, in a single layer on top of them and season. Put the rest of the sliced onions in a layer on top of the meat. Work the butter and flour together in a small bowl, divide it into tiny pieces and dot the mixture over the top of the onions. Cover with a layer of buttered parchment paper and a lid and cook for 2–2½ hours. The meat should be utterly tender when pierced with a skewer. Leave to cool overnight.

With a slotted spoon and copious amounts of paper towels, pick and scoop out every bit of solidified white fat you can. Mix the chopped parsley, minced garlic, olive oil, chopped anchovies, and vinegar together into a vinaigrette. Pour it over the casserole 1½ hours before you want to serve it, replace the paper and the lid, and cook for 1½ hours longer.

This grillade can be reheated as successfully as any stew. I would be hard pressed to think of a fuller-bodied, better-flavored winter dish.

This Polish recipe comes from my friend Ewa, whose restaurant in London's Shepherd's Bush is one of my favorite haunts, and a place where you go to celebrate. When you walk through the doors, you are no longer in England, you are in an eastern European salon. People play the piano and sing; there is a spirit of true generosity, bounty, plentifulness; the tables have bottles of Bison Grass vodka awaiting you; and there is matchless borscht, blinis, and soft crescents of pierogis. There is barley soup; veal paprikarz studded with red bell peppers and shredded pickled cabbage; great ham hocks marinaded, smoked, and roasted; and the mighty bigos, a hunters' stew that defines the word "hearty." With hunks of meat and smoked sausage, dried mushrooms, and sweet shreds of sauerkraut, this is a dish of deep-down earthiness and strength.

Bigos, or Hunters' Stew

SERVES 10—12

2¼lb sauerkraut
2¼lb cabbage
10 dried boletus or other dried
   mushrooms, or fresh
   mushrooms, if you prefer
2 onions
2 cooking apples
2 tbsp lard or speck, available
   from many supermarkets
18oz each of cold roast pork and
   cold roast beef, but any leftover
   meat will do, such as duck,
   venison, lamb
1¼lb sausage, Polish if possible
3 cups boiled ham cut into
   small cubes
10 prunes, pitted
10 juniper berries, crushed
10 peppercorns
2 bay leaves
⅔ cup dry red wine
1 tsp honey, salt and pepper

Drain the juice from the sauerkraut and chop it finely. Chop the cabbage finely. Pour boiling water over the cabbage and drain. Rinse the dried mushrooms, cover with a little warm water, and leave to soak for 15 minutes. Then cook them gently in their liquid in a pan for 30 minutes, drain, and cut into strips, keeping the juice. Peel the onions and chop them. Peel the apples and cube them, then fry with the onions in a tablespoon of lard or speck.

Put the cabbage and sauerkraut into a large Dutch oven. Add the onions, apples, mushrooms, mushroom liquid, prunes, juniper berries, bay leaves, and pepper. Add 3¼ cups boiling water, cover, and cook over a gentle heat for an hour.

Cut the meat into cubes. Slice the sausage and fry it lightly in the rest of the lard or speck. Add all the meats to the saucepan, pour in the wine and the honey, and cook for 40 minutes longer. Stir frequently, taking care not to let it burn.

Ewa says this dish tastes best on the third day, but it will keep for up to a week in the refrigerator. It is eaten in Poland in the cold months, between September and April. Serve with some kasha, if you like.

Buckwheat Kasha

1 cup of toasted buckwheat
4 tbsp lard
salted water

This is the most valued kasha in Poland, with a taste and aroma full of character. It is an indispensable addition, instead of potatoes, to all kinds of Polish beef dishes, and very good with Bigos. Ewa "dry roasts" it by pouring 1 cup of toasted buckwheat into a small pan in which the lard has been heated—it is much tastier cooked in lard than in butter. Stir until the grain has absorbed the fat and is slightly browned. Pour a cup of boiling salted water over the kasha, and cook over very gentle heat. When the kasha has absorbed the water, cover it, and place in a warm oven for 45 minutes.

A dish that comes from traditional Slavic cuisine and has acquired long-lasting popularity in Polish kitchens in both cities and villages.

Pierogi

For the dough:
3¼ cups all-purpose flour
a pinch of salt
1 egg

For the pork filling:
8oz cooked pork
1 onion, chopped
1 clove garlic, chopped
lard
salt and pepper

For the cream-cheese filling:
¾ cup cream cheese
1 cooked potato
1 onion, chopped
1 clove of garlic, chopped
lard
salt and pepper
1 egg

Mix the flour, salt, and egg and add some lukewarm water to make quite a slack dough, which does not stick to the hands or pastry board when well kneaded. Divide the kneaded dough into 4 parts, then roll each one out very thinly. Using a teacup or wine glass, cut out circles 2–2½ inches in diameter. Place a heaped teaspoon of filling in the center of each circle, fold over, and press the edges together firmly so they cannot open during cooking.

The most popular fillings are cream cheese and potato, and pork. For the meat filling, gently soften the onion and garlic in some lard and season. Process it through a food mill with the cooked meat. For the cream-cheese filling, process a cooked potato with the cream cheese, adding an onion cooked as above and seasoned, then add an egg to the mixture.

Drop the filled pierogi into a wide pot of boiling, salted water and bring it back to a simmer. When they rise to the surface, keep the pierogi in the water for 4–5 minutes longer, then take them out with a draining spoon and drain well.

You can sprinkle a few tiny cubes of pork fat over the pierogi, serve them with thick sour cream, or place two or three of them in your borscht.

Prunes and beef, lamb and apricots, pork and either—it is curious how meat and dried fruit form an alliance. This recipe, with obvious Arabic influence, is a classic Moroccan tagine. By all means substitute lamb and apricots if you would rather, and cook the dish at least a day before you want to serve it.

Beef and Prune Tagine

SERVES 4

12oz Agen prunes, soaked in
  ½ fresh orange juice, ½ water
  overnight
2¼lb shin of beef or chuck steak,
  cut into 2in cubes
olive oil
2–3 tbsp all-purpose flour
4 medium onions, finely sliced
3 fat cloves of garlic, finely sliced
3 stalks of celery from the heart,
  strung with a potato peeler and
  finely sliced
1 tsp coriander seeds
1 tsp cumin seeds
1 tsp ground cinnamon
1 tsp ground dried gingerroot
½–1 tsp cayenne
2 fresh bay leaves
2 pieces of orange peel, without
  pith
beef or chicken stock or water
sea salt and black pepper
a handful of fresh cilantro,
  chopped

Soak the prunes in the orange juice and water the night before you want to cook this dish.

While you warm 2–3 tablespoons of olive oil in a heavy-bottomed flameproof casserole, dry the meat with a paper towel and put it into a Ziploc bag with the flour, sea salt, and black pepper. Shake the bag until all the meat is lightly covered with flour, but not clogged. Put the meat straight into the pan, in a single layer, while it is still dry. Brown on all sides for a few minutes, then lift the meat out of the pan with a draining spoon and put it on a plate.

Add a little more oil to the pan, throw in the vegetables and sweat them gently. Toast the coriander and cumin seeds in a small skillet for a minute or so, until they exude their toasted spice smell, then crush them in a mortar with the cinnamon bark. Add them with the other spices to the vegetables when they have softened, after about 10 minutes, then add the bay leaves, orange peel, and prunes, without their soaking liquid, a couple of minutes later. Return the beef to the pan, and just cover with stock or water. Bring to a boil, cover, and simmer at a mere blip for about 1½ hours until really tender. Check the seasoning and, if possible, cool and refrigerate ready to heat and serve a day or two later. Sprinkle with chopped fresh cilantro before serving.

I serve my tagines, be they fish, flesh, or fowl, with couscous and some harissa, homemade or from a squeezy tube, which people can dollop into the meat juices as their taste buds dictate.

This will keep contentedly in the refrigerator for two or three weeks. Rather like preserved lemons, it is something that once you have, you will make use of, even *ad hoc* for things like pepping up a Bloody Mary. If you can't be bothered to make your own, the squeezy tubes, a Moroccan equivalent of tomato paste, are extremely good, and will spice up everything from tagine to mayonnaise.

Harissa

MAKES 1 JAR

3 red bell peppers, blistered on all
   sides under the broiler, seeded,
   cored, and skinned
2–3 red chilies, seeded
1 tsp tomato paste
1 tsp ground coriander
1 tsp ground cumin
4 tbsp best olive oil

Blend all the ingredients to a paste in a mortar or a blender. Put the harissa in a bowl to use immediately, or scrape it into a jar, cover with a thin film of olive oil, and put the lid on before keeping it in the refrigerator.

Harissa is not just for cranking up the heat of a meat, fish, or vegetable tagine; it is infinitely more versatile than that. Try it with some barbecued lamb shoulder, the pieces rolled in crushed coriander and black pepper before being suitably charred. Or, spread it on some good crusty ciabatta or Pugliese bread and add roasted vegetables and feta cheese. It is even good with a strong cheddar or a mature goat cheese.

This is perfect for a summer lunch you want to prepare the day before. All you have to do on the day is make the sauce, an easy five-minute job, and pour it over the chicken breasts removed from their overnight cold bath. Then leave them to languish in this most delectable black velvety liquid for three hours before lunch. It is a dish which, for me, conjures up an almost medieval world of food, the sweetness of the brown sugar and the lemon zest creating a Moorish feel. My friend George Morley wrote out the recipe for me three summers ago, and I have gazed at it hungrily ever since, waiting for the right occasion. This summer finally gave me one, with George as a guest, of course. It was only on reading the collected works of the most brilliant Italian food writer of them all, Anna Del Conte, that the origins of the dish became clear: it was one she, a historian by training, had unearthed. It is brilliant for when you have a lot of people, but you can adjust it for fewer. The one thing I have done is increase the sauce quantity from the original. And significantly. It needs it.

A 17th-Century Mantuan Chicken Dish

SERVES 12

10 large organic chicken breast
   halves, in fact mine were so
   large that 8 would still have
   been generous
4¼ cups chicken stock
1¼ cups dry white wine

For the sauce:
5 tbsp packed light brown sugar
½ cup dry white wine
½ cup golden raisins
grated zest of 2½ lemons
5 tbsp best balsamic vinegar,
   a well-aged, velvety 4-star
   vinegar; you want rich, mellow
   velvet, not sharp, thin acid
2 tsp sea salt
freshly ground black pepper
½ cup best olive oil

Put the chicken in a single layer in as many heavy-bottomed pans as you need, I used three, and cover each with the stock and white wine. Poach at a mere burble, turning every 5 minutes, until cooked through with a faint pink in the liquid when pierced with a skewer; 20–25 minutes should do large chicken pieces and they will continue to cook as the liquid cools. When cool, transfer to one pan with their liquid, cover, and chill overnight.

Just over 3 hours before you want to eat, take the chicken out of the refrigerator and make the sauce. Put the sugar and wine in a small pan and bring it very slowly to a boil, stirring to dissolve the sugar completely. Draw off the heat, and add the golden raisins and lemon zest to infuse. Leave to cool, while you cut the chicken into ½ inch slices, downward, reassembling them on a serving dish. Strain the sauce, reserving the zest and golden raisins in the strainer. Add the vinegar to the sauce, and the salt and pepper, then add the oil in a trickle, whisking as you go to form an emulsion. Return the zest and golden raisins to the sauce, taste, adjust the seasoning, and pour over the chicken. Cover with plastic wrap and keep at room temperature for 3 hours. Serve with new potatoes or rice and some cold white wands of leeks.

When I make fresh tomato sauce, I make huge quantities of it, particularly in the fall with my own tomatoes, and serve it with cod, spiced with chili; with pasta; stirred into soup; in gratins and tians; with zucchini and eggplants and anything I can think of. This recipe is the kind of assembly job that lasagne is, a layer-by-layer dish, but it has the advantage that you can make the tomato sauce and the crepes a day or two in advance, before building, stratum by stratum, this savory "cake." You sprinkle mozzarella and fresh Parmesan cheese between the layers before baking the dish like a pasta gratin. Only it isn't pasta, it is layers of soft crepes bubbling with tomatoey, oily juices and oozing fresh mozzarella. My children were as impressed as I was the first time I made it, and I then went on to experiment farther with a creamy pesto sauce. This is a substantial and unusual dish, beautiful enough for a party.

Crepes Layered with Mozzarella di Bufala and Tomato Sauce

SERVES 4

For the crepes:
1 cup all-purpose flour
salt
2 eggs
1¼ cups milk
a tiny pat of butter

CREPES:
This recipe makes thicker crepes than you would normally have, but you may add a bit more milk if the batter feels really thick. Leave the batter to rest for 30 minutes and then whisk again. Heat a tiny pat of butter in a heavy pan. Pour in a small ladle of batter, wait until it begins to bronze and bubble before flipping and repeating, then place on a plate with a metal spatula and repeat. For some inexplicable reason, the first crepe doesn't usually work. You should end up with 8 good-size crepes from this amount of batter.

For the tomato sauce:

1 onion, chopped

olive oil

about 2¼lb tomatoes, peeled
   seeded, and chopped

2 stalks of celery, chopped

2 cloves of garlic, chopped

1 bay leaf

1 teaspoon each of dark brown
   sugar and tomato paste

a splosh of red wine (optional)

For the béchamel sauce:

2 cups whole milk

3 tbsp butter

3 tbsp all-purpose flour

grated fresh nutmeg

salt and pepper

For the assembly:

2 x 2½-oz balls of fresh mozzarella
   di bufala, chopped into small
   dice

4 tbsp grated Parmesan cheese

a handful of fresh basil, chopped

TOMATO SAUCE

Sweat the chopped onion in some olive oil. Add the skinned, seeded, and chopped tomatoes, celery, chopped garlic, and bay leaf. Stir in the dark brown sugar and tomato paste and cook the whole lot down for at least 30 minutes until reduced, thickened, and jammy. You can add a splosh of red wine when you add the tomatoes. Pass your tomato sauce through the coarse disk of the food mill if you prefer your sauce less textured. Use canned tomatoes if it is not the time of year for good fresh tomatoes.

BÉCHAMEL SAUCE

Heat the milk. Melt the butter in a saucepan. Add the flour, cook for a few minutes, then stir in the hot milk. Cook the béchamel for at least 20 minutes so it no longer smells floury. Season with grated nutmeg, salt, and pepper.

ASSEMBLING THE DISH

Once you have made the tomato and béchamel sauces and the crepes, you are ready to assemble the dish.

Preheat the oven to 350°F. Stir the tomato sauce into the béchamel. Butter a gratin dish, place a crepe on the bottom, and spread a thin layer of the tomato and béchamel sauces over the top. Sprinkle with mozzarella, Parmesan, basil, salt, and pepper and cover with another crepe. Continue layering the crepes until you have a sort of leaning tower of Pisa, 8 crepes high. The top must be sauce, Parmesan, basil, salt ,and pepper, not mozzarella, which would turn to goo.

Cover the dish with a sheet of greased wax paper and bake for about 20 minutes. Remove the paper and continue to cook for 10 minutes longer until bubbling and gorgeous. Leave it to stand outside the oven before you cut into it just like a cake in triangular wedges. Serve with a plain green salad. This is substantial with a capital S!

I am an inveterate tinkerer, and I loved the idea of a baked pesto and béchamel gratin. It worked like a dream. Quantities for the crepes and béchamel as for the tomato sauce version on pages 196–97.

Crepes Layered with Pesto and Mozzarella di Bufala

SERVES 4

preheat oven to 350°

Ingredients for the crepes and
    béchamel (pages 196–97)

For the pesto:
2 handfuls of fresh basil leaves
1 tbsp pine nuts
1 clove of garlic, crushed
½ cup olive oil
1 tsp sea salt
2 tbsp grated Parmesan cheese,

There are three things you need to remember for this recipe. First, use fresh pesto. Second, don't add more than 3 tablespoons of it to the béchamel for this quantity of ingredients and people—it is extremely rich and olive oily. Third, if you add the pesto to the béchamel when the sauce has already begun to cool down, it will keep its magical brilliant green hue and not turn muddy khaki. I am not sure why, since once it goes into the oven it is going to be cooked. I can only imagine the layers of sauce and crepes somehow protect it.

You can make the pesto by grinding the basil, pine nuts, garlic, salt, and olive oil in a pestle and mortar, or whizz everything to a paste in a food processor. Either way, stir in the Parmesan afterwards.

This is a great vegetarian party dish. You can, of course, make your fresh pesto in advance and keep it in the refrigerator under a layer of olive oil that you then stir back into it when you are ready to use it. This time, try a tomato salad as a side dish, rather than an all-green feast.

Left: *Pancakes layered
with Mozzarella di Bufala
and Tomato Sauce*

In Sicily, this is called Pasta 'Ncasciata, the pie being encased—'ncasciata—in the fried eggplants. The Sicilians add salami to theirs, but I keep mine vegetarian. I feel the meat is not necessary since the dish already has a rich flavor and succulent texture. This is a stunning dish worthy of a celebration, and another thing to make when you have been cooking vats of tomato sauce. The huge dragons' tongues of the eggplants that arrive in my organic vegetable box make this a beautiful feast.

Sicilian Pasta Pie

SERVES 6
preheat oven to 375°F

1½lb eggplants, about 2 large
    specimens
salt
14oz penne or rigatoni
4 cups fresh tomato sauce, made
    with 2½ lb tomatoes as in the
    recipe on page 197
½ cup freshly grated Parmesan
    cheese
1 tbsp dried oregano
freshly ground black pepper
2 hard-boiled eggs, sliced
5oz Italian salami, thickly sliced
    and cut into strips (optional)
7oz fresh mozzarella di bufala,
    sliced
2oz caciocavallo cheese, sliced
2 tbsp brown bread crumbs
2 tbsp extra-virgin olive oil

Cut the eggplants lengthwise into thin slices and place them in a colander, sprinkling salt between the layers. Leave to drain for an hour. Rinse the eggplants thoroughly, pat each slice dry, and fry them a few at a time in plenty of hot vegetable oil. They shouldn't absorb a lot of oil and turn greasy if the oil is hot enough and you don't fry too many at a time. When they are golden on both sides, remove the slices and dry them well on paper towels.

Cook the pasta, drain it when *al dente*, and immediately dress it with the tomato sauce. Add the Parmesan and oregano, mix well, taste, and check the seasoning.

Line the bottom and sides of an oiled 8-inch springform pan with the eggplant slices. Cover the bottom with a layer of pasta, then add sliced egg, salami if you are using it, more eggplant, and mozzarella and caciocavallo slices. Repeat these layers until all the ingredients are used, finishing with a layer of pasta. Sprinkle with the bread crumbs and drizzle the olive oil over. Put in the oven to bake for 30–40 minutes, or until the dish is heated right through.

Remove from the oven and run a metal spatula between the pie and the inside of the pan. Place a round serving dish upside down over the pan and invert the pan onto it. Let the pie stand for a few minutes, then unclip the pan and carefully remove it. Take off the bottom of the pan and serve the pie immediately. Even if the pie collapses, it hardly matters; the flavor should overwhelm everyone.

Orzo with Seafood and Roasted Vegetables

SERVES 4

preheat oven to 425°F

12oz orzo (rice-shaped pasta)

1 small eggplant, cut into 1in cubes

1 onion, cut into thin wedges

1 red bell pepper, cut into 1in pieces

1 large plum tomato, cut into thin wedges

2 cloves of garlic, finely chopped

6 tbsp olive oil

½ tsp coarse sea salt

4oz prepared squid, cut into thin rings

8oz raw tiger prawns or jumbo shrimp, peeled and fried in olive oil until pink

3 sundried tomatoes in olive oil, sliced small

1 red chili, seeded and chopped small

1 tbsp white-wine vinegar

5 tbsp flat-leaf parsley, chopped

salt and freshly ground pepper

2oz arugula (optional)

Cook the pasta until *al dente*, drain, and let cool. A little slug of olive oil splashed over after draining prevents it from sticking unpleasantly. Put the eggplant, onion, red bell pepper, and fresh tomato in a bowl with the garlic, 2 tablespoons of olive oil, and the sea salt, and mix well. Roast, spread out in a small pan, for about 30 minutes until well colored around the edges. Let cool.

Heat 1 tablespoon of olive oil in a skillet. Add the squid, and fry over high heat for 2½ minutes until lightly browned. Season with salt and pepper and let cool.

When the pasta, vegetables, and squid are barely warm, put them in a large bowl with the rest of the oil, prawns or shrimp, sundried tomato, chili, vinegar, 4 tablespoons of parsley, a teaspoon of salt, and a few good scrunches of black pepper. Toss everything together lightly, then fold in the arugula if you've decided to use it. Spoon onto a large plate, and sprinkle with the remaining parsley.

When I went to lunch in Dorset with the incomparable Italian food writer Anna Del Conte, she had cooked the nearest equivalent to Italian pumpkin gnocchi she can make in England, using a combination of butternut squash and orange-fleshed sweet potato. These come close, she informed me, to the spicy sweetness and moist texture of a northern Italian pumpkin and are a traditional specialty of the Veneto and southern Lombardy. The first dressing is the classic dressing from Veneto, while the second one from Lombardy is the one that is generally used everywhere else.

Gnocchi di Zucca, or Butternut Squash Gnocchi

SERVES 4—5
preheat oven to 350°F

1 tbsp vegetable oil
1lb 2oz butternut squash
1lb 2oz orange-fleshed sweet
   potatoes
1⅔ cups flour, preferably
   Italian 00
2 tsp baking powder
2 large organic eggs
4 tbsp freshly grated Parmesan
   cheese
a generous grating of fresh
   nutmeg
salt

For the first dressing:
5 tbsp unsalted butter
2 tbsp grated Parmesan cheese
1 tbsp sugar
1 tsp ground cinnamon

For the second dressing:
5 tbsp unsalted butter
6 fresh sage leaves, snipped into
   pieces
½ cup Parmesan cheese

Line a baking tray with foil and brush it with oil. Cut the squash in half, scoop out and discard the seeds and fibers, and place the squash, cut side down, on the foil. Pierce the sweet potatoes with a skewer and place them on the foil. Bake for about an hour, until both vegetables can be pierced easily with a fork.

Peel the sweet potatoes and scoop the flesh out of the skin of the squash. Puree both vegetables through a food mill or potato ricer into a bowl. Mix in the flour and baking powder, and then break in the eggs. Mix very well to incorporate, then add the Parmesan and season with nutmeg and salt to taste.

Bring a large saucepan of salted water to a boil. Anna finds it easiest to make the gnocchi with a pastry bag and a large, plain tip, but you might prefer to make them by shaping them into small balls with floured hands. To pipe the gnocchi, fill the bag with the squash mixture and hold it over the saucepan, squeezing it with one hand and cutting the mixture as it comes out of the tip with the other. Cut short shapes about ¾ inch long, letting them drop straight into simmering water. Don't cook all the gnocchi together, do it in three batches. Cook them for a minute or two after they have come to the surface of the water. Lift out each batch with a slotted spoon and place in a large, shallow baking dish. Dress each batch separately and keep the dish in a low oven.

FOR THE FIRST DRESSING:
Melt 5 tablespoons unsalted butter and then pour it over each batch of gnocchi. Sprinkle with the Parmesan, sugar, and ground cinnamon

FOR THE SECOND DRESSING:
Put 5 tablespoons unsalted butter and the snipped sage leaves in a small pan and let the butter melt and begin to foam. Spoon over each batch of gnocchi and sprinkle with the freshly grated Parmesan.

It is funny how the inspiration of someone else's lunch, in this case Anna's gnocchi, should inspire and osmose into something intimately connected, yet utterly different. It might be linked by flavors, a method here, a texture there, but be a completely different dish in its own right. I often find, too, that an ingredient or combination of ingredients gets stuck on a sort of loop tape of consciousness, and I go on using them and experimenting over days, or occasionally weeks if they are in season. The roasted squash is great with roast pork or veal, or a pork chop. The skins of the red onion squash soften palpably into an edible texture that is brilliant with the mealy sweetness of the innards, so try them. The penne opposite was an utterly and unexpectedly delicious dish, made from some onion squash remaining unroasted from the previous night.

Spice-Roasted Red Onion or Butternut Squash

SERVES 2
preheat oven to 400°F

⅔ of a red onion squash
   or ½ a butternut squash
sprigs of rosemary and thyme,
   exceedingly finely minced
1 clove of garlic, finely minced
1 red chili, seeded and finely
   minced
good olive oil
sea salt and black pepper

Scoop the seeds out of the squash and cut it in melonlike slices. Put the minced rosemary, thyme, garlic, and chili into a little bowl of good olive oil, sea salt, and pepper to macerate, before spooning a little into the boat of each squash.

Bake the squash until cooked through, about 30–40 minutes, basting them a couple of times. You can add a pat of butter at the end if you feel like it.

Penne with Roasted Squash, Prosciutto, Sage, and Parmesan

SERVES 2

preheat oven to 400 °F

⅓ a red onion squash
    or ½ a butternut squash
olive oil
1 red chili, split down
    the middle and seeded
8oz penne
butter
4 slices of prosciutto
a good handful of
    fresh sage leaves
fresh Parmesan cheese
sea salt and black pepper

For this recipe, I think it is better to remove the skin of the squash before cooking. Cut the squash into small cubes. Roll them in about 4 tablespoons of good olive oil in a roasting pan, season, and add the split chili. Roast until the squash is tender, about 20 minutes. Remove the chili, which will have exuded enough warmth into the olive oil for this dish.

Cook the penne in plenty of boiling salted water. I favor the extra-large variety, which has apertures large enough to contain, as well as to be coated by the sauce. Make sure when you drain the penne that you return a little of the cooking water to the pan with it, then slather on a bit of butter.

Meanwhile, tear the prosciutto into bits and cook it separately in a couple of tablespoons of olive oil for a couple of minutes until crisp. Remove the prosciutto with a slotted spoon and throw in the sage, cooking until deliciously frizzled and browned.

Throw the squash, prosciutto, and sage into the pot with the penne, stir in a tablespoon or two of Parmesan, adjust the seasoning, and serve. Pass around some more Parmesan at the table. There is great contrast between the salty cheese, sweet, yielding, mealy-fleshed squash, crisp, salty prosciutto, and astringent sage.

Please see this dish as a suggestion rather than law. A couple of nights later I raided the refrigerator and cooked something not dissimilar, roasting more squash with chunks of red onion and half a remaining cauliflower. Cauliflower? Weird, but it worked, browning and intensifying in flavor as I turned it during the roasting. I had no meat, but added a tablespoon of crème fraîche and a cup of cubed Roquefort with the roasted vegetables to the final assembly. No Parmesan.

Since we are on the subject of sage, and it is something to which I seem to turn instinctively at the beginning of winter, the following gratin was a natural. Sage is the herb that has the greatest affinity with cheese; hard cheese that is—think of English Sage Derby. In the days when a lot of Welsh farms made their own Caerphilly, they often added sage to it. The following is a dish that I cooked entirely with what I found lurking in my refrigerator, but really any well-matured hard cheese will work well. This is the sort of comfort food that you will eat a lot more of than you think you will, but then what comfort food isn't?

Potato, Leek, Bacon, Sage, and Cheese Gratin

SERVES 2
preheat oven to 400°F

1½lb potatoes
3 or 4 fat leeks, well washed,
    trimmed of their dark green
    leaves ,and thinly sliced
6 slices of oak-smoked bacon
a generous handful of fresh sage
    leaves
4oz mature hard cheese, grated
    thickly
2½–4 cups chicken stock
butter
1 tbsp seeded mustard
about 4 tbsp crème fraîche
sea salt and black pepper

Slice the peeled potatoes on a mandolin or on the slicer disk of a food processor. Place them in a colander, wash to rid them of their starch, and pat them dry in a cloth. Butter a gratin dish and put in half the potatoes, then add all the chopped leeks in a layer. Snip the bacon into strips, removing the rind if necessary, and fry until crisply frazzled in its own fat. Remove it with a slotted spoon and dot it over the leeks. Frazzle the snipped sage leaves briefly in the bacon fat until browned and crisp, then dot them over the leeks with the bacon fat. Sprinkle the grated cheese over and add the rest of the potatoes. Pour the hot chicken stock over the potatoes, until it just reaches the top layer, but does not submerge them. Add seasoning, dot with butter, and place a layer of greased wax paper over the top of the dish.

Cook for 45 minutes. Remove from the oven, check with a skewer that the potatoes are nearly cooked through and add the mustard and crème fraîche that you have stirred together. Smooth over the top with a rubber spatula. Place the dish back in the oven, without the wax paper, for 15 minutes longer, when it should be golden, bubbling, and cooked right through.
A complete supper dish.

This, this like many dishes in my repertoire, is one I constantly play around with, each time thinking I have cracked the code and come up with the ultimate answer. But then I think of another twist, something to tempt the children with that is not going to be the self-same way they remember it from last time. So here is the most recent version of kedgeree I made, with Merchant Gourmet's red, wild, and white rice that all cooks miraculously at the same time.

Spiced Kedgeree

SERVES 2

7oz natural smoked haddock
2 large onions, peeled and sliced
    into thin rings
olive oil and butter
1 tsp cumin seeds
a pinch each of cayenne,
    fenugreek, and turmeric
1 sachet of Merchant Gourmet's
    red, wild, and white rice, or
    4oz organic basmati rice
4 eggs
a cup of frozen peas
2 tbsp crème fraîche
a handful of flat-leaf parsley,
    chopped
sea salt and black pepper

Place the smoked haddock in a gratin dish. Pour boiling water over to cover—the only cooking the haddock needs as it is already smoked. Leave for 10 minutes before draining off the water and gently pushing the flesh away from the skin with a spoon and fork into large translucent flakes.

Throw the onions into a little heated olive oil and butter in a large, heavy-bottomed skillet, along with the cumin seeds and some salt to draw the moisture from the onions. After a couple of minutes, add the other spices—the tip of a spoon end should be enough because you want warmth and spice, rather than real heat. Stir into the onions and cook gently for a few more minutes, before turning the heat down and covering with a lid to simmer for 20 minutes.

Cook the rice. Boil the eggs for 6 minutes and then run them under cold water until you can pick them up to peel them. Cook the frozen peas in boiling water for 3-4 minutes, drain, and add a little butter.

Check that the onions are softened before adding the rice, fish, and peas to them in the skillet. Stir gently to amalgamate and to prevent the rice from sticking. Add the crème fraîche. Transfer the kedgeree to a warmed shallow bowl, or serve it straight from the pan. Halve the eggs and place them around the edge and add a good scattering of parsley. This is a complete supper dish.

Another of those recipes that my friend George Morley lobbed my way one day, as she is prone, and highly encouraged, to do. She said she'd just done it for a party and it was sensational. I seem to have built up a deep-litter system of recipes that way, which I fully intend to keep until the occasion where the people suit the recipe, no small consideration, and then either it's the wrong season, I can't find the recipe or an ingredient, or something newer has risen to the surface of one of my Vesuvial agglomerations of things to be tried and tested.

The recipe came from Anna Del Conte's book *Entertaining all' Italiana*—George was the editor of the book, giving it a doubly immaculate pedigree. That fall I went to interview Anna about the reissue of her *Gastronomy of Italy*. On my return home, I thought, that's it—party or no, I'm going to cook this dish. I made one slight change: I added a little lemon zest and juice to the torta. And I think an extra couple of hours soaking of the rice in the mixture helps; you know how firm good risotto rice grains like arborio or carnaroli are in the center. I corralled two friends to come and eat the torta with my family—Brigid and Georgina, who is studying in Bologna, so steeped in good Italian food at the moment. Both pronounced it a triumph. I am promising myself that come the porcini season, I will attempt a Torta di Porcini. You will have to wait for that. The Torta di Porri is best served warm, but Anna also makes it a day in advance and serves it at room temperature, having kept it out of the refrigerator.

La Torta di Porri, or Leek and Rice Pie

SERVES 6

preheat oven to 350°F and heat a baking sheet

4 large organic eggs

1½lb leeks, washed thoroughly, green parts cut away, and white parts cut into very thin disks

¾ cup arborio or other risotto rice

¾ cup plus 2 tbsp extra-virgin olive oil

sea salt and freshly ground black pepper

7 tbsp freshly grated Parmesan cheese

lemon zest and juice

8–9 oz frozen phyllo pastry dough, thawed. I buy the longest I can find

Lightly beat the eggs and put them in a bowl with the leeks, rice, half the oil, two teaspoons of salt, plenty of pepper, and the Parmesan. Add the grated zest of an organic lemon and the juice of half of it. Mix very thoroughly with your hands. Set the bowl aside for 3 or 4 hours, mixing it whenever you remember to keep everything equally well lubricated.

Oil a 10-inch springform pan. Pour the rest of the oil into a small bowl. Carefully unfold the phyllo dough leaves, one at a time, taking care to leave the rest covered, because phyllo pastry dries out and cracks very easily. Lift out and lay one leaf over the bottom and up the sides of the prepared pan, allowing the ends to hang down over the outside of the pan. It will tear a little, but don't worry. Using a pastry brush, brush the leaf all over with a little of the oil and then cover with another leaf of the dough. Lay it across the previous one so the sides of the pan are covered all around. Brush with oil and lay two more leaves the same way.

Now fill the pan with the leek mixture. Fold the overhanging pieces of phyllo back over the top, one at a time, to make a lid. If the phyllo is not long enough, lay four more leaves over the top, brushing each sheet with oil. Cut them to fit inside the pan and fold the overlap over to form a ridge around the edge. Brush each one with oil before you place the next. Bake for 45–50 minutes on a preheated baking sheet, otherwise the base phyllo will not cook through and crisp. Let the pie cool for 10 minutes and then remove the side of the pan and turn it over onto an oven tray. Put the pie back in the oven, upside down, for 5 minutes to dry the bottom. Turn onto a round serving dish.

I've since remade this dish, with a larger amount of ingredients, so the torta was deeper, and I soaked the rice with the egg, oil, Parmesan, and leeks for 4 hours. The consistency was perfect. I used the whites of 2½lb leeks, ¾ cup plus 2 tablespoons olive oil to soak and more to brush with, 9 heaped tablespoons of Parmesan, and 6 eggs. Also, the zest and juice of a whole organic lemon, which I am convinced improves the dish. The same amount of arborio rice as above. Cooking time the same, but I allowed 10 minutes to crisp up the underside of the torta after I had turned it over and returned it to the oven. I served it with wedges of red onion squash baked in the oven with chopped red chili, and garlic, splashed with olive oil and seasoned with salt and pepper.

I think crab is at its best served chilled, but not icy cold. It is rich though, and you do not need a huge amount of it. The crab that I picked for this dish yielded 12 ounces of darker meat and a little less of white—enough for four.

Chilled Crab, Cucumber, and Avocado Salad

SERVES 4

3lb or so crab, cooked
a few bunches of watercress and
    some arugula or the heart of
    romaine
2 ripe Hass avocados
a cucumber
a mixed bag of herbs, ideally a
    tbsp of each of the following:
    chervil, dill, and chives
2 limes

Make a dressing with a tablespoon of homemade mayonnaise, a teaspoon of seeded mustard, a tablespoon of cider vinegar, and about 4 to 5 tablespoons of your best olive oil. Then sieve a couple of tablespoons of the darker crab meat into it and season to taste. You might like to add a tiny pinch of cayenne, instead of black pepper.

Put the white crabmeat onto a plate with the salad leaves. Add long slivers of avocado and chunks of peeled, seeded cucumber, the finely chopped herbs, and a few quarters of lime to squeeze on. Pour the dressing over, and serve the salad with a loaf of good country-style bread.

The following jellies and jams are a few of the things I make seasonally to be consumed in future weeks or months. A pot of crab-apple jelly, with its sparklingly brilliant, clear amber-red complexion and a squirl of lemon peel at its summit, makes a lovely present, as does a little bottle of damson and mulberry gin, made in September and matured by Christmas. The cakes, crackers, and cookies can be made a day or two ahead for puddings, birthdays, afternoon tea parties, or late-night kitchen raids.

These crackers are great with drinks, particularly a Sunday lunchtime Bloody Mary; see my homemade one on page 34.

Sesame and Roquefort Crackers

MAKES 20
preheat oven to 350°F

½ cup unsalted butter
1 cup self-raising flour
4oz Roquefort, Troupeau or
  Papillon are the best
4 tbsp sesame seeds

Process the butter and flour together in a food processor until they resemble crumbs. Crumble the cheese into the mixture and blitz for a second or two. Remove from the bowl and knead briefly by hand to distribute the ingredients evenly. Roll the dough into a long sausage shape, wrap in plastic wrap, and refrigerate until 20 minutes before you want to bake the crackers; up to a couple of days is fine.

When you are ready to bake the crackers, cut the dough into thin slices, coat with sesame seeds on both sides, and place on a greased cookie sheet, a little distance away from each other. Bake for 10 minutes or so. Do not remove the crackers to a rack to cool until you have let them firm up for a few minutes.

Quite simply, your kitchen should never be without this jam, and it keeps in the refrigerator for weeks if it is allowed the chance to do so. Great with a Montgomery Cheddar sandwich, in a toasted sandwich, or slicked onto bruschetta under a row of slices of goat cheese. Serve it with cold pork, on griddled scallops, or come up with your own idea. Versatile it is. I have upped the quantity from Peter Gordon's original recipe and this quantity of ingredients make enough for two large jars. Mine took double the cooking time he suggested, nearly an hour and a half, so don't panic if nothing seems to be happening after an hour.

Tomato Chili Jam

MAKES TWO LARGE JARS

1lb 10 oz very ripe organic
   tomatoes
4 red chilies, with their seeds
6 fat cloves of garlic, peeled
3 thumbs of fresh gingerroot,
   peeled and roughly chopped
3 tbsp Thai fish sauce (*nam pla*)
2¼ cups raw sugar
⅔ cup red-wine vinegar

Blend half the tomatoes, the chilies, garlic, ginger, and fish sauce to a fine puree in a blender. You need the chili seeds for the heat, which is not intense, and the tomato seeds for the pectin that will make the jam set.

Put the puree, sugar, and vinegar into a deep pan and bring to a boil slowly, stirring all the time. When it reaches a boil, turn down to a gentle simmer, and add the remaining tomatoes cut into tiny dice, about ¼ inch, skin and all. Skim off the foam and cook gently for 1¼ to 1½ hours, stirring every so often to release the solids that settle on the bottom and prevent them from burning. Be sure to scrape the sides of the pot too, so the entire mass of jam cooks evenly.

When the jam is done, pour it into warmed glass jars. Let it cool to room temperature before storing in the refrigerator or a cold pantry for later use.

I came to marmalade making late in life, after the odd abortive sojourn resulting in burned, caramelized offerings, or something that was over or under sweet, too runny, or set like a stone. After a whole day's instruction from my friend Gale last year, I can now face the annual boiling, when the kitchen is shrouded in steam and the tangiest, sharpest, most citrus of aromas for a whole day. Batten down the hatches and demand room service if you possibly can—after all, your family and friends will benefit for the rest of the year. This method is infallible, and sharp enough for me, which no store-bought marmalade ever is. And shreds should be shreds, not lumps of peel. Unrefined, or raw, sugar is as much of a must as Seville and organic oranges. Refined sugar seems to leave a toxic froth on the surface, which can only be the result of the 14 or so chemical processes to which it is subjected I assume. And unrefined tastes better.

Organic Seville Orange Marmalade

ENOUGH FOR 17 POTS OF
VARYING SIZES

4½lb organic Seville oranges
3 organic lemons
7lb organic raw granulated sugar
5½qt water

Wash the oranges and lemons, halve and squeeze them, reserving the juice and the seeds from the squeezing separately. Extract the remains of the pulp, pith, and seeds from the orange halves with your fingers and put them into a cheesecloth bag with the other seeds. Halve the halves, and pile the quarters into a stack that you can feed down the feeder tube of a food processor through the slicer disk. Trim any bits of peel that have not shredded properly.

Put the sliced peel into a large preserving pan, with the squeezed juice, water, and the cheesecloth bag tied to the side, and bring gently to a boil. Cover with a lid and simmer very gently on top of the stove. It will take about 2 hours for the peel to have absolutely no bite to it right the way through.

Remove the cheesecloth bag and suspend it over a bowl for the juice to drain through for about 30 minutes, then add the juice to the liquid in the pan. Now divide the mixture accurately into three batches for the next stage, because it sets better in small quantities. Put one-third of the mixture back into the preserving pan, with one-third of the sugar, and heat gently, stirring to dissolve the sugar completely. The mixture mustn't boil until the sugar has completely dissolved. Now boil hard until you reach setting point; ours took about 15 minutes, but start testing after 10. Put a small saucer in the refrigerator to cool, then place a teaspoon of boiling juice on the saucer, and put it in the freezer for a couple of minutes. While you do this, remove the marmalade from the heat so it doesn't cook any more. If the liquid on the saucer wrinkles when you push it with a finger, it has reached setting point.

Now leave the pan off the heat for 30 minutes before you ladle the marmalade into warm clean jars, otherwise the shreds will rise up the jar to the top, and you'll have half over-shredded, half gel marmalade. Don't fall at the last fence. Be patient, the waiting is all. Repeat with the remaining two-thirds of ingredients.

This recipe makes three puddings. Be generous, give a couple away. If you don't, I can guarantee they'll still be sitting in your kitchen reproachfully in June and you won't feel at all like cooking or eating them then. Try to force yourself to make them a couple of months in advance. I didn't this year, I made them only two weeks before Christmas. It was a new recipe, stuffed full of Agen prunes—a real plum pudding this—dried apricots and fresh dates. I wanted more fruit than vine fruit. I gave one to my friend Nick Welsh, Harry's erstwhile tutor at Eton and a mighty keen cook. He doesn't make a Christmas pudding because although he loves them, his wife Sal and children don't. When they arrived to spend New Year's Eve with us—the first I haven't spent in Ireland for a decade, so the food HAD to be good to compensate— Nick declared that it was the best pudding he'd ever tasted, that Sal now loved Christmas pudding, and perhaps I should make a tradition of it and give them one every year. I guess I better had. Everything in this pudding was organic, except the Guinness and Cognac.

Christmas Pudding

MAKES 3 PUDDINGS

1⅔ cups all-purpose flour
1 tsp ground cinnamon
1 tsp ground mace
1 tsp ground cloves
1 tsp ground dried gingerroot
1 tsp allspice
7oz each of golden raisins, raisins,
    and currants
8oz each of Agen prunes,
    unsulfured dried apricots, and
    pitted dates
2 cups packed dark brown sugar
1 cup each of Brazil nuts and
    blanched almonds, chopped
4 cups fresh brown bread crumbs
½ cup butter, chopped into tiny
    bits from a cold stick, I do not
    use suet in the pudding, but use
    6oz of beef or vegetarian suet if
    you want to
3 sharp eating apples, grated with
    their skin into the mixture
1 large carrot, peeled and grated
6 eggs
1¼ cups Guinness
¼ cup Cognac
juice and grated zest of an orange
a bit of milk to mix

Grease three English pudding basins. Sift the flour into an exceptionally large bowl, add the spices and dried fruits, then the sugar, nuts, bread crumbs, other fruits and carrot, the chopped butter or suet, followed by the eggs, Guinness, Cognac, and orange zest and juice that you have beaten together with a whisk. Stir the liquid well into the dry ingredients. Add a little milk if you need to, to make a soft dropping consistency.

Fill the pudding basins just over three-quarters full. Cover with a layer of wax paper and a layer of foil on top of it, both pleated in the middle to allow for the pudding to rise. Tie securely with string, making a handle as you go, and place in large saucepans on a trivet or layer of foil. Fill half way up the sides of the puddings with boiling water, put a lid over each pan, and bring to a boil. Then allow to cook at a gentle blip of a simmer for 6–7 hours, topping up with water every couple of hours.

Take the puddings out of the water, remove the foil and wax paper, and allow to cool. Re-cover with foil and wax paper in the same way, ready for blast-off on Christmas Day, when they will need 2–3 hours more cooking.

This year I used Julian Temperley's wonderful 10-year-old Somerset Cider Brandy for my brandy butter. It may not be allowed to call itself calvados, but it is up there with the best of them. I also used it to ignite the pudding.

Somerset Cider Brandy, Brandy, or Rum Butter

MAKES A GOOD BOWLFUL

1 cup best unsalted butter
1 cup unrefined confectioners' sugar for brandy butter, or half unrefined confectioners' sugar, half light brown sugar for rum butter
2–3 tbsp Somerset Cider Brandy, Cognac or dark rum
grated zest of an orange
a small grating of nutmeg
a squeeze of lemon juice

Start with soft butter, which you can cream more in a bowl with a wooden spoon, before adding the sifted sugar and all the other ingredients. Now work the butter, sugar, and alcohol with your fingers, the aim being to incorporate all the liquid and end up with a slushy, alcoholic mixture. It will firm up in the refrigerator. Add a suspicion of nutmeg only. Good with the pud and the mince pies.

Enough for two enormous jars, or about four dozen mince pies. This, too, should be made weeks in advance, but yet again, I made mine three days before I used the first of it this Christmas. I nearly relented and bought some I was so busy, then I thought guiltily of how the children would never forgive me. It takes longer to buy the ingredients than it does to make if you need a spur. With Miranda and Charissa weighing and stirring, chopping, and putting into jars, it was done in minutes. There is something tremendously satisfying about using the largest wooden spoon you possess to stir the largest tonnage of ingredients you are ever likely to fill a bowl with.

Homemade Mincemeat

MAKES TWO BIG JARS

about 2 cups each of organic
  golden raisins, raisins, and
  currants
1½ cups finely chopped blanched
  almonds
3 eating apples, cut into dolls'-size
  dice
2 cups packed dark brown sugar
1⅓ cups organic mixed peel,
  finely chopped
grated zest and juice of 1½ organic
  lemons, and the zest of an
  organic orange
1 tsp fresh nutmeg, finely grated
¼ tsp ground cloves and
  cinnamon
⅛ tsp ground mace and dried
  gingerroot
6oz beef or vegetarian suet
4 tbsp dark rum
½ cup Cognac or Somerset Cider
  Brandy

Simply mix all the ingredients together really well in a colossal bowl. Decant into sterilized jars, cover, and keep at room temperature. Turn the jars upside down every so often so the liquid permeates the mixture constantly.

When Sally Edwards used to bake this cake at her River Café in Taunton, England, the strongest-willed noncake eater would have weakened. She gave me the recipe to cook on camera, about three minutes before I had to make it, when she joined me to cook on *Tamasin's Weekends*, which I made for UK Food recently. I've never made a cake faster in my life, and thank God the result was every bit as good as hers. The crew hoovered it up instantly. It is really a dessert cake, and should be eaten with a memory of warmth to it, alongside some spiced plums, apricots, or pears. The top should be both crunchy and gooey at the same time. A cross between macaroon and meringue was the production team's verdict.

Almond Macaroon Cake

SERVES 6—8
preheat oven to 350°F

1½ cups unsalted butter
¾ cup vanilla superfine sugar
a pinch of salt
zest of an organic lemon
2 organic eggs
4–5 tbsp crème fraîche
1 cup plus 2 tbsp unbleached
    self-rising flour
¾ cup freshly ground blanched
    almonds

For the topping:
2 egg whites
1 cup plus 2 tbsp vanilla
    superfine sugar
¾ cup freshly ground blanched
    almonds

Grease a 7in cake pan, then place a circle of greased wax paper in the bottom of it. Cream the softened butter and sugar together thoroughly. Add a pinch of salt, the lemon zest, and the eggs, one by one, beating as you go. Fold in four tablespoons of crème fraîche, the sifted flour, and the almonds. If the batter is a little heavy, slacken it with another tablespoon of crème fraîche. Bake in the middle of the oven for 30 minutes.

Five minutes before you are due to take the cake out, whisk the whites stiffly, incorporate half the sugar, and whisk again until stiff. Fold in the almonds and the rest of the sugar lightly and quickly. Take the cake out of the oven and gently but swiftly pile the macaroon mixture on top and spread it across. Return the cake to the oven for about 20 minutes. The top should be pale gold in color and crisp to the touch. Cool for 10 minutes, turn out, and serve warm with crème fraîche. You can also leave the cake to cool completely, and warm it gently a few hours later when you want to eat it.

This wonderfully old-fashioned cake is best made a couple of days before you want to eat it, cut into squares, rather like treacly-black, molasses-laden gingerbread. Curiously, it is as good eaten with a good fruity slice of Montgomery cheddar as it is served for tea or dessert, with a delicious butterscotch sauce. Any which way you please.

Parkin

MAKES 12—16 SQUARES
preheat oven to 350°F

½ cup butter
scant ½ cup light brown sugar
1 cup organic blackstrap molasses
1¾ cup all-purpose or
    wholewheat flour
2 tsp baking powder
1 tsp ground ginger
1 tsp apple-pie spice
salt
4 tbsp milk
flaked almonds (optional)

Melt the butter, sugar, and molasses together in a pan over gentle heat. Remove from the heat and add to the remaining ingredients in a bowl, beating them together lightly until well amalgamated. Grease and line a roasting pan with wax paper, pour in the batter, and bake for about 40 minutes, until just firm to the touch. You can add flaked almonds to the top about 15 minutes into the baking time if you like.

Cool on a wire rack with the paper still attached, then wrap in wax paper and foil and keep for a couple of days before cutting into squares. You can always go down the clotted-cream route if you prefer it to the idea of butterscotch sauce, and you are going to eat the parkin warm.

Butterscotch Sauce

SERVES 6

1 cup light cream
¾ cup light brown sugar
½ cup butter

I find light cream, light brown sugar, and butter melted together in a pan and whisked until well amalgamated and hot, makes the kind of sauce that is utterly irresistible to the toothed and toothless of all ages.

Citrus works wonderfully with cardamom. This is a light, sticky pudding of a cake, perfect with crème fraîche or orange ice cream.

Lemon and Cardamom Cake

MAKES A 9IN CAKE
preheat oven to 350°F

2 heaped tsp cardamom pods
¾ cup unsalted butter
⅔ cup packed light brown sugar
3 large eggs
1⅔ cups all-purpose flour
1½ tsp baking powder
½ tsp baking soda
½ cup fine yellow cornmeal
10 tsp Greek-style yogurt
grated zest and juice of 2 large
    organic lemons
demerara sugar to sprinkle

Grease and line a 9-inch springform cake pan. Crush the cardamom pods with a mortar and pestle to split them, remove the husks, and crush the seeds.

Cream the butter and sugar until light and fluffy, then beat in the eggs, one by one, adding a little sifted flour if the mixture begins to curdle. Sift the flour, baking powder, and baking soda into the batter, then add the cardamom seeds. Fold in the cornmeal and yogurt, add the lemon zest and juice, and plop the batter into the pan, smoothing the top. Bake for 35 minutes, then gingerly open the oven door, pull the cake toward you, and throw a handful of demerara over the top of it. Carry on baking for 15 minutes longer, then test with a skewer. Almost clean means that it is baked—you want a slightly damp center with a crust of crunchy sugar on top.

Cool for 10–15 minutes, then finish cooling on a rack. Eat it, if your timing is impeccable, with a memory of warmth to it.

This is my take on the classic lemon cake, whose top you attack with deep skewer holes and trickle down a sticky, tangy lemon syrup. This is the same with ginger and lemon, but the ginger's heat and strength does not overwhelm the citrus. The top ends up looking rather like a glossy, caramel-colored brandy snap.

Drenched Ginger and Lemon Cake

SERVES 6—8
preheat oven to 350°F

¾ cup unsalted butter
¾ cup light brown sugar
2 large eggs
grated zest and juice of 2 lemons
1 tsp baking powder
a pinch of salt
scant 1½ cups self-rising flour,
    I used ½ whole wheat,
     ½ organic white
3—5 tbsp milk
4 pieces of ginger from a jar
    of preserved ginger in syrup
3 tbsp demerara sugar
2 tbsp ginger syrup

Butter a 7in cake pan and line the base with a circle of buttered wax paper. Cream the butter and light brown sugar until light and fluffy, then beat in the eggs one at a time. Grate the lemon zest into the batter, then sift the baking powder, salt, and flour over and fold them in lightly with a metal spoon. Stir in enough milk to give a dropping consistency, then add the finely chopped ginger and fold in lightly. Plop into the pan, smooth the top, and bake in the middle of the oven for about 40–50 minutes, until springy to the touch in the center.

Remove from the oven and leave for 15 minutes before turning out onto a rack. When still warm, place on a plate, and with a long skewer, pierce holes all over the cake from the top through to the bottom. Put the demerara sugar, lemon juice, and ginger syrup in a pan, stir as it heats to dissolve the sugar, then bubble it up fiercely for a minute or so. Pour it as slowly as you can over the top of the cake, allowing it to seep down the holes. Serve warm or cold with crème fraîche.

This is a delicious, densely fruited moist loaf, which needs no more than spreading with a thick slice of unsalted butter.

Malt and Apple Loaf

MAKES A 1LB LOAF
preheat oven to 325°F

⅓ cup golden raisins
⅓ cup raisins
2 tbsp apple juice concentrate
1¼ cups hot water
¼ cup unsalted butter
2 tbsp malt extract
2¼ cups plus 2 tbsp all-purpose or
   whole wheat flour
½ tsp baking soda
1 tsp ground apple-pie spice
½ tsp ground cloves
a sharp eating apple, peeled,
   diced, and spritzed with fresh
   lemon juice

Soak the golden raisins and raisins in the apple juice concentrate mixed with the hot water for 30 minutes. Then place them in a saucepan with the butter and malt extract, and heat through until the butter and malt are melted and dissolved.

Combine the dry ingredients and the diced apple in a bowl, then pour on the hot ones, and stir together thoroughly. Plop the batter into a greased 8 x 4-inch loaf pan and bake for 1–1½ hours, when a skewer comes out clean. Turn out after 15 minutes and cool on a wire rack.

I have always found red-currant jelly just too sweet for lamb, equally so for venison and hare, but add some spice and apple cider vinegar, and you have something with the sharpening effect of mint sauce, but with the fruity strength and acidity of the red currant. Red currants set blissfully easily, so this is a very satisfying jelly to make.

Spiced Red-Currant Jelly

MAKES 3 OR 4 JARS

3lb 5oz red currants
4 cups water
3 cloves
a short length of cinnamon stick
1 cup apple cider vinegar
3lb 5oz raw granulated sugar

Throw the red currants into a large preserving or enamel pan as they are, with their stalks. Add the water and spices, bring to a boil, and simmer until the red currants are soft. Strain the juice through a cheesecloth or jelly bag into a bowl, suspending it above the bowl and leaving it to drip overnight. You do not want to squeeze or hurry any of the juice through; this will make your jelly cloudy instead of sparkling.

Add the vinegar and sugar to the liquid in the pan, and boil until it reaches setting point. To test for the setting point, put a small saucer in the refrigerator to cool, then place a teaspoon of boiling juice on the saucer, and put it in the freezer for a couple of minutes. If the liquid on the saucer wrinkles when you push it with a finger, you have reached the setting point.

Pour into clean, warm jam jars. Top each one with a circle of waxed paper while the jam is still hot and let cool. When the jam is cold, cover each pot with a circle of cellophane secured with an elastic band. Store in a cool, dark place.

This was my father's favorite breakfast treat, and now it is mine. On the odd years I pine. On the even years, when my tree is glutted with the waxy glow of crimson and primrose, I pick baskets of the fruit, drape cheesecloth from the beams of the kitchen and let the amber juice drip into bowls for days. I then proudly pot dozens of jars, with a sprig of lemon peel adorning each summit. I even dared to give pots to chefs Richard Corrigan and Simon Hopkinson this year, so good it was. Crab apples should be picked when they are just ripe, but the odd bruise from falling to the ground will not hurt.

Crab Apple Jelly

as much fruit as you can pick
water
unrefined sugar, 1lb for each
   2½ cups of juice

Wash the fruit, put it in a huge preserving pan, and just cover with water. Bring to a boil and simmer slowly, covered, until the apples are softened to a pulp. Strain the juice through a cheesecloth jelly bag into a bowl, suspending it above the bowl and leaving it to drip overnight. You do not want to squeeze or hurry any of the juice through; this will make your jelly cloudy instead of sparkling.

Measure the beautiful pink juice in a glass measuring cup, and add 1lb of unrefined sugar to each 2½ cups of juice. Bring to a boil, remove the scum, and keep boiling until you reach setting point. I start testing after 10 minutes. Put a small saucer in the refrigerator to cool, then place a teaspoon of boiling juice on the saucer, and put it in the freezer for a couple of minutes. If the liquid on the saucer wrinkles when you push it with a finger, the jelly has reached the setting point.

I scald the jars with boiling water in the sink as I wait for the setting point. Ladle the jelly through a funnel into the jars as soon as you have reached setting point. Cover with waxed discs and cellophane covers (see page 227). Store in a cool, dark place.

This year, my little mulberry tree fruited for the first time, providing just enough to make a breathtakingly good sorbet and to add to my homemade damson gin. This is a fall treat of a job: I pick the sloes or damsons in late September, prick them with a fork, add the sugar, gin, kernels from the damson pits, the heart of the fruit, and seal the purple brew in a huge Ball jar, to shake rumbustiously every week before the first tasting at Christmas. The sweet purple stickiness reminds me of childhood cough syrup—if only that had tasted so good. I filled the last quarter of my jar with mulberries and didn't take the top off until Charlotte and Bill Reynolds, of Swaddles Green Organic Farm arrived with my Bronze turkey, goose, and ham on Christmas Eve. It was four in the afternoon, and they'd been flat out with Christmas orders for weeks, including 1,100 organic turkeys. I sat them down with smoked eel, homemade granary toast, and shot glasses of my mulberried damson gin. Bill was most taken by it and felt suitably mellowed after the first three glasses.

Damson, Sloe, or Mulberry Gin

MAKES A LARGE JAR

4 cups damsons or sloe berries, put them in a large measuring cup as you pick, or, if you make mulberry gin, use equal measures of mulberries and gin
1¾ cups unrefined sugar
5 cups good gin
either half a dozen kernels from inside the damson pits, which you crack open with a hammer, or a few drops of bitter-almond extract

Prick the damsons, sloes, or mulberries and put them into a large Ball jar. Add all the other ingredients, seal the jar, and give it a good shake. Shake every week until Christmas, when you can strain and bottle the gin. The fruit will be delicious with a bit of the sticky purple syrup eaten with some homemade vanilla ice cream.

This recipe also works well for "moonshine," which Stephen Markwick of the brilliant restaurant Markwick's in Bristol, England, makes. Moonshine is vodka based, filled with cherries, and a lot of the kernels from the cracked cherry pits.

Shamelessly rich and
indulgent, tiramisu is not
difficult to make and is best
prepared the day before
you need it so the flavors
can blend and mature.

a lingering end

4

Francesco Zanchetta's peerless rendering of this classic Italian pudding. Make this the night before you want it so the cream has time to bind with the layer of biscuit and the flavors develop.

Tiramisu

SERVES 6

1 organic egg and 3 organic egg
    yolks
¼ cup white wine
¼ cup Marsala
2 tbsp amaretto, use Cognac and a
    drop or two of Culpeper's bitter
    almond extract if you can't get
    amaretto
½ cup raw vanilla sugar
1 cup mascarpone cheese
1 tsp espresso powder

For the biscuit layer:
3 small cups of espresso coffee
1½ tbsp sugar
2 tbsp Marsala
6oz Italian savoiardi biscuits, or
    good boudoir biscuits
2 tbsp best organic, unsweetened
    cocoa powder for sifting over
    the top

Whisk together the egg yolks and whole egg, white wine, Marsala, and Amaretto in a double boiler; I have my grandmother's old enamel one. The top pan should not touch the water simmering in the bottom pan. Whisk until the mixture becomes very thick; you are making zabaglione. Once it is firm and fluffy, remove the bowl from the pan and carry on whisking for a few minutes longer. Now add the sugar, which will dissolve very quickly. Gently fold in the mascarpone with the espresso powder, and then beat everything together for another minute or so to lighten the cream.

Mix together the cups of espresso, sugar, and Marsala in a dish deep enough to soak the biscuits. Dip in the biscuits so they absorb the liquid but do not start to break up. Hot coffee helps.

Cover the bottom of a large, shallow rectangular dish with a layer of soaked biscuits, laid tightly together in the same direction, then pour half of the cream over before adding a second layer of biscuits, placed at right angles to the layer beneath. This helps to hold the tiramisu together when you serve it. Cover with the rest of the cream and sift the cocoa powder thickly over the surface. Cover and chill in the refrigerator overnight.

Chocolate

This could so easily turn into a chapter, a book, a magnum opus. I am, let us say, not immune to the pleasures of chocolate, and only grateful that there is no closed season for it. If there were, the term stockpiling would hardly be sufficient. I greet the discovery of a new bar, cake, dessert, or ice cream as just that, an important discovery for the happiness and wellbeing of man, but I would not want to burden those of a dissimilar disposition with the finer details that clearly identify and typify the truly obsessed. Instead, I offer you a token few of my latest recipes, including a few classics and long-time favorites, without which many a Sunday lunch or dinner for friends and family would have been infinitely the poorer.

This is a magical cake, which you can make without the raspberries, if you are of the purist chocoholic bent, or simply don't agree with chocolate and fruit, which some don't. You can make the cake well in advance—it will keep for a week in a tin—and then add your ganache. This cake is flourless, but moist with freshly ground almonds.

Chocolate and Raspberry Pudding Cake with Chocolate Ganache

SERVES 8—10
preheat oven to 325°F

4 organic eggs, separated, plus one whole egg
¾ cup plus 2 tbsp vanilla-flavored superfine sugar
8oz best bittersweet chocolate, minimum 70% cocoa solids
1¼ cups blanched almonds, freshly ground
1 tsp heaped ground coffee
7oz fresh raspberries

For the ganache:
½ cup heavy cream
8oz semisweet chocolate

Whisk the egg yolks and egg together with half the sugar, until pale and doubled in volume. Melt the chocolate in the top of a double boiler. Whisk the egg whites, adding the remaining sugar a bit at a time, until they are at the satiny, soft peak stage. Add half of them to the egg-and-sugar mixture, folding them in gently. Add the chocolate and the rest of the whites, folding as you go. Then do likewise with the almonds and coffee. Last of all, add the raspberries, which need folding in with extreme gentleness so they don't break up.

Scrape the batter into a greased and floured 8-inch springform pan, with a circle of greased parchment paper laid on its bottom. Bake for 30 minutes. Then turn off the oven and leave the cake in for another 15 minutes, or until a skewer comes out clean from the center. Remove from the oven and leave to cool in the pan.

Scald the cream in a small pan, remove from the heat, and stir in the broken up chocolate. Stir until smooth. Cover the cake with the ganache and leave to cool.

A delicious birthday cake, which needs little more than a perfectly made vanilla ice cream with fresh Madagascan vanilla beans.

Chocolate Mocha Cake with Irish Whiskey

MAKES A 8IN CAKE
preheat oven to 350°F

6oz semisweet chocolate,
  minimum 70% cocoa solids
4 tbsp freshly made strong
  mocha coffee
2 tbsp Irish whiskey
7 tbsp raw vanilla-flavored sugar
½ cup unsalted butter, soft
  enough to cream
3 organic eggs, separated
½ cup freshly ground blanched
  almonds
a few drops of natural bitter-
  almond extract
6½ tbsp all-purpose flour, sifted

For the frosting:
2oz best bittersweet chocolate
2 tbsp Irish whiskey
¼ cup unsalted butter

Butter and flour an 8-inch cake pan. Melt the chocolate in the top of a double boiler with the coffee and whiskey. Remove the top pan and allow them to cool. Cream together all but a tablespoon of the sugar with the butter until it is pale and fluffy, then beat in the egg yolks, one at a time. Whisk the egg whites with a pinch of salt to soft peak stage, then add the last tablespoon of sugar and beat to firm peaks. Blend the chocolate mixture into the creamed butter and sugar with a rubber spatula, then stir in the ground almonds and bitter almond extract. Fold in a spoonful of the egg white, followed by a spoonful of flour, and continue until it's all blended in.

Scrape the mixture into the cake pan and bake it in the center of the oven for 25–30 minutes. A skewer should come out clean. Cool in the pan for 10 minutes, then run a knife round the edge of the pan and turn the cake out on to a rack.

Ice it when it is completely cool. Melt the chocolate and whiskey in the top of the double boiler until satiny smooth. Remove from the heat and beat in the butter, a tablespoon at a time. Stand the bowl over iced water and continue to beat, otherwise the butter and the chocolate will separate. You can always add a little cream if this happens—whisk and the mixture will cohere. Spread the icing over the cake, leaving a rough finish.

This is a fabulous dessert, which you turn out in a block rather like a gold ingot and cut into thin slices. I found very good organic Spanish chestnuts to make it with; they come vacuum packed and the flavor is strong enough not to be overpowered by the chocolate. Disarmingly simple to make.

Chocolate and Chestnut Marquise

SERVES 10

3 x 7-oz packs of vacuum-packed chestnuts, the best you can find
½ cup unsalted butter, melted in a pan
½ cup plus 2 tbsp raw vanilla-flavored sugar
7oz best semisweet chocolate, minimum 70% cocoa solids
1 tbsp Cognac
1 tbsp water
4 organic eggs, separated

Put the chestnuts in a food processor with the melted butter and all but a tablespoon of the sugar. Blend until well mixed. Melt the chocolate in the top of a double boiler with the brandy and water. Add the melted chocolate to the chestnut mixture and blitz briefly. Stir in the egg yolks, one by one, then whisk the egg whites to soft peak stage. Add the remaining tablespoon of sugar and whisk until stiff. Stir the first tablespoon into the chestnut mixture, then fold in the rest as well as you can; the mixture will be very thick and sludgy at this stage. Plop it into a loaf pan, which you have greased lightly with an unobtrusive oil such as almond oil, and smooth down the surface. Leave to cool and put it in the refrigerator when cold.

I think this is best eaten after a day or two, so you can make it in advance. It will turn out beautifully onto a flat dish. Serve with cream, to which you can add a tablespoon of freshly made coffee, if you like. A couple of slices each are all you will want. The other route would be to serve it with a whipped, sugared crème chantilly. Killer.

Sally Edwards was forbidden by her customers to take this dessert off the menu at her River Café in Taunton, Somerset. I found it very difficult ever to choose anything else as a result. It is simply one of the best cakes I have ever come across, and it needs no more than a yielding spoonful of crème fraîche and a pile of fresh sweet berries to smarten it up.

Chocolate Espresso Cake

SERVES 8—10
preheat oven to 375°F

1 cup plus 1 tbsp unsalted butter, diced, plus extra for greasing the pan
6½oz best semisweet chocolate, broken into pieces
¼ cup very strong freshly brewed coffee
6 eggs, separated
scant 1 cup raw superfine sugar
heaped 1 cup blanched, roast, and coarsely ground almonds,

Melt the butter and chocolate together with the coffee in a bowl over a pan of barely simmering water.

While they are melting, cream the egg yolks and sugar in an electric mixer until pale and light, 8–10 minutes. Continue to whisk, adding the melted chocolate and butter. Stop the machine, remove the whisk, and fold in the almonds with a metal spoon. In a clean glass or metal bowl, whisk the egg whites to stiff peaks. Stir a spoonful of egg white into the chocolate mixture to lighten it before folding in the rest.

Grease the sides of a 10-inch springform pan and line the bottom with a circle of buttered parchment paper. Pour in the batter and bake for 20 minutes. Turn the oven down to 325°F and continue baking for 40 minutes longer.

Remove the cake and leave in the pan set on a rack until completely cool. Turn out of the pan and remove the paper. Delicious served with crème fraîche as a cake or dessert.

Quite the best, just don't overcook them,. Brownies are meant to have a "sad" middle, above which there is a thin, dry, slightly crunchy crust.

Rich Chocolate Brownies

MAKES 12—16 SQUARES
preheat oven to 350°F

7oz best semisweet chocolate,
  minimum 70% cocoa solids
½ cup softened unsalted butter
1 cup plus 2 tbsp raw vanilla sugar
2 eggs and 1 yolk
4 tbsp freshly made strong coffee
1 cup plus 3 tbsp all-purpose flour
1 tsp baking powder
a pinch of salt
a handful of fresh whole
  hazelnuts

Line the bottom and sides of small roasting pan or gratin dish, about 12 x 9 inches, with foil. Gently melt the chocolate in the top of a double boiler or in a bowl over, but not touching, simmering water in a pan. Cream the butter and sugar until really light and fluffy. I do this in my KitchenAid. Add the eggs, one at a time, then the extra yolk, with the mixer running. Pour in the melted chocolate, then the coffee. Transfer the mixing bowl to the work surface and sift in the flour, baking powder, and a pinch of salt.

Pour into the pan, then push hazelnuts into the top of what you will later cut into 12–15 squares. Bake for about 25 minutes. Test with a skewer, you don't want it to come out completely clean, but the mixture should not feel raw. The brownies will go on baking when you take them out of the oven. Leave to cool before you cut them into squares and remove from the pan.

Quite the best, too, so which ones are you going to do? I suggest you try them both. Size is your business, but this mixture fills a small roasting pan.

Rich Chocolate Chip and Hazelnut Brownies

MAKES 12—16 SQUARES
preheat oven to 350°F

1½ cups raw sugar
4 eggs
1 cup unsalted butter
9 tbsp organic unsweetened cocoa
⅔ cup all-purpose flour
⅔ cup roasted hazelnuts
4oz best bittersweet chocolate chunks

Grease the roasting pan. Beat the sugar and eggs together really well, until they have thickened and the sugar has totally dissolved. Melt the butter and pour it into the sugar and egg mixture. Sift the cocoa and flour together into the mixture, then melt the chocolate in a bowl over hot water and stir it in.

Put the hazelnuts and chocolate in a Ziploc bag, and whack them as hard as you dare with a rolling pin, keeping things a little chunky. The nuts will be more pulverized than the chocolate. Fold into the batter and scrape it into the pan. Bake for about 25 minutes. Test with a skewer. You don't want it to come out completely clean, but the mixture should not feel raw.

Leave to cool before you cut the brownies into squares and remove them from the pan.

Our second lunch at Riva in Barnes, in south London, the other day, was, I think Simon Hopkinson would agree, true to form, as perfect a symphony as the first last year. The three movements were rather shorter and more eclectic than our previous one—far too long and shamelessly greedy to go into here—but this time it was the week before Christmas and a little self inflicted abstinence was the plan. The fritto misto that the exceptionally talented chef Francesco Zanchetta made for us consisted of the airiest and crispest of golden batters, encasing everything from a single sage leaf to squid, shrimp, and the most divinely battered balls of salt cod, one of my favorite things in the world. Then Simon suggested the fresh ricotta gnocchi with chanterelles. I was powerless to resist, what with the joy of having Simon unbossily absolving me of all decisions, and NOT insisting that we had to have something different. That, too, was about as delicious as you could ever imagine it to be from the simple description above. I was not going to eat dessert. Well, that lasted about a minute, until Simon got into conversation with Francesco about his budino. It turns out that Simon has been trying to make a chocolate budino as stratospherically delicious as Francesco's for some time now, and still hasn't quite succeeded. Undaunted and single-minded, he is still refusing the recipe, trying to see if he can create the same silken-textured, creamy chocolate pudding, tremblingly light, the gelatin barely holding its rich, soft, smooth soothingness together. You think I exaggerate? Go to Riva and try it for yourself. And, as Simon insisted I did, accompany it with a white slice of equally trembling and perfect panna cotta. Simon refused the recipe again. I asked for it and have been trying equally hard to reach Francesco's perfection with his minimal instruction, but I will give you what I have arrived at to date. And then Simon insisted that I try the tiramisu, that trat dessert that took over the dessert cart in all Italian restaurants when the zuppa inglese was finally consigned to the morgue. None so good as this. You will never be sniffy about tiramisu again if you make Francesco's (see page 234). As to the moral of the story, vis à vis Simon struggling on without the recipe and me taking it home with me, I would have thought it rather obvious. He is, of course, the better cook.

Budino

8oz best semisweet chocolate,
   70% cocoa solids
1 short espresso, or the equivalent
   strong small cup of fresh coffee
2 egg yolks
½ cup superfine sugar
2¼ cups milk
4 leaves of gelatin soaked in
   2–3 tbsp of water for about
   10 minutes

Melt the chocolate with the espresso in the top of a double boiler. Take it off the heat and whisk in the egg yolks. Heat the milk with the sugar until it is dissolved. Add the milk and sugar mixture little by little to the chocolate, whisking all the time, without creating any foam. Once the gelatin has completely dissolved, add it to the mixture and continue whisking. Pour into small molds, I used my little plastic steamed-pudding molds. Leave them to cool and leave to set in the refrigerator.

You can serve them several hours or a day later. A metal spatula worked around the molds enables you to plop them out onto plates. Light cream is a must. It slicks the chocolate tops beautifully before cascading down the sides.

I served these at my New Year's dinner, as well as the clementine, passion fruit, and muscat jelly, and Nick and Sally Welsh were in raptures. My budinos were good, but they still weren't as good as Francesco's. Mine seemed to be more solid, less quakey. I will try one leaf of gelatin less next time.

A simply delicious chocolate pudding that you can serve hot or chilled, depending on your mood and what timing suits you. Both are equally good, although the cold tends to be richer, since I add a layer of lightly whipped cream and finely grated chocolate to shroud the chocolate beneath.

Hot or Cold Chocolate Pudding

SERVES 6—8
preheat oven to 400°F

5oz semisweet chocolate,
   70% cocoa solids
10 tbsp unsalted butter
1 tsp of pure vanilla extract
⅔ cup warm water
½ cup plus 2 tbsp vanilla sugar
4 organic eggs, separated
3 tbsp self-rising flour
cream for serving

Grease a 2 quart soufflé dish. Melt the chocolate, butter, and vanilla in the top of a double boiler over simmering water. Add the warm water and sugar and keep stirring until all the sugar has dissolved. Pour the mixture into a bowl and stir in the egg yolks, one by one. Stir in the sifted flour and whisk until the mixture is free of lumps. Whisk the egg whites to stiff peaks, stir the first tablespoon into the mixture, then fold the rest lightly in with a metal spoon.

Boil a kettle, put the soufflé dish inside a roasting pan, and pour in scalding water to come half way up its sides. Cook for 10 minutes, then turn the oven temperature down to 325°F and cook for 30 minutes longer.

Serve hot with cream, or leave to cool completely. To serve the cold version, softly whip 1¼ cups cream, cover the pudding with it, and finely grate a dusting of bittersweet chocolate over the surface. Serve at room temperature—the pudding is lighter that way than if you chill it in the refrigerator.

This recipe doubles up perfectly, so if you have a party, just make double the amount in a larger soufflé dish.

This is one of the best winter Sunday lunch desserts—incredibly simple to make, and it will burble away on the stovetop while you tackle the roast. Being flourless, it is a whole lot lighter than you would suspect a steamed pudding to be, and not something any child or grownup could say "no" to. Another of my cousin Deborah's good desserts.

Steamed Nut and Chocolate Pudding

SERVES 8

7 tbsp softened butter, plus extra
    for greasing
½ cup vanilla-flavored superfine
    sugar
6 eggs, separated
½ cup ground hazelnuts
3½oz organic semisweet
    chocolate, chilled
2 tbsp brandy
a pinch of salt
whipped cream for serving

Butter and sugar a 1½ quart English pudding basin or bowl. Cream the butter until soft, add the sugar and beat until fluffy and light. Add the egg yolks, one at a time, then fold in the ground hazelnuts. Grate the chocolate on the coarse side of a grater or on the big disk of a food processor. Fold the chocolate into the batter with the brandy. Whisk the egg whites with the pinch of salt until stiff and fold into the chocolate-and-nut mixture

Pour into the sugared and buttered bowl. Cover with foil and secure with string and steam for 1 hour over simmering water.

Let stand for 5 minutes before turning out. Serve with whipped cream with a little extra brandy in it.

Another wonderful recipe from a recent marathon cooking weekend with my friend George Morley, her husband Shawn, and small son Charlie. Usually George and I, unreformable greedies, decide who's going to cook what and when, and what we're going to be drinking with it, in slavering telephone conversations. As the two bossiest women either of us know ever to set foot in a kitchen, it is all the more extraordinary that we never seem to come to blows. Greed and mutual respect are no small levelers here, and the culinary laboratory of the kitchen hums with our fairly suspect brand of caustic wit as we dissect everything from bone to body politic over many a fine glass and hot stove. George found this particular recipe the weekend she came down to "guest" on my television series. I think I probably did the guesting that day. She had found the recipe in an American book, *Walking on Walnuts* by Nancy Ring. I devised the cookies to go with it, using the last of my fabulous roast hazelnuts from Piedmont. A zenlike combination.

If you need further endorsement, here it is—courtesy of an article written by the illustrious historian Paul Johnson. The subject, "A rhapsody on puddings that would not have disgraced Belshazzar's chef." At the end of the piece he writes: "The other day I dined at the home of Tamasin Day-Lewis, the *Daily Telegraph* expert, and was served the best ice cream I've ever eaten, made of burnt orange according to a most complex and esoteric recipe. I don't know what Richard II would have made of it, but I had three helpings—unheard of!" Praise indeed, but how on earth do I top it next time?

Burnt Orange Ice Cream

SERVES 6—8

*quantities are in US cups—we used an
ordinary teacup*

2 tbsp sugar

1 cup heavy cream

1 cup whole milk

2 tbsp grated orange zest

2 cups freshly squeezed orange
juice; George has also made it
with blood oranges

¼ cup plus 1 tbsp Cointreau

¼ cup plus 2 tbsp sugar for the
caramel

¼ cup egg yolks, about 10 large
ones

Place the 2 tablespoons of sugar in a mixing bowl. In a medium saucepan, scald the cream and milk with the orange zest, then steep them together off the heat with a lid on the pan for about 30 minutes.

Simmer the orange juice and Cointreau until reduced to one cup. Whisk into the cream mixture and strain, then return it to the pan and keep warm over very gentle heat. In another pan caramelize the ¼ cup plus two tablespoons of sugar until very dark (just past the color of an Irish setter). Do not stir at any time. Swirl gently in the pan, if necessary, to ensure even color. Remove from the heat, protecting your stirring hand with an oven mitt, and immediately temper the caramel with a small amount of the warm orange cream while stirring vigorously. Keep adding cream slowly until the caramel stops bubbling violently. Whisk all of the tempered caramel back into the remaining cream and place on the stove over medium heat to scald once more.

Add the yolks to the sugar in a mixing bowl and whisk together when the cream scalds, but not before. Temper the yolks with the scalded cream by pouring a small stream of the hot cream into the yolks while whisking continuously. Pour back into the pan and return to the stove over medium heat. Stir continuously with a spatula until the mixture thickens to a perceptible custard and a line can be drawn through it with your finger. Cook only until it is just thickened or it will curdle. Immediately strain the finished ice-cream base and stir to cool, then churn in an ice-cream machine or put into a freezer tray. If you use a tray, remember to stir the setting walls of the ice cream into the middle of the tray after the first hour, and then again an hour or two later, to prevent crystals forming. Serve with the hazelnut and orange cookies on page 250.

Once you have made the dough for these delicious cookies, you can keep it wrapped up like a fat sausage in wax paper in the refrigerator. Slice it like a salami and cook the cookies whenever you want them—warm for tea, as petit fours with coffee, or to go with desserts like the burnt orange ice cream on page 249 or a fruit fool.

Hazelnut and Orange Cookies

preheat oven to 375°F

¾ cup plus 2 tbsp unsalted butter
¾ cup raw superfine sugar
1 large egg
1¾ cups self-rising flour
finely grated zest of an organic
    orange, use a nutmeg grater
a few drops of sweet orange oil
¾–1 cup whole roasted hazelnuts,
    the freshest you can find,
    bashed into bits with a
    mezzaluna or sharp knife

Cream the butter and sugar thoroughly in a KitchenAid or by hand. Then add the egg, sifted flour, zest, oil, and nuts and amalgamate. Form the mixture into two balls and roll each one out on a lightly floured surface with both hands, until you have a sausage about 2 inches in diameter. Wrap these in wax paper and foil, and refrigerate. Overnight is best.

Slice the sausage into as many cookies as you want, place them on a greased cookie sheet or two, not touching, and cook in the middle of the oven for about 8 minutes. They should not have colored significantly. Remember, a minute too far and they will burn.

Using a metal spatula, transfer the cookies immediately to a rack. Be careful, they are soft and bendy and can break at this stage, but they firm up very quickly. They should be beautifully crisp and nutty and scented with orange. Serve them warm with the burnt orange ice cream, which you should transfer from freezer to refrigerator 30 minutes before you want to eat it.

You can make these unfussy puddings well in advance, and they are as good in the winter with dried fruit as they are with summer berries or fruits.

Vanilla Cream Pots with Armagnac and Orange Apricots

MAKES 6 RAMEKINS
preheat oven to 325°F

2¼ cups heavy cream
7 tbsp whole milk
1 fresh vanilla bean with its
   scooped-out innards
6 egg yolks
⅓ cup raw vanilla-flavored
   superfine sugar

Put the cream and milk in a pan, add the vanilla bean and seeds, and bring just to scalding point. Cover the pan, remove from the heat, and infuse for 30 minutes or so.

Whisk the egg yolks together with the superfine sugar until thick and pale, then remove the bean from the cream mixture and pour the liquid over the yolks, whisking them together. Strain the cream into the ramekins, set them in a roasting pan with hot water to come half way up their sides, and cover them with a sheet of wax paper to prevent a skin forming as they cook.

Bake until quiveringly set. They will continue to cook outside the oven. Test after 40 minutes by nudging them. Remove from the *bain-marie* and leave to cool completely.

Three of these apricots in their gloopy, citrusy alcohol make a spectacular top to the vanilla cream pots on page 251. Or you can serve them on their own or with the carrot, apricot, and cinnamon cake on page 256. Remember to soak the fruit in half the orange juice the night before you cook it. The dish will keep well in the refrigerator for several days.

Armagnac and Orange Apricots

SERVES 6

18 dried unsulfured
   organic apricots
¾ cup plus 2 tbsp freshly squeezed
   orange juice
½ cup raw superfine sugar
7 tbsp water
a few drops sweet orange oil
   (optional)
the peel of an organic orange,
   all pith removed, sliced into
   matchstick shreds and
   blanched in boiling water
   for a minute
Armagnac, Cognac, Cider
   Brandy, or Calvados

Soak the apricots overnight in half the orange juice. Next day, put the rest of the juice into a pan with the sugar, water, and shreds of blanched peel. Simmer for 10 minutes, then add the apricots and their juice and simmer until tender, about 15 minutes. Cool them in a glass bowl, add a generous slug of alcohol, and stir it in well.

If you are keeping the fruit in the refrigerator, bring it back to room temperature again for half an hour before you place two or three apricots with some juice and peel on top of each vanilla cream.

This is the lightest of cakes, made with potato flour, the ricotta strained to aerate it. I add a touch of Grand Marnier and orange-flower water to the batter, and serve it alongside strawberries and clotted cream in the summer.

Orange-Scented Ricotta Cake

SERVES 8
preheat oven to 350°F

6 tbsp unsalted butter
¾ cup vanilla-flavored superfine
    sugar
2 large organic eggs
grated zests of half an organic
    orange and lemon
3 tbsp potato flour
1½ tsp baking powder
a pinch of salt
2 cups ricotta. If you are lucky
    enough to find fresh, drain it
    through a cheesecloth-lined
    strainer overnight
⅓ cup organic raisins soaked in a
    little hot water to plump up for
    15 minutes
2 tbsp Grand Marnier or
    Cointreau
2–3 tsp orange-flower water
confectioners' sugar

Beat the butter and all but a tablespoon of the sugar together until pale and creamy, then add the eggs, continuing to whisk. Add the zests, potato flour, baking powder, and salt. Push the ricotta through the small disk of a food mill or a strainer, and blend into the other ingredients. Add the plumped-up raisins, Grand Marnier or Cointreau, and sprinkle the orange-flower water over. Butter a springform pan, then scatter the rest of the sugar into it and roll it around the bottom and sides, discarding any extra.

Scrape in the cake batter and bake in the middle of the oven for 55 minutes, or until a skewer comes out clean; leave to cool. Turn out onto a plate, and sprinkle over a little confectioners' sugar if you like. This is a habit that I refuse to get into, it is so overworked on restaurant desserts, alongside sprigs of this and that and solitary fanned fruit. If in doubt, leave well alone.

I can't pretend I reach for the suet regularly, even in a cold snap, but once or twice a year when the mood strikes, there is no substitute. If you are loath to part with your own homemade marmalade, store-bought will do, but go for a top-quality brand.

Steamed Apple and Marmalade Pudding

SERVES 6

about 2¼lb cooking apples
juice of a lemon
1⅔ cups self-rising flour
a pinch of salt
6 tbsp grated beef suet
¼ cup packed dark or light brown
  sugar (depending on quite how
  dark and treacly you like
  things)
6 tbsp good, bitter marmalade

Peel, core, quarter, and cut the apples into thickish wedges, then sprinkle them with lemon juice to prevent them from discoloring. Put the flour into a bowl, add a pinch of salt and the suet, then add water, a tiny bit at a time, and mix to a stiff dough. Roughly 6 tablespoons of water should do, but go easy, you don't want a sticky ball of slime.

Divide the dough into two pieces, one three-quarter lump, the other the remaining quarter. Roll the large one out first and fit it into a buttered 1-quart English pudding basin or ovenproof bowl. Roll the apple in the sugar, then add the marmalade and coat thoroughly before piling into the pudding basin. Roll out the small piece of dough, wet the edge of the dough in the basin, and stick the dough top to it, pressing them together to seal tightly.

Cover with pleated wax paper, then foil, and tie. Place the pudding in a large, heavy-bottomed pan and pour in scalding water to come halfway up the sides of the basin. Cover with a lid and steam at a simmer for at least 2 hours—2½ will be fine. Turn out the pudding onto a large plate and serve with homemade custard. Flavor the custard with a bit of Seville orange juice.

This is a recipe I adapted from the winning entry to a competition I held in my *Daily Telegraph* column after my trip to India. The entrants had to devise a dessert to complement a spice ice cream. Malcolm Kennedy won with this delicious cake, which is not too aggressively or diffusely spiced. It works wonderfully with my ginger and spice ice cream, and with the Armagnac and orange apricots (page 253) as a third element. That way you just need a thin slice of warm cake, always great with ice cream.

Carrot, Apricot and Cinnamon Cake

SERVES 8—10
preheat oven to 350°F

1 tbsp ground almonds
10 tbsp unsalted butter
¾ cup packed light brown sugar
2 eggs
2 tsp ground cinnamon
6 tbsp freshly squeezed orange juice and the zest of 2 oranges
2¼ cups self-rising flour
1 tsp baking powder
a pinch of salt
scant 1 cup grated organic carrot
½ cup chopped unsulfured dried apricots

Butter a 1½ quart gugelhopf pan or fluted mold, and dust it with ground almonds. Cream the butter and sugar in a KitchenAid or by hand until light and fluffy, then whisk in the eggs. Add the cinnamon, orange juice, and zest, then sift in the flour, baking powder, and salt, and fold in well. If the batter is heavy and hasn't quite achieved dropping consistency, add more orange juice. Stir in the grated carrot and apricots.

Scrape into the prepared mold, tap on the work surface to eliminate air bubbles, and smooth the top. Bake in the middle of the oven for 1–1¼ hours, or until a skewer comes out clean. Cool in the pan for 10 minutes, then turn out onto a rack and serve while still warm.

It is the frisson of very hot with very cold that does it. These doughnuts were the runners-up in the competition and they worked beautifully with green cardamom ice cream, as they do with ginger and spice ice cream. The tiny doughnuts double in size as they fry and are then rolled in sugar, cinnamon, and allspice, an inspirational detail.

Mrs. Golumbina's Hot Spicy Doughnuts with Fresh Mangoes and Lime

3 tbsp unsalted butter
¾ cup sugar
2 eggs, well beaten
4 cups all-purpose flour
crushed seeds of 3 or 4 green
    cardamom pods
⅔ cup whole milk
1 tsp ground cinnamon
½ tsp ground allspice
vegetable oil for deep-frying
1 ripe mango, sliced
1 lime

Cream the butter into 6 tablespoons of the sugar, then stir in the eggs, the flour, and the crushed cardamom seeds. Add the milk, bit by bit, until you have a soft dough that leaves the side of the bowl.

Divide the dough and roll it into small, walnut-sized balls. Drop them into very hot oil for about 4 minutes. Keep spinning them as they cook until they are golden all over. Remove from the pan and drain well on paper towels. Cook the doughnuts in batches so you don't overcrowd the pan, which will lower the heat and make them greasy.

Spread the remaining sugar, cinnamon, and allspice on a plate. Roll the cooked doughnuts lightly in the mixture until completely covered.

Serve with slices of fresh mango, over which you have squeezed the juice of a lime, and a scoop of spiced ginger or green cardamom ice cream.

I first ate this pudding as an undergraduate. I was lucky enough to have a boyfriend who was also a keen cook. He had found the recipe in one of his mother's tomes under the heading "lemon bomb pudding" before I ever came across it in Jane Grigson's classic *English Food*. I guess the lemon does explode like a bomb, sending a brackish-black moat of sugary liquid around the dome of suet. The term "rib-sticking" was made for it. For students, it was perfect—cheap and brilliant to leave for four hours in our little "gyp" room, where we had a small Belling stove, while we got to grips with *Pericles* or *Gawain and the Green Knight*. Both demanded something epic to tuck into afterward.

Sussex Pond Pudding

SERVES 6

1¾ cups self-rising flour
4oz grated suet
⅔ cup milk and water
½ cup slightly salted butter,
    chopped into pieces
⅓ cup molasses or demerara
    sugar, depending on how black
    and how treacly you can take it
1 large organic lemon

Mix the flour and suet together in a bowl. Add the half milk, half water to mix them into a soft dough. Roll the dough out into a large circle, and then remove a quarter with a knife to use as a lid.

Butter a 1½ quart English pudding basin or ovenproof bowl, drop the three-quarters piece of dough into it and press it together to line the basin. Put half the chopped butter into the basin with half the sugar. Prick the lemon all over with a fine sharp skewer or larding needle to help the juices escape. Place the lemon on top of the butter and sugar and cover with the remaining butter and sugar. Roll out the remaining quarter of dough and lay it on top to seal the filling inside.

Cover with pleated wax paper, then foil, and tie. Make a string handle, then lower the pudding into boiling water in a large saucepan, making sure the water comes halfway up the pudding basin. Cook for 3–4 hours. Turn the pudding out onto a large plate with plenty of room for the moat; you will have to ease it with a metal spatula first. Make sure everyone gets some of the lemon, all of which will be edible. Serve with clotted or thick cream, naturally.

Will there ever be a successor to the decadently becaloried sticky toffee pudding? I think this is as close as it gets, and I like it equally well with or without the nuts. What I prefer about this pudding is the fact that when you turn it out you have a tidal moat of butterscotch pouring down from its summit, coating everything in sight. Slightly different principle to the sticky toffee sauce that basks underneath the sponge of the original.

Steamed Apricot and Pecan Pudding with Butterscotch Sauce

SERVES 6—8

For the sauce:
1 cup packed light brown sugar
½ cup unsalted butter
½ cup plus 2 tbsp organic crème fraîche
1 tsp organic vanilla extract

For the pudding:
1¼ cups boiling water
7oz unsulfured organic dried apricots, chopped into small pieces
1 tsp baking soda
1 cup plus 2 tbsp vanilla-flavored superfine sugar
¼ cup unsalted butter
1 egg
1⅔ cups all-purpose flour
1 tsp baking powder
½ cup pecans, bashed up but not crushed to death

Melt all the ingredients for the sauce together in a saucepan. Let them bubble for 3 minutes or so longer before pouring them into the bottom of a large, greased English pudding basin or ovenproof bowl.

Pour the boiling water over the apricots and baking soda and leave to cool. Cream the sugar and butter until light and fluffy, then beat in the egg. Sift the flour and baking powder over, and throw in the pecans. Stir in the apricot mixture, and scrape the batter into the pudding basin on top of the butterscotch sauce.

Cover with foil and secure with string, then steam in a saucepan of water that reaches halfway up the pudding for 1½ hours. Check that the water level remains constant throughout. Turn the pudding out onto a large, warm serving plate, not too flat for the moat of butterscotch, and serve with more crème fraîche, if you dare.

Another of those lovely dessert cakes, you can also make this with pears. More pudding than cake, this can be served with crème fraîche laced with Somerset Cider Brandy, Calvados, or rum.

Caramelized Apple Cake with Calvados Crème Fraîche

SERVES 8—10
preheat oven to 350°F

2¼lb sharp eating apples
1 cup unsalted butter, plus an
    extra ¼ cup to cook the apples
    in
⅓ cup good honey
scant 2 cups raw confectioners'
    sugar
4 eggs
1¾ cups plus 2 tbsp all-purpose
    flour
½ package active-dry yeast
a pinch of sea salt
demerara sugar

Peel the apples and cut them into small dice. Brown them in the ¼ cup of butter, adding the honey after a few minutes

Remove from the heat and drain the juice from the apples, keeping it to pour over the cake later. Cream the cup of butter and the confectioners' sugar until white and fluffy, then whisk in the eggs, one by one. Add the yeast, sifted flour, and salt and fold in the apples.

Grease a large springform pan and line the bottom with a disk of greased parchment. Sprinkle a thin veil of demerara around the sides. Pour in the batter and scatter a bit more demerara over the surface of the cake. Bake for about 1½ hours, or until a skewer comes out clean.

Cool for 15 minutes before removing from the pan. Serve warm with the crème fraîche and a small pitcher of the reserved apple-cooking juice.

Of all nursery puddings, this has to be the best and most comforting. It should not be known under any other name; it is a classic and should be treated as such. The other lovely thing about it is that it was the first pudding my nine-year-old daughter Miranda made by herself when I was away filming one Sunday. She followed the recipe to the letter, and my brother Daniel pronounced it "as good as your mother's." Just as it should be.

Queen of Puddings

SERVES 6
preheat oven to 350°F

1 cup day-old brown bread bread crumbs
heaped 1 tbsp vanilla-flavored superfine sugar
grated zest of an organic lemon
2½ cups milk
¼ cup unsalted butter
4 large eggs, separated
a jar of best-quality apricot or raspberry jam or bramble jelly
heaped 1 cup vanilla-flavored superfine sugar

Put the bread crumbs into the deep, buttered baking dish you intend to cook the pudding in, with the tablespoon of vanilla-flavored sugar and lemon rind. Scald the milk with the butter, stir them into the crumbs, and leave to cool for 10 minutes. Now beat in the egg yolks, one at a time. Bake in the oven for about 25 minutes until the custard has set.

Heat the jam gently with a teaspoon of two of water, and pour it over the custard. Whisk the egg whites until stiff, stir in a spoon of sugar, then whisk in half of the remaining sugar until it is satiny. Fold in all but a spoon of the remaining sugar, pile the meringue on top of the pudding, and sprinkle the rest of the sugar over the top. Put back in the oven for 15–20 minutes or until the meringue is golden and crisp. Serve hot with plenty of cold, light cream. You can make the pudding up to the meringue stage a few hours earlier, if it suits you.

If you still find a degree of childish pleasure in dunking a warm toast soldier into a softly boiled egg and watching the crocus-colored yolk splurt down the sides of the egg cup, the chances are you also love crème brûlée: The tap with the back of the spoon on the mahogany surface; the splintered shards of glassy, bitter sugar as the thick ivory cream breaks through the barrier; the combined tastes and textures. This autumn I had a glut of apples and thought their sharp-scented fragrance and a hint of spice could transform the classic brûlée. There was always the danger that the apple would destroy the custard's unctuousness, but liquid they were not. They were divine.

Spiced Apple Brûlée

SERVES 6–8
preheat oven to 375°F

4 medium-size cooking apples
2½ cups organic heavy cream
a little piece of cinnamon stick,
    or 1 tsp ground cinnamon
5 cloves
5 egg yolks
unrefined superfine sugar
demerara sugar

Core the apples and score them around their circumference with a knife tip. Place them on a baking tray, pour in a little cold water and bake them in the oven until soft right through.

Meanwhile, scald the cream in a saucepan just to boiling point. Peel the apples, making sure you have cored all the tough bits, and chuck the puree in the food processor. Grind the cinnamon stick and cloves in a mortar and add them to the apple. Add the egg yolks and process briefly until everything coheres. Add sugar to taste, but leave the puree tart, because you are going to brûlée the top with demerara sugar. Lastly, pour the hot cream into the food processor with the blade still running.

Spoon the apple mixture into ramekins and place them in a roasting pan. Pour boiling water around the ramekins to come halfway up their sides, and cook them on the middle shelf of the oven for about 40 minutes. The custards should be set, but with a tremble. They will take longer than conventional custards because of the liquid content of the apples, but hold your nerve.

Remove from the pan and cool, then put them in the refrigerator overnight. In fact, they will keep for several days if you want to get ahead. Sprinkle a thin layer of demerara sugar over the surface of each ramekin and spray with a mist of water to help the torch scorching. Bubble with a blow torch, using a mild flame as close as you can get to the surface. Once you have a beautiful, even mahogany-colored top, leave to cool before serving.

There are times when only the best, childhood-memory food will do, and you want something you can cook almost blindfold and one-handed. The three sugars add flavor and texture to the top, and the orange-oily spiced sugar turned into the fruit to macerate delivers a keen whiff of the Orient that is somehow right for the time of year. This is a winter pudding.

Spiced Three-Sugar Crumble

SERVES 6—8
preheat oven to 375°F

8 apples, I used 6 firm cookers
    and 2 sharp eating apples
a blade of mace, 6 cloves, and
    a couple of small pieces
    of cinnamon stick
4 tbsp or so of raw superfine sugar
the finely grated zest of an
    organic orange
scant ½ cup organic all-purpose
    or whole wheat flour
¼ cup each of raw granulated,
    light brown, and demerara
    sugar
½ cup unsalted butter

Peel, quarter, and core the apples. Cut them into slices and place them in the bottom of a baking dish. Grind the spices together in a mortar—fresh spices make all the difference, the ready ground have lost their intense flavor. Add the superfine sugar to the spice mixture in the mortar and stir to mix well until the sugar is freckled with brown. Add the fine zest of the orange, and stir it in, then pour the mixture over the apples and turn them well to coat. Doing this an hour or so in advance of cooking really helps the spice rub to penetrate.

Process the flour, sugars, and cold butter cut into small pieces briefly, or do this by hand, until the mixture is sandy textured. Pile over the top of the apples, smooth the surface, and bake for 45 minutes until browned, with little geysers of bubbling juice escaping here and there. Rest for a few minutes before serving with light cream.

Great cold, too, with a scoop of vanilla or the preserved ginger and spice ice cream (page 268). You can prepare this several hours in advance of cooking it.

This is a lovely dessert-cake, the sharp, orange orbs of Cape gooseberry bursting onto the tongue, the sponge moist with almonds. Perhaps because of their decorative quality, with their veiny, dry-textured leaves, Cape gooseberries are not always taken seriously as an ingredient. Yet their acid sharpness and explosion of flavor would grace a gooseberry sauce for mackerel, or even a scented summer fool. Experiment.

Upside-Down Cape Gooseberry and Almond Cake

MAKES AN 8-INCH CAKE
preheat oven to 325°F

12oz Cape gooseberries, weighed
    after removing their leaves
1 cup raw superfine sugar
¾ cup plus 2 tbsp unsalted butter
¾ cup organic ground almonds
a few drops vanilla extract
3 organic free-range eggs
finely grated zest and juice of
    an organic orange
1 tbsp crème fraîche
1 cup soft pastry or cake organic
    white flour
1 tsp baking powder
a pinch of salt
demerara sugar to sprinkle

Butter an 8-inch springform cake pan. Cover the bottom with a layer of Cape gooseberries, leaving just under a third of them to add to the cake batter.

Cream the sugar and butter until light and fluffy, then stir in the ground almonds and vanilla extract. Beat in the eggs, one at a time, fold in the orange zest and juice, then the crème fraîche, sifted flour, baking powder, and salt. Fold the remaining gooseberries into the mixture. Sprinkle a bit of demerara sugar over the layer of gooseberries in the pan, then plop the batter over them and smooth it down with a rubber spatula.

Bake in the middle of the oven for 1 hour and 10 minutes, but check with a skewer every five minutes after 1 hour. Leave to cool in the pan on a rack until just warm, then turn out upside down onto a large plate, and serve warm with crème fraîche.

I wanted to come up with a Christmas ice cream, full of warming spices, that would coldly slide from the summit of your pudding or pies, but would also work well with crumble. I pureed the globes of ginger through a food mill, but it would be easier to blitz them in a blender with the custard and cream base. The very finely chopped bits of ginger are a matter of taste. I like the texture; you might prefer to have a silken-smooth ice cream.

Preserved Ginger and Spice Ice Cream

SERVES 6—8

2 cups whole milk
2 vanilla beans, split and the
    insides scraped out
6 organic egg yolks
¾ cup plus 2 tbsp raw
    superfine sugar
1¼ cups heavy cream and
    1¼ cups crème fraîche, or all
    heavy cream
6–8 globes of preserved ginger,
    put 6 in the blender
    to begin with
1 tbsp ginger syrup
2 very finely chopped globes
    of preserved ginger
6 or 7 cloves and a few little bits
    of cinnamon stick crushed
    together in a mortar

Scald the milk with the split vanilla seeds and beans. Whisk it into the egg yolks and sugar that you have put into a bowl. Return the mixture to the pan, and cook it over low heat, whisking as you go, until it thickens perceptibly. Do not boil the mixture; you do not want it to curdle into scrambled egg.

As soon as the custard has thickened, remove from the heat and whisk in the creams thoroughly. Whizz in a blender with the whole globes of ginger, ginger syrup, and half a teaspoon of the spice mixture. Taste until you have the right strength: The ginger should predominate, but you want a musky breath of spice.

Churn in an ice-cream maker for 30 minutes and then add the tiny ginger bits to the setting mixture. You can put the mixture in a ice tray and freeze, but remember to stir the setting walls of the ice cream into the middle of the tray after the first hour, and then again an hour or two later, to prevent crystals forming.

Little warm shells of spicy sponge, spiced madeleines are delicious with the preserved ginger and spice ice cream (opposite), or the poached Armagnac and orange apricots. You will need to buy a madeleine tray to get the classic shape.

Spiced Madeleines

preheat oven to 350°F

2¼ cups ground almonds
1 cup all-purpose flour
1 cup raw superfine sugar
1½ cups unsalted butter, softened
7 tbsp honey
10oz egg whites
a pinch each of 5-spice,
    cinnamon, nutmeg,
    and star anise
1 tbsp mixed grated orange and
    lemon zests

Mix the ground almonds, flour, sugar, and spices in a large bowl, then add everything else and beat together well. Put in the refrigerator for 20 minutes.

Grease some madeleine molds and pour in the batter. Bake for 10–15 minutes, when a skewer should come out clean. Turn out and leave to cool on a wire rack.

I serve the following two ices together in the summer, the contrast of pistachio green and pale peachy orange, of water ice and ice cream, both delicate and subtle. You may find the idea of ice cream served in a melon shell kitschly redolent of those frozen atrocities of orange and lemon sorbets that are the province of the 80s' trattoria or the more contemporaneous Indian restaurant. I would disagree, on the grounds that it is really about the quality of what is inside it. And if you place your scooped-out melon on some pretty leaves it should offend neither the eye, nor the good-taste arbiters.

Charentais Water Ice

SERVES 6

½ cup plus 2 tbsp vanilla-flavored superfine sugar
1 cup water
2 Charentais or canteloupe melons
lemon and/or lime
1 egg white

Simmer the vanilla-flavored sugar with a cup of water for a few minutes. Puree enough melon pulp to give you 1¼ cups of juice, two melons maximum. Add the cooled syrup slowly, tasting as you go, then sharpen with a spritz of lemon juice, and, if you like, one of lime, which makes melon taste more melony (and, incidentally, mango more mangoy).

Freeze until the outside is set, but the middle still slushily liquid. Gently fold in a stiffly whisked egg white before returning the mixture to the ice tray and to the freezer. You can make this a couple of days before you wish to serve it, but it does tend to lose flavor after that.

Galia Melon Ice Cream

SERVES 6

1 Galia melon
½ cup plus 2 tbsp raw vanilla-
   flavored superfine sugar
4 egg yolks
kirsch
lemon juice
1¼ cup heavy cream

Cut a lid off the top of a Galia melon and transfer the seeds to a strainer with a bowl placed under it to catch the juice. Carefully scoop out the flesh and stew it gently in a pan with the juice and the raw vanilla sugar for 2–3 minutes. Blitz in the blender briefly, return it to the pan with 4 beaten egg yolks, and cook over very gentle heat until it thickens.

Cool the mixture, then add a splosh of kirsch and a good squeeze of lemon juice to taste. Fold in the whipped but slightly slack heavy cream, and freeze in an ice-cream machine or in an old-fashioned ice-cube tray. If you use a tray, remember to stir the setting walls of the ice cream into the middle of the tray after the first hour, and then again an hour or two later, to prevent crystals forming.

When the ice cream has set, scoop it out in balls and return it to the melon shell, the bottom of which you may have to shave slightly with a knife so that it will stand upright. Place the filled melon on a white dish lined with fig leaves or any large leaves you happen to have in the garden, and serve.

Magpie that I am, it was while watching a heat of *Masterchef* that I registered one of the contestants cooking a rhubarb and passion fruit tart and I began to wonder about the sanity of pairing these two intensely tart, sharp ingredients together. Reckoning on the softening effect of brown sugar, cream, and a proper home-made vanilla-ey custard, I got to work.

In fact, I got to work twice, the first time with whole chunks of rhubarb, the second with a briefly mashed puree. It was a triumph, the mashed version even better than the jeweled, since the little frozen pieces of rhubarb didn't release their taste so well. With mark 2, both fruits rang out strong and clear. The best ice cream I have dreamed up to date. A clean-fruited dessert that you can make at the end of January when the first fragile wands of forced rhubarb appear and the rigors of Christmas make it all the more desirable.

Rhubarb and Passion Fruit Ice Cream

SERVES 8
preheat oven to 300°F

8 thin wands of rhubarb
light brown sugar, about 4 tbsp
4 large or 6 small passion fruit
2¼ cups milk
1 vanilla bean
6 egg yolks, save the whites for macaroons to serve with the ice cream, if you like
1 cup plus 2 tbsp raw superfine sugar
1¼ cups heavy cream

Chop the rhubarb into small chunks, turn it in the sugar in a baking dish, and bake in the oven until softened, 20–30 minutes. Test for sweetness. Drain and reserve the juice, you can pour it over the ice cream or drink it! Mash the rhubarb with a fork. Halve the passion fruit, scoop out the contents into a small pan, and heat very gently until warm, which makes the fruit easier to strain. Keep the juice and the seeds separately.

To make a custard, first scald the milk with the split vanilla bean and its innards, then pour the hot milk over the well-whisked egg yolks and sugar, whisking as you go. Return the mixture to the pan and continue to whisk over gentle heat until you have a thickened custard. Decant into a bowl to cool. Whisk the cream until thickened, but by no means rigid. Fold the cream into the cooled custard, then stir in the passion-fruit juice and rhubarb. Finally, fold in a spoonful of passion-fruit seeds, more would overwhelm with crunch. Churn in an ice-cream maker and freeze, or freeze in an ice-cube tray. Place in the refrigerator 20–30 minutes before you want to serve it.

Macaroons

MAKES ABOUT 30
preheat oven to 375°F

1½ cups ground almonds, Spanish
    organic ones are the best
1½ cups superfine sugar
3 egg whites
2½ tbsp all-purpose flour or
    arrowroot
vanilla extract
rice paper or baking parchment
a handful of split almonds

Mix the ground almonds and sugar in a bowl, add the egg whites, and cream together thoroughly. Add the flour or arrowroot and flavor to taste with vanilla extract, a few drops.

Place the rice paper or baking parchment on baking sheets, and spread the mixture out in little circles with a teaspoon. Press a split almond into the middle of each one and bake for about 20 minutes. Cool thoroughly on a rack before storing.

Apple and Carrot Shortbread

MAKES ABOUT 20 WEDGES
preheat oven to 350°F

½ cup semolina
1¼ cups plus 2 tbsp unbleached
    all-purpose flour
¼ tsp baking powder
a pinch of salt
10 tbsp unsalted butter, softened
½ cup raw superfine sugar
⅓ cup grated carrot
2 tbsp grated apple
milk

Sift together the semolina, flour, baking powder, and salt. Cream together the butter and sugar until light and fluffy. Throw the grated carrot and apple into the flour mixture, then fold into the creamed butter. Knead into a soft dough. Rest for half an hour in the refrigerator.

When you're ready to cook the shortbread, roll into two 9-inch disks, ½ inch thick. Mark the disks into wedges, being careful not to cut through the disks. Fork the edges, brush with a milk wash, and bake on a nonstick surface for about 10 minutes. Leave to cool before cutting.

The Jelly

Curiously, I crave jelly as much in midwinter for its refreshing, fruited zestiness
as I do when there are piles of soft-berried summer fruits to play with.
Christmas is a great time for jelly, as is the New Year, when the palate is jaded
and wearied from the rich, buttery, creamy, sugary, fatty delights of feasting. I
cannot understand why most people don't seem to bother with jellies, and why
they have become a bastardized childrens' party food, quivering, sugared lumps
of primary-colored hue and phoney fruitiness, which come set in dinky party
plates with store-bought ice cream.

I have been making different jellies throughout Christmas, from the jokily
frivolous mimosa to orange, grenadillo, and muscat; and, unanimously the best,
a clementine, passion fruit, and muscat jelly. Come the blood-orange season,
I mean to experiment with spice, too—a sunset-colored, blood orange jelly
spiked with cardamom. Ice cream if you must, something homemade, but
I think a clean palate, no cookies, no cake, no cream is best. A good jelly takes no
longer than 10 minutes to make, even if you are squeezing an orchard of
oranges. Just remember not to experiment with pineapple. There is an enzyme
in the fruit that prohibits it from setting.

I know champagne isn't cheap, but you've got the rest of the bottle to drink and no other killer ingredients to buy—and this is for Christmas, or birthday, or something special

Mimosa Jelly

SERVES 6—8

2½ cups champagne
2½ cups of freshly squeezed
   organic orange juice
8 leaves of gelatin, broken in half
   and soaked in 2–3 tbsp cold
   water for 10 minutes

Measure the champagne and pour it into a bowl. Put the orange juice into a small saucepan with the leaves of soaked gelatin and their water—8 sheets should set 1¼ quarts liquid, but check the package. Gently heat the orange juice, stirring as you go to dissolve the gelatin completely. You do not want the liquid to become very hot or it won't taste so fresh, but using a wooden spoon, make sure that there isn't a stringy trace of gelatin to be seen. Pour the orange-and-gelatin mixture into the champagne, stir it all together, it will fizz as you do, and then pour everything through a strainer into a jelly mold. Mine is big enough for 2 quarts, but I never seem to make a jelly quite that big. Leave to cool, before putting in the refrigerator to set.

You can make a jelly from four hours to two days before you want to eat it. It will keep for longer in the refrigerator, but the freshness of the fruit starts to diminish. Turn out by dunking the base half of the mold briefly in boiling water and inverting the jelly onto a plate, or serve from the mold.

On a recent trip to the Far East I got hooked on exotic fruits for breakfast. They don't seem quite so attractive away from their native tropical island, served icy cold like the weather you come home to. But when I returned, I found the tangerine-shelled grenadillos, with their milky, moonstone-white fruit, gluey and black seeded, and turned them, with a delicious organic muscat wine and some oranges, into jelly.

Orange, Grenadillo, and Muscat Jelly

SERVES 6—8

2 grenadillos

8 leaves of gelatin soaked in 2–3 tbsp cold water for 10 minutes

1½ cups Bonterra organic muscat wine, or something similar

8–10 organic oranges squeezed to make the level of liquid just under 1¼ quarts

Halve the grenadillos and scoop out the innards and seeds. Heat them gently in a pan and strain into a large measuring cup—it is easier to separate seed from fruit if it is warm.

Put the gelatin and its soaking liquid into a small saucepan with the orange juice. Heat through gently, stirring as you go. Make sure the gelatin is completely dissolved and then pour the contents of the pan into the measuring cup with the muscat and grenadillo fruit and stir everything together.

Pour the mixture through a strainer into a jelly mold, leave to cool, then set in the refrigerator for four hours to two days.

This was the triumph. I served it after the New Year's goose, with the either/or option of a divine chocolate budino (see page 245). Well it wasn't an option really; both were impossible to resist. I used large, somewhat underripe passion fruit. The skins had not crinkled and the sharpness won through gloriously. The sweet clementine and fruity muscat flavors were not clouded and were a marriage of three that transported. Sugar unnecessary.

Clementine, Passion Fruit, and Muscat Jelly

SERVES 6—8

3 large, underripe passion fruit
about 20 organic clementines
1½ cups Bonterra organic muscat
   wine, or something similar
8 leaves of gelatin soaked for 10
   minutes in 2—3 tbsp cold water

Scoop the insides of the passion fruits into a small saucepan, and heat to warm so that the seeds will separate more easily from the fruit. Strain them into a pitcher or bowl with the muscat. Squeeze the clementines until the pitcher contains just under 5 cups of liquid.

Stir in the gelatin, and pour the liquid into the saucepan, heating it through very gently to just warm enough to dissolve the gelatin completely. Pour the mixture through a strainer into the jelly mold, cool, and then put in the refrigerator.

The jelly will be ready to eat from between four hours to two days later, depending on when you want it. Serve with some thinly sliced oranges.

Raspberries and red currants, fortuitously, ripen together in late July and to my mind are THE summer dessert fruits. They also make a magical jelly, with little hanging lanterns of red currants suspended in the jelly alongside bruise purple blueberries and soft seeded raspberries. A heap of fruits around the plate and you have a summer dessert as toothsome to the very young as it is to the very old. And the fruit is all raw, even in the jelly. I find it a near sacrilege to cook midsummer fruit.

I use individual plastic bowls, the lidded steamed pudding kind, from which the jellies turn out with minimum resistance, so there are no last-minute panics. You can, of course, use a large mold or glass bowl.

Raspberry and Red Currant Jellies with Summer Berries

MAKES 7

1lb fresh raspberries
5oz red currants
raw confectioners' or superfine
    sugar to taste, about 4 tbsp
6 leaves of leaf gelatin
water
an extra pint each of raspberries
    and red currants and a pint of
    blueberries

Soak the gelatin for 5 minutes in 2–3 tablespoons of cold water. Blitz the fruits in a food processor, then strain them into a measuring cup. Sweeten to taste, stirring in the sugar to dissolve. Err on the tart side. Top up with water to the 1 quart mark, but remember to fall short of it by the same number of tablespoons of water you have got soaking the gelatin. Heat the fruit liquid gently until hot, stir in the gelatin in its liquid, and stir off the heat until the gelatin has totally dissolved.

Pour the mixture into the rinsed but still wet molds and leave to cool. The liquid will start to thicken as it cools. Then pop in the berries one by one, about three raspberries, six blueberries, and four or five red currants to each bowl. Put in the refrigerator to set.

Eat a few hours or up to two days later. To turn out, dip the bottom of each bowl in boiling water for 10 seconds, go round the edge of the bowl with a knife point, turn upside down, and squeeze. Arrange on a large dish with extra fresh berries or on individual dishes.

First published in the United Kingdom in 2002
by Weidenfeld & Nicolson
an imprint of the Orion Publishing Group
Wellington House
125 Strand
London WC2 0BB

For information address:
Hyperion
77 West 66th St
New York, NY 10023-6298

ISBN 1-4013-5233-2

Design director David Rowley
Editorial director Susan Haynes
Designed by Clive Hayball and Nigel Soper
Edited by Jinny Johnson
Proofread by Gwen Rigby
Index by Elizabeth Wiggans

Pots, bowls, plates and linen used in the photographs were kindly lent
by Divertimenti, 139-141 Fulham Road, London SW3 6SD
Tel: 020 7581 8065. Fax: 020 7823 9429. E-mail: fulham@divertimenti.co.uk

Acknowledgements

I almost dread writing this bit more than the horror of conceiving the introduction that will give the book its shape and form and send it on its way. But this bit I dread for different reasons. First, it's like putting the book to bed, as curiously recalcitrant a thing, I find, as a small unwilling child. Second, I have said it all before, and several times now, since I have had the great good fortune to work with the very same individuals on this book as on the last. And, in most cases, the previous two as well.

What I would like to say, and this is in no small measure due to the main protagonists, is that they have done it again. They have produced an even better book, and that is because they are now even better at their jobs than they were this time last year, and the book reflects that. If I had detected even the slightest sense that David Loftus, the most talented photographer I have worked with, was going to coast this book and rely on what we had achieved in the past, it would have been time to try someone new. But the joy of working with David is that he isn't like that. We can talk through the look of a book, and go on developing it until the last shot. I wanted something more abstract, less reliant on endless brush strokes of colour than a lot of the current cook books, but something that allured through its glamorous simplicity and beauty, and still made you want to scrape the food off the page. David, you have shot the most beautiful pictures of my food yet, not always easy with me as cook and with the insanely short schedule we had to work to, but made a trifle easier by the beautiful pots, bowls, plates and linen lent by the lovely kitchen shop Divertimenti.

Susan Haynes, my editor, is, like the best football supporter, always at the match cheering and shouting from the terraces and utterly loyal and committed to the game. She treats the emergent work with a degree of love and care that goes well beyond the confines of professionalism. She really minds about the end result and its attaining, which, in turn, forces authors to give of their best. Thank you for being as good an editor as you are a friend.

This time, the publisher, Michael Dover and his wife Ruth invited us to their house to shoot the photographs. Michael's support, advice and encouragement have always been of the best, but this time, the joys of his lovely kitchen and garden have made the feel of the finished book what it is. It wouldn't have been the same without his generosity. And all for a few leftovers that we hadn't hoovered up with our customary greed. Michael, I owe you a serious Dover Dinner.

George Capel, my agent, is chief cheerleader. She listens to the earliest ramblings of an idea, then encourages, cajoles and enthuses as the glimmer takes shape and the fledgling flies. How lucky I am, knowing that each doubt, uncertainty and questioning is met with serious attention, an honest response and her inimitable sense of fun.

David Rowley's cooking has probably not improved during the shoots for this book, due to the degree of unseriousness with which his attempts at whisking and stirring were taken. But it is not every art director who will come on a shoot and be told that he is there to do more than eat and primp. His is the brilliant eye that has conceived the shape and form of *Good Tempered Food*, alongside designer Nigel Soper, and I know how lucky I am to have both of them for their sensitivity, attention to detail and ability to capture the visual beauty and style that is the essence of the book.

Jinny Johnson has, yet again, edited the text intelligently, coherently, minutely in a way that is always a pleasure rather than a chore, and helped cook for the shoots, making herself so indispensable that it would now be impossible to imagine doing them without her. Bar the chocolate cake that is. She is a first-class cook and skilled navigator, clearing a path through any culinary imprecision and suggesting just where suggestion is needed.

TAMASIN DAY-LEWIS, MAY 2002

Index